Sailing directions for the South-Eastern Coast of England, etc.

Alexander Findlay

Sailing directions for the South-Eastern Coast of England, etc.
Findlay, Alexander
British Library, Historical Print Editions
British Library
1857
8°.
10496.aaa.6.

The BiblioLife Network

GUIDE TO FOLD-OUTS, MAPS and OVERSIZED IMAGES

In an online database, page images do not need to conform to the size restrictions found in a printed book. When converting these images back into a printed bound book, the page sizes are standardized in ways that maintain the detail of the original. For large images, such as fold-out maps, the original page image is split into two or more pages.

Guidelines used to determine the split of oversize pages:

• Some images are split vertically; large images require vertical and horizontal splits.
• For horizontal splits, the content is split left to right.
• For vertical splits, the content is split from top to bottom.
• For both vertical and horizontal splits, the image is processed from top left to bottom right.

SAILING DIRECTIONS

FOR THE

SOUTH-EASTERN

COAST OF ENGLAND,

BETWEEN

BEACHY HEAD AND FLAMBOROUGH HEAD;

AND THE

COAST OF FRANCE AND BELGIUM,

BETWEEN

BOULOGNE AND OSTEND.

TO ACCOMPANY THE CHART.

PUBLISHED BY R. H. LAURIE,

No. 53, FLEET STREET, LONDON.

Price, with the Chart, 10s. 6d.   Separately, 2s. 6d.

SAILING DIRECTIONS

FOR THE

SOUTH-EASTERN

COAST OF ENGLAND,

BETWEEN

BEACHY HEAD AND FLAMBOROUGH HEAD;

AND THE

COAST OF FRANCE AND BELGIUM,

BETWEEN

BOULOGNE AND OSTEND.

TO ACCOMPANY THE CHART.

By ALEX. G. FINDLAY, $\mathcal{K}$

Fellow of the Royal Geographical Society.

LONDON:

PRINTED FOR RICHARD HOLMES LAURIE,

CHART-SELLER TO THE ADMIRALTY, THE HON. CORPORATION OF TRINITY HOUSE, ETC.
No. 53, FLEET STREET.

1857.

J. & W. Rider, Printers, 14, Bartholomew Close, London.

CONTENTS.

———

MR. LAURIE

BEGS TO CALL ATTENTION TO THE FOLLOWING WORKS, IN CONNECTION WITH THE PRESENT.

THAMES AND MEDWAY, &c., from the new Surveys of Captains Bullock and Washington, and the late Captain Hewett; with the Coast from Folkestone to Orfordness, and the Rivers to London and Rochester; with particular Plans, on enlarged scales, of the SOUTH CHANNELS, ISLE OF THANET, &c. (Honoured by the special approbation of His late Majesty William IV.) With a Sailing Directory, 8*s.*; or, continued Eastward to the Gabbards, &c., 10*s.*

RIVER THAMES, WITH THE STRAIT OF DOVER, &c., between Hastings and Harwich, and Boulogne and Ostend. Price 4*s.*

EASTERN COAST OF ENGLAND.—*A new Survey of the* EASTERN COAST *of* ENGLAND, from Orfordness to Flamborough Head; with plans, on enlarged scales, of Yarmouth Roads and the neighbouring Channels, Boston and Lynn Deeps, the River Humber, &c., with Views of the Land, elegantly engraved. On two sheets. With a Sailing Directory. Price 8*s.*

THE EAST COAST OF ENGLAND AND SCOTLAND, from Flamborough Head to the Orkney Islands, and thence to Cape Wrath. Three sheets of atlas paper. From the Admiralty Surveys of Captains Hewett, Slater, Johnson, Otter, and Commander George Thomas. By ISAAC PURDY. The first sheet contains enlarged Plans of Newcastle and the Tyne River, Scarborough Bay, Whitby Harbour, Blythe, Hartlepool and Tees Bay, Seaham Harbour, Sunderland Port, Berwick Harbour, Holy Island, Farn Islands, &c., and Holy Island Harbour. The second sheet contains Leith Roads, Dundee Harbour, Arbroath Harbour, Montrose Harbour, Aberdeen Harbour, Banff and Macduff, Fraserburgh, and Peterhead. The third sheet contains the Frith of Inverness and Thurso Bay. With a Book of Sailing Directions, by ALEX. G. FINDLAY. Price 10*s.* 6*d.*

THE ENGLISH CHANNEL on a large scale, with particular Plans of the Downs, &c.; Shoreham, Newhaven, Boulogne, &c.; Ushant, Brest Harbour; with Description of the Tides. By A. G. FINDLAY. With a Book of Sailing Directions. Price 12*s.*

THE ISLE OF WIGHT, with the adjacent Coast between Bognor and Hurst Point, including Selsea, Portsmouth, Southampton, &c., with separate Plans of Portsmouth Harbour, Southampton Docks, and the Needles Channel, from the recent Admiralty Survey by Captain Sheringham, &c., 1851. Price 5*s.*

THE NORTH SEA, *upon a large scale;* constructed from a great variety of original and accurate Surveys; more particularly those of the respective Governments, adjusted by the best astronomic observations: with particular plans of the Pentland Frith, the Channels to Bergen, and the Harbour of Christiansand; accompanied by *a new Sailing Directory* for all the Harbours, &c. By JOHN PURDY. With numerous Appearances of the Land, Lighthouses, &c. Price 8*s.*

THE COASTS OF HOLLAND, GERMANY, AND DENMARK, from the Texel to the River Hever; including the River Ems to Emden, with the Elbe, the Weser, and the Eyder; including Husum, Frederichstadt, Tonningen, Hamburgh, and Bremen. Composed from the recent Surveys made by order of the Dutch and the Danish Governments. With a new Sailing Directory. Price 6*s.*

THE COASTS AROUND IRELAND, with the ST. GEORGE'S and BRISTOL CHANNELS. With Plans of Waterford, Cork, Liverpool, Holyhead, Dublin, and Belfast. With a Sailing Directory. By A. G. FINDLAY. *Nearly ready.*

THE PHAROLOGY;

OR, DESCRIPTION OF THE LIGHTHOUSES OF THE SOUTH-EASTERN COAST OF ENGLAND, ETC.

*** THE more detailed description of the lights, and their uses, is given hereafter in the pages indicated in the last column.

The lights are bright, or of the natural colour, when not otherwise expressed.

Coast or principal lights are indicated thus, NORTH FORELAND. Harbour lights thus, MARGATE. Tide lights thus, *Ramsgate*.

RIVER THAMES.

Name and Description of Light.	Situation.	Geographical Position.	Height above High Water.	Height of Build-ing, base to vane.	Visible in Miles.	Year completed.	Page of Work.
HOPE POINT. Lantern light for Colliers.	In the Fort on a flagstaff.	° ′ ″				1852	2
MUCKING FLAT. One bright or *red* light.	A pile lighthouse, painted white. A bell in fogs.		40	53	10	1849	3
CHAPMAN HEAD. One bright or *red* light.	A pile lighthouse, painted red. A bell in fogs.		40		10	1849	3
SOUTHEND PIER. One *red* light.						1840	4
NORE LIGHTVESSEL. One revolving light every half minute.	East end of the Sand. Moored in 3 fathoms.	51 29 0 N 0 48 0 E	38		10	1734	5
MARGATE PIER. One *red* light.	West end of the Pier.	51 24 0 N 1 23 0 E	85	70	10	1829	10
MOUSE LIGHTVESSEL. One fixed light.	On West end of the Sand. Moored in 4½ fathoms.	51 32 0 N 1 0 0 E	38		10	1838	13, 14
GIRDLER LIGHT-VESSEL. One revolving light every half minute.	West Girdler Sand. Moored in 3½ fathoms.	51 29 0 N 1 7 0 E	33		10	1848	14
PRINCES CHANNEL LIGHTVESSEL. One *red* revolving light every 20 seconds.	On the North side, in 3½ fathoms, near the Spit of the Girdler Sand.					1856	14
TONGUE LIGHTVESSEL. Upper light bright; Lower light *red*.	At East end of the Tongue Sand, moored in 10 fathoms.	51 29 0 N 1 19 0 E	38 14		10	1848	14
NORTH FORELAND. One fixed light.	On the Head.	51 22 29 N 1 26 47 E	184	70	18	1790	19

THE PHAROLOGY.

KENT.

Name and Description of Light.	Situation.	Geographical Position.	Height above High Water.	Height of Building, base to vane.	Visible in Miles.	Year completed.	Page of Work.
NORTH SAND HEAD LIGHTVESSEL. Three fixed lights.	Off North end of the Sand. Moored in 9 fathoms.	51 19 0 N 1 35 0 E	28 42 28		10	1793	21
GULL STREAM LIGHT-VESSEL. Two fixed lights.	Near western edge of the Sand. Moored in 8½ fathoms.	51 17 0 N 1 30 0 E	14		7	1809	21
SOUTH SAND HEAD LIGHTVESSEL. One fixed light.	Off South end of the Sand. Moored in 13 fathoms.	51 10 0 N 1 28 0 E	38		10	1832	23
Ramsgate. A *red* light while 10 feet water. A green light while less than 10 feet A *green* lt. on W. Cliff.	West Pierhead.	51 20 0 N 1 26 0 E	37				25
SOUTH FORELAND. Two fixed lights.	On the Head.	51 8 26 N 1 22 22 E	372 275	69 49	25 22	1793 1842	28
Dover. One small *red* light with 7 to 10 feet water.	South Pier.	51 7 0 N 1 19 0 E	12			1842	29
Two large *red* lights and one small red light, with above 10 ft. water.	North Pier.		60	12	12	1852	29
One *green* light toward the entrance.	Near the Clock Tower.					1852	29
A *blue* light from the end of the Admiralty pier.					2	1849	29
Folkestone. One *red* lt. while 10 ft.	South Pierhead.	51 5 0 N 1 11 0 E	36	26	6	1848	29
DUNGENESS. One fixed light.	Extreme Point.	50 54 59 N 0 58 0 E	92	103	14	1792	30

SUSSEX.

Rye. Two lights while 10 feet. Two thwart lights.	Camber, North side of Entrance.	50 57 0 N 0 44 0 E	26 16	20 10	4 3		31
HASTINGS. One bright, one red light for the fishermen.	Upper light in the town; Lower on the Beach.	50 52 0 N 0 36 0 E	60 30	25	7 4		31
Eastbourne. A fishing light.		50 45 0 N 0 17 0 E	10				32
BEACHY HEAD. One revolving light every 2 minutes.	Bellet out Cliff.	50 44 0 N 0 13 0 E	285	45	22	1828	32

COAST OF FRANCE AND BELGIUM.

Name and Description of Light.	Situation.	Geographical Position.	Height above High Water.	Height of Building, base to vane.	Visible in Miles.	Year completed.	Page of Work.
Boulogne Tide Lights. One *red*, two bright fixed lights.	A *red* light, with 9 feet water, on N.E. Jetty head. Two lights on the S.W. Jetty head.	50 43 54 N 1 35 6 E	16 43 33		11 9	1835	35 35
CAPE GRISNEZ. A bright revolving light every half minute.	A Tower, 46 feet high, on the summit of the Cape.	50 52 12 N 1 35 0 E	193		22	1842	36
CALAIS. A fixed light, varied by a flash every 4 min.	On a new Tower, 167 feet high, and 1,312 feet East from the old tower.	50 57 50 N 1 51 6 E	100		21	1848	37
CALAIS HARBOUR. A *red* fixed light.	A *red* light on West Jetty.	50 52 12 N 1 35 5 E	16		2	1842	37
Calais Tide Light. A bright light, with 8 feet water.	A bright light on Fort Rouge, to the right of the entrance.		33		10		37
GRAVELINES. 1. One bright fixed light. 2. Two bright fixed lights.	1. A red column on Fort Philippe, East side of the entrance. 2. On the S.W. Mole of Fort Philippe.	51 0 18 N 2 6 30 E	102 20		15 6	1843 1854	38
DUNKIRK. One bright revolving light, visible every minute.	A Tower, 180 feet high, at half a mile S.E. by E. ¼ E. from the end of the West Jetty.	51 3 0 N 2 21 48 E	193		24		38
DUNKIRK HARBOUR. Two bright fixed lights.	1. On the North end of the West Jetty. 2. On the Heuguenar Tower, only visible in the direction of the entrance.		23 85		6 15		38
Nieuport. One fixed tide light.		51 8 25 N 2 43 0 E	32	28	16	1825	42
OSTEND. One bright fixed light. One *green* light on West pier. One *red*, two bright tide lights.		51 14 0 N 2 55 0 E	77 25	72	12 7	1771 1849	43

ESSEX.

Name and Description of Light.	Situation.	Geographical Position.	Height above High Water.	Height of Building, base to vane.	Visible in Miles.	Year completed.	Page of Work.
MAPLIN. One bright light.	S.E. part of Sand. (*Red* light to S. by W.)	51 35 0 N 1 3 0 E	36		10	1838	
SWIN MIDDLE LIGHT-VESSEL. One revolving light every minute.	West end of the Sand. Moored in 4 fathoms.	51 39 0 N 1 7 0 E	38		10	1837	46

Name and Description of Light.	Situation.	Geographical Position.	Height above High Water.	Height of Building, base to vane.	Visible in Miles.	Year completed.	Page of Work.
GUNFLEET. One *red* revolving lt.	A pile lighthouse on S.E. part of Sand.	51 45 50 N 1 20 0 E	41		10	1856	47
SUNK LIGHTVESSEL. One fixed light.	Fairway of East Swin. Moored in 11 fathoms.	51 47 0 N 1 28 0 E	37		10	1802	
CORK LEDGE LIGHT- VESSEL. One revolving light every half minute.	Near the Cork Ledge. Moored in 4 fathoms.	51 50 0 N 1 23 0 E	38		10	1844	50
SHIPWASH LIGHT- VESSEL. One fixed light.	Off N.E. end of the Sand. Moored in 9½ fathoms.	52 1 30 N 1 38 0 E	38		10	1837	50
ORFORDNESS. Two fixed lights.	On the Ness.	52 5 0 N 1 34 30 E	83 63	87 68	12 12	1792	52
HARWICH. Two bright fixed lights. A lower light.	At entrance of the har- bour S.W. of the town.	51 56 39 N 1 17 23 E	69 25	84 40	12 9	1818	55
LANDGUARD FORT. One *red* or bright light.	From one of the barracks in Landguard Fort.	51 56 15 N 1 19 0 E				1848	55
GALLOPER LIGHT- VESSEL. Two fixed lights.	S.W. part of the Shoal. Moored in 19 fathoms.	51 45 0 N 1 56 0 E	36		10	1803	59
KENTISH KNOCK LIGHTVESSEL. One revolving light every minute.	East side of the Sand. Moored in 12 fathoms.	51 40 0 N 1 39 0 E	37		10	1840	60

SUFFOLK.

Name and Description of Light.	Situation.	Geographical Position.	Height above High Water.	Height of Building, base to vane.	Visible in Miles.	Year completed.	Page of Work.
PAKEFIELD. One *red* light.	South part of Cliff.	52 26 0 N 1 44 0 E	68	33	9	1832	61
LOWESTOFF. Two fixed lights.	High light is on the Cliff; Lower on the Beach.	52 29 10 N 1 45 30 E	119 45	52 45	18 10	1609 1676	62
LOWESTOFF HARBOUR. Two red & 2 green lights.	On each Pier of harbour.					1847	62
STANFORD LIGHTVESSEL. Two fixed lights.	Near North end of New- come Sand, off Lowestoff. Moored in 3 fathoms.	52 29 0 N 1 47 0 E	23		9	1802	63
ST. NICHOLAS GAT LIGHTVESSEL. One fixed light. Low *red* light.	North end of Kettle Bottom Sand. Moored in 10 fathoms.	52 34 0 N 1 47 0 E	40 12		10	1837 1856	65
YARMOUTH. One *red* light.	South Pier at Gorleston.	52 34 25 N 1 44 20 E			2	1852	62, 67
COCKLE GAT LIGHTVESSEL. One revolv. lt. every mt.	N. entrance, Eastern side. Moored in 6½ fathoms.	52 41 30 N 1 47 0 E	36		10	1844	65

NORFOLK.

Name and Description of Light.	Situation.	Geographical Position.	Height above High Water.	Height of Building, base to vane.	Visible in Miles.	Year completed.	Page of Work.
WINTERTON. One fixed light.	On the Point.	52 43 0 N 1 41 30 E		59	14	1790	68
NEWARP LIGHTVESSEL. Three fixed lights.	Near North end of the Sand. Moored in 19 fathoms.	52 45 0 N 1 53 0 E	22 36 22		10	1791	66
HASBOROUGH. Two fixed lights.	S.S.E. of Hasborough Church.	52 49 0 N 1 32 0 E	137 100	93 72	18 15	1791	69
HASBOROUGH LIGHTVESSEL. Two fixed lights.	Near North end of Sand. Moored in 15½ fathoms.	52 58 0 N 1 36 0 E	38		10	1832	69
LEMAN AND OWER LIGHTVESSEL. One revolving and one fixed light.	Between Leman and Ower Sands. Moored in 16 fathoms.	53 8 30 N 2 2 7 E	38 27		10	1840	72
CROMER. One revolving light every minute.	On Foulness, near the Cliff.	52 56 0 N 1 19 0 E	274	61	22	1719 1833	70
HUNSTANTON. One fixed light (red to W.N.W.)	On the Point.	52 56 54 N 0 29 50 E	109	61	13	1677 1840	74
LYNN WELL LIGHTVESSEL. Two fixed lights.	Off the Hook of the Long Sand, Lynn Deeps. Moored in 25 fathoms.	53 1 40 N 0 25 0 E	34		10	1828	77
DUDGEON LIGHTVESSEL. One fixed light.	Near the Shoal. Moored in 8 fathoms.	53 15 0 N 0 56 0 E	38		10	1736	73

YORKSHIRE.

Name and Description of Light.	Situation.	Geographical Position.	Height above High Water.	Height of Building, base to vane.	Visible in Miles.	Year completed.	Page of Work.
HUMBER RIVER:— SPURN LIGHTVESSEL. One revolving light every half minute.	Off the Point. Moored in 8 fathoms.	53 34 0 N 0 13 0 E	38		10	1820	82
SPURN. High light fixed. Low light fixed.	On the Point.	53 34 44 N 0 7 9 E	93 54	108 60	15 11	1770 1851	82
BULL SAND LIGHTVESSEL. One fixed light.	S.E. end of the Sand. Moored in 4½ fathoms.	53 34 0 N 0 5 0 E	21		10	1832	83
STALLINGBOROUGH. One fixed light to W.S.W.	At the Ferry.	53 37 0 N 0 10 0 W					

Name and Description of Light.	Situation.	Geographical Position.	Height above High Water.	Height of Building, base to vane.	Visible in Miles.	Year completed.	Page of Work.
KILLINGHOLME. Three fixed lights.	South Killingholme.	53 39 0 N 0 12 0 W	68 35 37	77 45 45		1836 1836 1852	84
PAULL. One fixed light.	Near the S.W. end of the Village.	53 43 0 N 0 13 0 W	36	20	7	1836	84
HEBBLES LIGHT-VESSEL. One red light.	South side of Channel. Moored in 5 fathoms.	53 44 0 N 0 16 0 W	16		5	1839	86
Bridlington. One fixed light while 9 feet water.	North Pierhead.	54 5 12 N 0 11 42 W	21		8	1852	88
FLAMBOROUGH. One revolving light every two minutes; twice bright, once red.	On the Head.	54 7 0 N 0 5 0 W	214	86	19	1806	88
Scarborough. One red light, while 10 feet water.	Vincent Pier.	54 17 0 N 0 23 0 W	58	56	13	1806 1843	89

THE SOUTH-EASTERN COAST OF ENGLAND, ETC.

The VARIATION of the COMPASS, in 1856, in the Thames Mouth and the Downs is about 21° 36'; off Yarmouth, 21° 0'; and off the Humber, 22° 22'. These variations *decrease* about 6° 27' annually.

SECTION I.

THE RIVERS THAMES AND MEDWAY, BETWEEN GRAVESEND AND ROCHESTER AND THE NORE.

THE RIVER THAMES, whose estuary may be considered to commence with Sea Reach, drains an area of 5,000 square statute miles. The jurisdiction of the Corporation of the city of London extends between the highest water mark on every side, from above the village of Staines, in Middlesex, 20 miles West of London Bridge, to the Crowstone, a mile below the town of Leigh, on the Essex shore, and to Yantlet Point, on the Kentish shore. The limit on the Medway is below Upnor castle.

The LIMITS of the Port of London are,—on the West, London Bridge; and on the East, a line extending from the North Foreland in a true N. by W. direction to the Naze of Essex, and nearly touching the Gunfleet lighthouse.

The soil of the river between London Bridge and the main sea is vested in the Trinity House, who are the conservators, for the benefit of poor and decayed seamen, their wives, widows, and orphans, and no ballast may be raised without its authority.

A description of and directions for the river between London Bridge and Gravesend will be found in our "Piloting Directions for the Thames and Medway," 1854, Section I.

GRAVESEND was formerly more important in a mercantile view than now, for vessels sailing from the Port of London were obliged to clear out at Gravesend; but as it is still the starting point for sea voyages, it maintains some importance. It is now chiefly noted as a pleasure and watering place, of easy access from London.

Gravesend has a very commodious and handsome pier, 160 feet long, consisting of columns or piles of cast iron, supporting a floor or stage, extending outward nearly 50 feet beyond low water mark. At a quarter of a mile lower is another pier, that of the *Royal Terrace*.

At half a mile below the Town Pier was formed the station of the *Gravesend and Rochester Railway*, parallel to the canal to Rochester, but the canal has been filled up, and the railway connected with the North Kent line to London. From the river is seen the rural church of *Milton*, with a cluster of trees about it. The village of Milton, now incorporated with Gravesend, was for many years extinct. The town of Gravesend has very much increased of late years, from the facility of railway and steamboat communication with London, and, with Milton to the East, extends along the river for above 1 mile.

B

Directly opposite to the eastern part of Gravesend is *Tilbury Fort*, having a strong battery, garrisoned by a small detachment, or a company of invalids.   There is a regular ferry to this place from Gravesend, and a railway is constructed from London, which connects Tilbury (and of course Gravesend, by the ferry) and Southend with the metropolis.

Outward bound vessels are obliged to stop here, in order to land the customhouse officer; and a sentinel at the block-house, on the eastern extremity of the town, gives notice, by the firing of a musket, to vessels coming up the river, that they may receive on board the necessary customhouse officers, who are here in waiting for the purpose. The spot beyond which no vessel is allowed to pass, without its clearance, is denoted by an obelisk, erected on the bank, a little above the site of the canal basin.

The shores of GRAVESEND REACH are shoal to a considerable distance from shore, but the water in mid-channel is deep, and the tide is rapid.   If it be intended to anchor here, when the shipping is numerous, your vessel should have a good scope of cable at once, lest the anchor come home, and you get athwart-hawse.   In the night, especially, keep well over towards the North shore.*

You proceed downward with Gravesend church open to the northward of the Block-house, until Denton and Gravesend mills become a sail's breadth open, or the two mills and Milton church at equal distances.   These marks will lead clear of the bank called the *Oven*, stretching out from the *Coal-house Point*, more than half a cable's length from shore, and lying with the coal-house on with the East end of *East Tilbury church*.   A *black nun buoy*, of large size, surmounted by a ball, has been placed on the Oven spit, with Hope Point battery and East Tilbury church in a line.   By night you will know when you are to the eastward, by the light of Mucking being of the natural colour, while to the westward of the line of direction, or bearing N.E. by E., it is red.   Here you enter the *Hope*.

HOPE REACH.—The HOPE begins at the *Coal-house* or *Upper Hope Point*, and extends between marshes on each side, to the *Sea Reach*, N.E. and N.E. by E.   At its entrance, on the left, is the *Oven*, before mentioned; and the shelf continues along shore to Mucking Flat, which fills all the bight between the creeks of Mucking and Stanford-le-Hope, and extends one-third over the river.

. In proceeding down this Reach, you see to the *eastward* the conspicuous church of *Cliff*, with a chalk pit below it; and to the *westward* and N.W. the churches of *East Tilbury, Mucking, and Stanford-le-Hope*: more to the N.E. are those of *Corringham* and *Fobbing*.   Mucking church may be known by having a shingled spire on a tower steeple.   That of Stanford-le-Hope has a tower on its North side.   Corringham church has a high shingled spire, and Fobbing an embattled tower steeple.   *Pitsey church*, which stands to the N.E. of all these, has a shingled spire.

In proceeding from Gravesend Reach you enter the Hope with the mark above mentioned, Gravesend mill a little open to the left of Denton mill.   With the Hope Point Battery small house and East Tilbury church in one, N.N.W., you will be below the Oven, and the course thence down the Hope will be N.E. ½ N., towards Fobbing church, which should be kept in this direction until Mucking church bears N.W. ½ N., and Cliff church S. by E., whence the course into Sea Reach is E. by S.†

Off Mucking Flat, when turning, you may stand into 5 fathoms, or until you bring Pitsey church about a ship's length on the eastern part of some trees to the East of Fobbing church.

On the East side of the Reach the flood tide is slack; and, close to the shore, no tide sets at all: vessels therefore, when working upward, must not stand too far over to the eastward; because, if the head gets into less water than the stern, it may occasion missing stays, and running on shore.   Near Mucking Flat the ebb sets strongly toward the North shore.

---

* There are several buoys near Gravesend and Tilbury Fort, but they are merely transporting buoys, and not intended as a direction for the navigation of the river.

† A *measured nautical mile*, for the purpose of exactly ascertaining the speed of steamers or other vessels, has been marked on the East side of the Hope.   The westernmost marks are two beacons, at the eastern point of Cliff Creek, near the Coast Guard station; the eastern-most mark is a beacon close to the house on Lower Hope Point; staff and chimney in one, to the two western beacons in one, is the measured mile.

SEA REACH.—This Reach extends from the Hope to the Nore, a distance of 13 miles. Its general direction is E.S.E. between the extensive marshes on either side: both sides are shoal to a considerable distance, but in the channel way the water is deep; from 5 to 7, 8, and 10 fathoms; but again shoaling eastward, to 4½ and 4 fathoms.

The whole of the Kentish shore, from the Lower Hope Point to the islet called Yantlet, a distance of 7½ miles, is bordered by an extensive flat called the *Blythe Sand*, a great portion of which is uncovered at low water. At 3 miles below the Hope Point, opposite to *Hole Haven*, the bank extends nearly one-half over the river; although not far from its edge are 7 fathoms of water. The mark leading clear of it, in the best water, is West Tilbury mill W.N.W. ½ W. in a line with Chadwell church, and the course E.S.E. ½ E. may be continued to Holy Haven.

LIGHTS.—The Corporation of Trinity House have established two lights for the service of the navigation through Sea Reach, which were first exhibited on October 1st, 1849, in temporary structures. And in September, 1851, the permanent lighthouses having been completed, the lights were shown as follows:—

The *Light* at *Mucking* stands on the North side of the river, and the light burns at an elevation of 40 feet above the level of high water spring tides, and is of the usual or natural colour, except in the following directions, in which the light is coloured red, viz.:—1st. In the direction E. by S. ¾ S. which clears the Scars and Chapman Head. 2nd. On the line of bearing S.W. by W. from the lighthouse, in which direction it strikes the Spit of the Oven's Shoal, a short distance outside the 9 feet mark of low water spring tides. 3rd. On the line of bearing S. ¼ E. from the lighthouse, a narrow strip of red light is shown for the purpose of marking the direct line of bearing of the West Blyth buoy.

The light at *Chapman Head* is a structure similar to that on the Maplin, consisting of iron piles, and standing on the edge of the sand. The light burns at an elevation of 40 feet above the level of high water spring tides, and is of the usual or natural colour; except that upon the line of bearing of the East River Middle Buoy, viz., S.E. by E. ½ E. from the lighthouse, it is coloured *red*, which colour extends to the northward to the lighthouse, on Southend pier, in the direction E. by S. ¼ S.

These two lights, both on the North side of the river, will serve to keep vessels, going up or down, away from the dangerous Blythe Sand. For having arrived off the upper light, a direct course toward that off Chapman Head, about E. by S. ¾ S., will lead clear of the edge of the Blythe; and from the Chapman light, a direct course to the Nore light, S.E. by E., will carry a vessel through the middle of the fairway.

In sailing down you leave on the larboard hand the inlet called *Shell Haven*, which may be known by a house, with some trees about it, standing on its eastern bank.* *Holy* or *Hole Haven* is 1¼ miles lower, and known by the houses called the *Checkers* and *World's End*, on the *Isle of Canvey*. At three-quarters of a mile beyond the latter are the *Skar Houses*. The Isle of Canvey, hence eastward, to Leigh Creek, is very low and marshy.

On the north-western Spit of the Blythe Sand a standing beacon was placed; it was in 6 feet, at low water, spring tides, with Pitsey church tower, in line with a farmhouse next eastward of the Thames Haven Cottages, N.N.E. ¼ E.; and the Blythe lower beacon next described, E. by S. ½ S. But this beacon having been repeatedly run down, it was found necessary to take down the remains of it, and a green buoy was moored near its foundation, and a *black buoy* of large size was moored a short distance to the northward of it. (*May*, 1852.)

The *Blythe Lower Beacon* stands just opposite and below the entrance of Holy Haven. A black buoy marked its situation until June, 1847, when a new standing beacon, of a triangular form, coloured black, and surmounted by a staff and cage, was placed upon the *eastern* part of the Sand, with Fobbing church, its width on the West end of Shell Haven Trees, N.N.W. ¾ W.

The southern shore of Canvey Island is bordered by the bank called the *Chapman*, which extends to a mile beyond its eastern point. The greater part is dry at low water,

---

* Within the extent of a mile above Shell Haven is the site of the 'THAMES HAVEN,' with its tide dock, and closed docks for colliers and merchandize, as described in the prospectus of the Company, 1840. A branch railway now connects it with the Southend and London line.

and it extends, generally, more than half a mile from shore. On the edge of it stands the *lighthouse* before described.

Upon this bank a clump of rocky spots, called the *Skars*, stretches along shore from Holy Haven to below the *Skar houses*. The Skars extend a cable's length from shore, and are steep-to. The Haven's mouth, kept well open, leads clear of them. The edge is indicated by a strong rippling of the tide.

The courses from off Holy Haven to Leigh Road are S.E. by E. ¼ E. 1¾ miles, and E.S.E. ¼ E. 3½ miles. This leads down between the Blythe and the Chapman, within a quarter of a mile of the latter, and in the best water, 10 to 8, 7½, 5, and 4½ fathoms. Throughout this tract the flood sets nearly true West; it is very rapid, and the courses must be regulated accordingly.

LEIGH ROAD.—The shoals which encumber the navigation of Sea Reach have varied in their form and situation very considerably at different periods. From the last examination it appears that the shoal now called the Leigh Middle has shifted to the northward and eastward of the former site of the River Middle Ground, thus narrowing the channel to the North of it, called the Leigh Road, or Channel.

At present the Leigh Middle Shoal extends from a little below the line of the pier at Southend for above 2 miles in a N.W. by W. direction, having on its shoalest parts from 8 to 12 feet least water. The southern face of this shoal part is marked by two buoys, the East River Middle, *red and white striped*, and the River Middle *red* buoy.

The former mark for leading through the Leigh Channel to the northward of the Middle Ground, viz., the lighthouse on the extremity of Southend pier, in one with the extreme tree on Shoeburyness, E. by S. nearly, now leads over the flat in from 14 to 16 feet least water. Therefore a more northern course should be taken. There is also a channel along the edge of the Chapman, separated from the Leigh Channel by the Little Middle Ground. This has a depth of from 10 to 20 feet, being narrow, and the banks on each side steep-to. By night the Leigh Middle Sand is indicated by the Chapman Head Light appearing of a *red* colour, as previously stated.

Leigh Ray and *Hadleigh Ray*, two channels which lead across the mud flats to the respective towns, have their entrance about half a mile to the N.W. of Southend pier; a *black buoy*, marked Spit, has been placed to mark this entrance on the South side.

On the South side of the Fairway Channel, between the western end of the Leigh Middle Ground and the flats off Yantlet Creek, is a shoal of 15 and 16 feet least water, called the Yantlet Middle Ground. This is nearly 1½ miles in length, running parallel with the course of the channel, which is about three-fourths of a mile in breadth. There is also a channel South of the Yantlet Middle Ground. A *black buoy*, marked *Yantlet*, has been placed on the West end of Yantlet Flats, in 3 fathoms at low water, with Minster church S.E. by S., and St. Mary's church, S.W. ½ W. (*March*, 1851.)

On the South side of the river, opposite the buoy of the "East River Middle," and 1½ miles S.S.W. from it, is a *black buoy*, called that of the *Jenkin*, which is designed to facilitate the navigation of the swash called the Jenkin, lying between the Nore Sand and the Isle of Grain, noticed hereafter in the directions for the Medway. At 1½ miles below the Jenkin buoy is the white buoy on the Nore Sand; and at 2 miles S.E. by E. ½ E. from the latter is the Nore Light. Therefore, in proceeding eastward from Leigh Road, you leave the black buoy of the Jenkin, the white buoy on the Nore Sand, and the Nore light on the starboard, while the striped buoy of Leigh Middle, and the Shoebury buoys (*black*), are to be left on the larboard side.

From Leigh Road, with 4 fathoms of water, a direct course to the Nore light vessel is S.E. ¼ E. 5 miles; and to the West Shoebury buoy S.E. by E. ¼ E. 4¾ miles. The depths will be best understood by reference to the chart.

SOUTHEND.—This fashionable bathing place is nearly 2½ miles to the eastward of the eastern extremity of Canvey Island. The houses extend in a continuous line, and have a handsome appearance from the river. The upper part of the town is elevated; it stands on a high bank of clay and gravel, and commands extensive views. Here is a spacious hotel, adapted to attract numerous visitors to this favorite spot. As noticed on a previous page, this town is connected with the metropolis by a railway passing Tilbury, &c.

A pier has been constructed, which, from the East end of the Terrace, extends 5,500 feet from shore, over a firm bank of hard sand, and on the extremity of it is the *pier-house*, on which is a *red light*.

The little town of LEIGH is 2¼ miles to the westward of Southend. Its ancient church, with a lofty square tower, is conspicuous, being situate on the rising land. It is inhabited chiefly by fishermen engaged in the shrimp trade. On the shore, at less than a mile to the eastward of it, is the *Crowstone* or *London Stone*, which marks the eastern termination of the conservatorial jurisdiction of the city of London, as we have shown in the chart, and in page 1.

The MAPLIN.—The bank called the *Western Maplin* extends from off Southend to the distance of 7 miles eastward, and its breadth off Shoebury-ness is a mile from shore. The black buoy, called the *Middle Shoebury buoy*, which formerly lay off the *Ness*, has been removed rather more than a mile eastward from its former station.

On the West end of the Maplin a black buoy has also been placed, in 4 fathoms, and called the *West Shoebury* or *Shoebury-ness* buoy.

The sand between the East Shoebury buoy and the Blacktail Spit buoy having grown out to the southward and eastward, the East Shoebury buoy has been moved about half a mile E. by S. from its former position, into 6 fathoms low water.

The NORE LIGHTVESSEL is the first of the kind which was established. It has one lantern only, but displays a light of great brilliancy, which may be seen from every direction; it was formerly fixed, but now *revolves* once in half a minute, to distinguish it from the masthead lights of the numerous vessels which usually are anchored near it. The vessel is painted *red*, with the word NORE, in white letters, on each side. The height of the lantern above the level of the water is 33 feet, and the light may be seen at 10 miles off. During the day a *red* ball is shown at the masthead, and a gong is sounded in foggy weather. The vessel lies with the Garrison Point of Sheerness W.S.W. ¾ W. 3¼ miles; Minster church, on with the easternmost part of a triangular field, called *Mizzen-hedge*, bearing S.S.W. ¼ W.; and Great Wakering church, N.N.E.

The lightvessel lies on the eastern extremity or spit of the *Nore Sand*, which is situate at the distance, by water, of 41 miles (47 *statute*) from London Bridge. It is from this point that vessels usually take their departure both for the North and South Channels in the mouth of the river. Between it and Sheerness is the anchorage commonly called THE NORE, and the Bar of Sheerness Harbour, on the shoalest part of which there are 12 and 15 feet at low water.

SHEERNESS.—The Nore Sand extends about 4 miles N.W. by W. ½ W. from the lightvessel. Its middle part, lengthwise, is narrow, and dry at low water, with common tides.

Jenkin Swash lies to the South of the Nore sand; at its entrance is from 4 to 5 feet at low water. In order to facilitate the navigation through the Swash from the Thames to the Medway, a black buoy is laid at the entrance. This buoy is to be left on the larboard or eastern side, when coming in from the northward. At the S.E. end of the Swash there is now a *red buoy*, in 9 feet water, marked *Grain Spit*, which is to be left on the westward or starboard side.

The Passage into the Medway lies between the *Cant* on the larboard side, and the *Nore*, with *Sheerness Middle Ground*, on the starboard. The Cant is that extensive flat which extends from the Isle of Sheppey, and which is uncovered to a very considerable distance from shore. *Sheerness Middle Ground* forms the bar of the Medway, and has on its edge a *black buoy*, in 2¼ fathoms, which, on entering, is to be left on the starboard side. At 1¼ miles W. by S. above the buoy is the anchorage of the *Little Nore*.

The Anchorage at the Nore is either to the eastward or westward of the light, between the bar and Nore Sand, in from 6 to 9 fathoms. The best marks are Minster church S.S.W. ¾ W., and the Nore light N. ¾ W.

The anchorage at the Little Nore is at nearly a mile E.N.E. from Sheerness or Garrison Point, and 2¼ miles W. by S. from the Nore light, and lies with Queenborough church S.W. ¼ W., on the West end of the Turf Redoubt, a little to the eastward of the town of Sheerness, and the New church at Mile Town in one with the mark trees on the Furze hills S. ½ W.

In proceeding from the Great to the Little Nore, you will bring Minster church S.S.W. on the first hollow or depression of land eastward of the westernmost cliff of Sheppey, and should stand toward it until a beacon, with Sheerness Point, appears a short handspike's length open to the northward of a chimney with a white top, in the second buildings to the southward of the Garrison Point at Sheerness. Then steer more to the westward, and when so far advanced as to have Minster church upon the western declivity of the West Cliff, steer West, northerly, and bring the beacon midway between the first and second buildings to the southward of the Garrison Point. When Queenborough church comes to the East end of Mile Town, bring the beacon to touch the South side of the first buildings to the southward of the Garrison Point. These marks lead up in the best water, until Queenborough church bears from the anchorage as above. A common mark for anchoring at the Little Nore is, the outer Lazaret in Stangate Creek just open of the Garrison Point.

On the eastern point of the Isle of Grain there are two black beacons and one white beacon. These marks are serviceable for proceeding from the Great to the Little Nore, above described. When to the South of the Nore light, bring the Cockleshell boathouse on the S.E. point of the Isle of Grain on with Garrison Point, which will lead in. To clear the Middle ground, do not bring the southern tree at the foot of the hill, open North of the outer or northern black beacon above mentioned; and the white beacon and inner black beacon in one clear the coast.

The *Common Roadstead* for ships that ride windbound within the Medway is at *Blackstakes*, or below the West spit of Queenborough Swale, in from 3 to 5 fathoms.

With the ebb tide there is a strong eddy within, on the western shore; and at Sheerness another, equally strong with flood.

Between Sheerness and Queenborough is a shelf of mud, called the *Lapwell* or *Lappel*, which dries at low water. From the town, at the South end of the Royal Dock and mast pond at Sheerness, is a pier or wharf; there is also on the Lappel a tide pier. It is improper for any vessel to sail over or near the tide pier, there being no depth of water for vessels of more than 4 feet draught, when the tide is over the same.

RIVER MEDWAY.—In the Medway, as in the Thames, the several bends are denominated Reaches, as follows:—

1. *Sheerness Reach.*—This Reach extends S.W. by W. and W.N.W. 2 miles, to the South side of the Isle of Grain. The breadth of the river is here three-quarters of a mile, and the depths, in the channel way, vary from 12 to 10, 6, and 5 fathoms. The Garrison Point is steep-to, but the Isle of Grain side shoal to a considerable distance, and the shoal extends eastward so as to form *Sheerness Middle Ground.* Over the latter, with the tide, you may pass W. $\frac{1}{2}$ S., with the Garrison Point in a line with Cockle Shell house, on Corner Point, on the Isle of Grain; leaving the *Cant* on the larboard side, and thence rounding into the river.

The majestic line of ships moored off the Isle of Grain, at *Blackstakes, &c.*, sufficiently indicate the moorings. To the eastward and southward you have the *Lapwell Bank*, mentioned, and the entrance of *Queenborough Swale.* Off the last is a bar of 12 feet.

2. *Salt Pan Reach*, in continuation of *Sheerness Reach*, bisects the lowest depression of the marshes in the valley of Medway. It is 2 miles in length, from the mill at the Salt Pans to *East Hoo Creek*, and extends W.N.W. The eastern side bounds the noted quarantine station, *Stangate Creek*. Both sides of this Reach are shoal to a very considerable distance from shore, the depths in midchannel are 7, 10, 8, and 6 fathoms.

A mark for the anchorage at Blackstakes is, West Hoo church, having a spire steeple, just open of Sharpness.

3. *Kit's Hole Reach*, extending S.W. more than a mile, is nearly half a mile in breadth. Rainham church, nearly S.W. $\frac{1}{4}$ W., leads down in the best water, 6, 7, 8, 6, and 5 fathoms.

4. *Long Reach*, between the Beacon Point of Oakum Marsh and West Hoo Creek, extends nearly W.N.W. 2 miles. The North side of the channel is limited by an extensive shoal, called the *Muscle Bank*, which contracts the channel to one-third of the distance between the two shores. The depths in the best water are from 4 to $3\frac{1}{2}$, 2, $2\frac{1}{2}$, $3\frac{1}{2}$, 4, and 5 fathoms. The leading mark through the Reach is Minster church, in Sheppey, a sail's breadth open of the beacon upon Oakumness; or, in the contrary direction, Frindsbury upper mill, on with a white house, a ship's length to the southward of *Upnor castle.*

5. *Folly or Pincup Reach*, extends nearly S.W. by S. two-thirds of a mile. Its western point is *Hooness* or *Folly Point*, which bears from Darcnetness W. by S. rather more than half a mile. The Reach is bounded on the N.W. and West by the *Hoo*

Flats, on the East by *Bishop's Marsh* and *Nor Marsh.* In the upper part is a Middle Ground, having in one or two spots only 4 feet over it at low water, and the southern extremity of which lies with *Upnor castle* just clear of Hooness.

You steer about S. by W. until the easternmost windmill on the South shore, bearing nearly S.W. by W., comes on with a barn on which a target is conspicuously painted. This mark leads to the S.E. of the Middle Ground; and when Frindsbury upper mill comes a little open of *Cat'sness*,[*] you will be to the southward of it, and should steer towards Hooness in order to enter the next Reach, with Hoo church N. by W.

The flood in this Reach sets upon the Hoo or western shore, and the ebb in the opposite direction, running strongly into and through South Yantlet into Bartlet and Rainham Creeks.

6. *Gillingham Reach.*—On entering this Reach, you will see before you, to the West, the ancient church and village of *Gillingham*, from which the Reach derives its name; and beyond these a fort, originally intended to annoy the ships of an hostile invader. The Reach extends 1¼ miles W.N.W., and the course through, halfway up, is in this direction along the North shore, until you advance toward Gillingham Fort, where the best water is more to the southward, the ground toward *Cat'sness*, the western point of Hoo marshes, being shoal. The South side of the Reach is altogether shoal, and the bank in the lower part extends more than halfway over the river.

7. *Short, or Sovereign's Reach*, from *Cat'sness* to *Finsboroughness*, extends N. by E., and is bordered by a sandy flat on each side, shelving from the marshes. The western side is buoyed, so as to mark the best channel, and here three-decked ships are commonly moored.

8. *Cockham Wood Reach*, between *Finsboroughness* and the *London Stone*, is three-quarters of a mile in length, and lies in a N.W. by W. direction. Its depths are from 12 to 15 feet at low water, and buoys indicate mid-channel. The best water is toward the Finsboro' or western shore.

9. *Upnor Reach*, from the London Stone to Chatham dockyard, is three-quarters of a mile long. Its direction is S.W. by S., between the castle and village of Upnor, on the West side, and the marshes on the East. The remains of the castle, so called, now constitute a powder magazine, and are an ornament to the shore. The depths in mid-channel are from 12 to 16 feet, and the buoys indicate the best water. The flood sets with some degree of strength upon the western shore.

St. Mary's, or Finsboro' Creek, between Gillingham Fort and Upnor Reach, makes an island of the Finsboro' marshes, and serves with the tide as a passage for craft, &c.

10. *Chatham Reach* extends S.S.W. from Upnor Reach to the town of CHATHAM, and in the greater part of its eastern shore is that of the Royal Dockyard, Ordnance Office, &c. The western shore is a low marsh. From St. Mary's Creek to Chatham Jetty the shore is flat and driest; but the lower shore is bolder, and the buoys show the proper course. The depths are 3, 3½, 2⅓, and 3 fathoms to the Ordnance Office, above the Dockyard: but in the bend of the river along the town they suddenly diminish, and form a bar across the river of only 4, 5, and 6 feet at low water.

11. *Limehouse Reach*, in a North and South direction, extends from Chatham to Frindsbury, nearly a mile. Having passed the bar just noticed, you will find the water deepen to 18, 15, 18, and 12 feet. Here you have, on the left over the marshes, the city of ROCHESTER. The river as below continues buoyed, and the buoys are therefore a sufficient guide to the next Reach.

12. *Bridge Reach* extends from Rochester Point to the bridge, three-eighths of a mile; the depths at low ebbs are from 12 to 9 feet. A mud flat from the North shore extends nearly one-third over the river, and the best water is toward the South shore. The bridge is in length 560 feet, and 15 feet in breadth. It is formed with eleven arches; the starlings of which occupy so much of the course that there is left but 230 feet for the tide of flood and ebb to act in. The new railway bridge crosses the river close to the ancient bridge. The entrance of the *Tunnel* constructed for the Thames and Medway Canal, now used for the North Kent Railway to Gravesend and London, is at one-quarter of a mile above the church of Frindsbury, on the North shore; and the station of the North Kent Railway is close to the shore.

* *Cat'sness* is the S.W. point of the Hoo marshes, in the next or Gillingham Reach.

TIDES IN THE RIVERS THAMES AND MEDWAY.

In the river Thames the time of flowing and the perpendicular rising of the first tide after the full and change of the moon are nearly as follow :—At London Bridge the time is 2^h 15′; and at the Docks, 2^h 10′; at Blackwall and Woolwich, 2^h 5′; at Purfleet, 1^h 45′; at Gravesend, 1^h 30′; at Holy Haven, 12^h 45′; and at the Nore, 12^h 30′. At London spring tides rise from 17 to 18 feet; at Purfleet, nearly 17; at Holy Haven, 15; and at the Nore, about 14 feet. Allowance must, however, be made for the wind, which frequently affects the tide considerably.

It appears, therefore, that the tide flows at the Nore $1\frac{3}{4}$ hours before it is high water at London Bridge; and after it flows there, by the ground, it runs upward, in the middle of the river, for nearly half an hour; at which time the water, perhaps, has fallen a foot in height. In the same manner it rises 1 foot before the flood appears to run.

It has been remarked that, during strong N.W. gales, the tide marks high water earlier in the river Thames than otherwise, and does *not give so much water*, whilst the ebb tide runs out later, and marks lower; but upon the gales abating and the weather moderating, the tides put in and rise much higher, whilst they also run longer before high water is marked, and with more velocity of current, nor do they run out so long or so low.

In this river, as in other winding rivers, the stream passing from one reach to another does not immediately wind round the point between; but, setting *directly forward*, it first, and with greater force, strikes against the shore which immediately opposes it. The distance to which the stream then runs along the opposing coast, before it acquires the direction of the new channel, depends on the velocity of the stream, the relative width of the river, and the difference in the course or direction of the two reaches. In those parts where the river is narrow, the stream rapid, and the difference in the course considerable, the water will strike with violence against the shore lying as above described: when the resistance which it meets with, and the greater elevation thereby occasioned, will be the means of repelling it back toward the opposite side, above or below the point, according to the ebb or flood; and it appears that this action of the tide, in its ebb and flood, has, in the process of ages, given to the river its present configuration in different reaches.

At Rochester the mean time of high water, on the first tide after full and change, is 1^h; at Chatham, 12^h 54; and in Sheerness Dockyard, 12^h 40′; the vertical rise at the bridge is 20 feet; at Sheerness, 14 feet.[*]

Ships drawing 20 feet, and bound down the river from Chatham, should not get under way until the last quarter-flood of spring tides, and with the wind at West, W. by N., W.N.W., or N.W. by W.

SECTION II.

THE NORE TO MARGATE ROADS.

The COAST.—From SHEERNESS POINT the coast of the Isle of Sheppey trends irregularly $6\frac{1}{2}$ miles S.E. to WARDEN POINT on the *Land's End*. At halfway between are the church, mill, and village of MINSTER; which, standing on the rising ground, are conspicuous from sea. Warden Point is the most elevated part of the coast: and the land drops suddenly towards *Shellness*, a low point which terminates the island at 3 miles more to the S. by E. To the northward of the Isle of Sheppey is an extensive flat, stretching $2\frac{1}{2}$ to 5 miles to the deeper channels to the entrance of the Thames. These flats, called the *Cant* to the West, and the *Spaniard, &c.*, to the East, are the remains of the island of Sheppey, which, entirely formed of clay, is washed away by the action of the sea to such an extent that the church of Minster, a century since in the centre of the island, is not more than two-fifths of a mile from the shore. The outer edge of this flat is marked by buoys, presently described.

---

[*] In the Medway the flood stream runs up, in mid-channel, from 15 to 20 minutes after high water at Sheerness Dockyard; but at the Nore lightvessel the flood stream runs up the Thames for half an hour after high water at the Dockyard.

EAST SWALE.—The EAST SWALE is a portion of the river which forms Sheppey Island. Its entrance lies between a hard sand called the *Columbine* on the North, and *Whitstable Flats* on the South; and it forms an excellent harbour for small vessels, more especially since it has been regularly buoyed. Westward of the Columbine is the southern part of the *Cant*, having on it an extensive oyster ground, and a mussel bank, and beyond this is *Shellness*, the S.E. point of Sheppey Island, having two dwelling houses upon it, called *Paul's houses*, and a signal beacon.

At 3 miles above Shellness, on the South or larboard side, is the entrance of *Faversham Creek*, distinguished by its beacon. Opposite to this, on Sheppey, is *Harty church* and village: and in the river, between these, nearly two-thirds from the South shore, is a bank, called the *Horse*, which is partly dry at low water, and 1¼ miles in length. On the East end of the latter is a *red buoy*, which lies with the church of Herne hill, nearly South, just open to the eastward of that of Graveney.

WHITSTABLE.—At 3 miles S.E. by E. from Shellness are the town and harbour of Whitstable. This harbour, formed as shown on the chart, was first opened in April, 1832. It was constructed by the spirited proprietors of the Canterbury and Whitstable Railway, being very commodious for the loading and unloading of commercial vessels; but it is to be regretted that, on the oyster ground in front of it, there is a depth of only 3 feet at low water.

The EAST SWALE is one of the best small harbours in this kingdom: and vessels losing their cables and anchors, or meeting with any other accident in the navigation between the River Thames and the Downs, may here find a secure retreat until their damage is repaired.

FOR SAILING OUT OF THE EAST SWALE you must have a leading wind; and, if your ship draws 15 or 16 feet of water, you are to wait till the water is so high as to reach the foot of the beacon at the mouth of Faversham Creek, which will be about the first third of the flood; at that time there are 3 fathoms on the East end, which part of the channel has less depth of water than the rest.

In thick weather, when the marks are invisible, if you can see the point of Shellness, steer in for it, and bring it to bear W. by S., which will carry you in safely. Or, if Paul's houses can be seen, steer for them until they bear W. by N., and Shellness W. by S. Then proceed as above directed.

BUOYS, &c.—Four buoys are placed in the entrance; that is to say, two on the Columbine, one between the East end of the Columbine and Whitstable, and one near the spit of the Pollard, on the South side, to be left in entering, as follows:—

The Outer Buoy of the Columbine lies in 9 feet; to starboard.

The second, or Spit buoy of the Columbine, red, lies in 6 feet; to starboard.

The Ham Gat Buoy, on the West end of the Columbine, red, lies in 6 feet of water; to starboard.

Whitstable Street Buoy, black, *with staff and ball*, in 12 feet; to port.

The Pollard Spit buoy, black, in 8 feet; to port.

Between the buoys of the Columbine and Whitstable Flats the course in mid-channel is W.S.W. ¼ W. Having passed the Columbine Spit, bring Judd's hill and Ore mill in a line bearing W.S.W. ¼ W., and keep them so until you are 2 miles above Shellness. There is good anchorage all the way up, in from 3 to 5 fathoms, clay bottom, with mud on the surface.

HERNE BAY.—This town is situated at the distance of 4 miles eastward from Whitstable, and 2¾ miles westward from Reculver. From its agreeable situation, and proximity to London, it has lately become a considerable watering place, and now extends about a mile in length, parallel with the shore. The principal feature of the town is the pier, which is constructed of piles; is more than 1,300 yards in length, extending over the sands in a N. ¼ W. direction, and having at its head a depth of 7 feet at low water, spring tides, affording the means of landing at all times. It is provided with cranes and other conveniences for landing goods and passengers, and has a railway down it to the shore, along which goods and passenger cars are propelled by means of a sail. At the western extremity of the town is the coastguard station, and at about a quarter of a mile East of the pier is a low white windmill, used as a seamark; and at a short distance further is a lofty clock tower, built by Mrs. Thwaites, in 1837: off these buildings is a mussel bank of hard gravel. The village of Herne lies enbosomed in trees at 1¼ miles inland, in the direction of the pier; on the high land to the left of the village stands Herne mill (black, with white top), also used as a mark.

The direct course to this place, by the *Overland Channel*, from the white buoy on the West end of the Spaniard, is S.E. by S., and the distance 7 miles; from the black buoy on the East end of the Spaniard the course and distance are S. ¼ E. 5¼ miles; and from the West or beacon buoy of the Last, or Horse Channel, W.S.W. ¼ W. 2½ miles. The water is altogether shoal, as shown by the chart, and the sand is uncovered at low water, to 3 cables' lengths from shore.

RECULVER CHURCH is 3 miles eastward of Herne Bay pier. It is a well known sea mark, preserved by the Trinity House. It is in ruins, and stands close to the shore, which has much washed away. Its two spires are also known as the " Sisters," from a tradition.

MARGATE.—The harbour of Margate is situate in a small bay between two extensive flats of chalk rocks, the *Nayland* on the West, and the *Fulsam* on the East, both of which are covered before high water. The artificial harbour is formed by a stone pier, which commences on the eastern side of the bay, around which the town is situate, and extends 800 feet to the westward, in an irregular curve, leaving the entrance open to the N.W.

MARGATE LIGHT.—A stone lighthouse stands on the pier head, upon the larboard side in entering. This lighthouse is in form of a handsome fluted column, 70 feet in height, and exhibits a *red light*, at 85 feet above the level of high water, which, in clear weather, may be seen at 3 leagues off. The light is kept up from sunset to sunrise, and by day a *blue flag* is kept hoisted during the time that vessels may enter. On the extremity of the jetty, or Jarvis's landing place, is a lantern light for the use of the fishermen, to prevent their running foul of it.

NORE TO MARGATE ROADS, THROUGH THE FIVE-FATHOM AND HORSE CHANNELS.

Buoys, &c.—The following are the names of the buoys, &c., which mark out the tracks through these channels; to which are annexed their number, colour, and the side on which they are to be left in sailing downward.*

NORE LIGHTVESSEL, revolving light, in 4 fathoms, as described on page 5.

WEST SPILE BUOY; *black*, in 12 feet, on the port side, at S.E. 3¾ miles from the Nore light.

The *Spile, Red Sand*, and *Shivering Sand*, now constitute one ridge; which, from the buoy of the Spile to the beacon buoy of the Shivering, extends E. ¾ S., 7½ miles. Some parts are nearly dry at low water.

BUOY OF THE MIDDLE GROUND; *squared black and white*, in 10 feet, on the port side, at 1¼ miles S.E. from the buoy of the Spile.

WEST BUOY of the SPANIARD; *white, with a black staff and ball*, in 10 feet, on the starboard side.

BEACON on the SPIT OF THE MIDDLE GROUND.—A standing beacon stands 10 fathoms from the southern edge of the sand, where it dries at low water spring tides. On the port side.

The MIDDLE BUOY of the SPANIARD; *white*, was first laid down in May, 1837, and lies at 1½ miles E.S.E. from the West buoy in 13 feet, on the port side.

EAST BUOY of the SPANIARD, *black, with a staff and inverted cone*, in 10 feet, on the starboard side. Having passed this on the starboard side, the course to the *Queen's Channel* is S.E. by E. ¼ E. 3 miles; and to the Horse Channel, S.S.E. ¼ E. 5¼ miles.

The MIDDLE GROUND, with the GILLMAN, forms the North side of the FIVE FATHOM CHANNEL, the South side of which is formed by the Spaniard. Upon the middle of the Spaniard there is a depth of only 6 feet at low water, and upon several spots less. In the Channel the depths are from 12 to 18 feet.

* The marks for all these buoys, &c., are given in the Directions which accompany our large Chart of the River Thames, to which the attention of the reader is directed.

THE NARROWS, HORSE CHANNEL, ETC.

The HORSE CHANNEL has been buoyed, with three black buoys on the South side of the *Last*, which forms the North side of the channel, and a red one on the *Horse*, on the South side of the channel. The buoys lie as follow :—

WEST BUOY *of the* LAST; *black*, with a *staff and ball*, in 11⅓ feet, on the port side.

TAIL *of the* HORSE; *red*, in 10 feet, on the starboard side.

MIDDLE BUOY *of the* LAST; *black*, in 10 feet, on the port side.

EAST BUOY *of the* LAST; *black*, in 10 feet, on the port side, and on the southernmost part of the East end of the sand.

GORE PATCH BUOY; *striped black and white*, in 6 feet, on the port side.

HOOK BEACON, surmounted by a staff and globe, is placed on a spot which dries at low water, spring tides, on the S.W. Spit of Margate Sand, on the port side.

The MARGATE SAND has extended lately to the eastward on the South side, consequently the white beacon buoy on the South side has been removed, and the two following substituted.

S.E. MARGATE SAND.—A *black* nun buoy, marked "S.E. Margate," in 4 fathoms water, on the port side.

SOUTH MARGATE BUOY.—A *black* can buoy, marked "South Margate," in 4 fathoms water, on the port side.

THE EAST BUOY OF MARGATE SAND.—*Black*, with *staff* and inverted cone, to the North or port hand.

DIRECTIONS.

FIVE-FATHOM CHANNEL.—The recent extension of the sands to the westward, and general diminution of depth, render former instructions for proceeding from the Nore to the Five-fathom Channel worse than useless. The passage over the Cant, from the Nore lightvessel, will now be S.E. ¼ S. 5 miles; thus leaving the black buoy of the *Spile* and the buoy of the *Middle Ground* (black and white) on the larboard side.

On crossing the Cant you may keep the Nore lightvessel in the middle of the valley between the high land of Fobbing and the high land to the N.E. of Holy Haven. This leads across the Cant, in 9 or 10 feet at low ebbs, and to near the West buoy of the Spaniard.

The course from the Middle Ground buoy to the middle buoy of the Spaniard is E.S.E. ⅓ E. 2¼ miles; and from the middle buoy to the eastern or beacon buoy, E. ¼ S. 2 miles. When in the Channel, tack upon the first shoal cast on either side, and remember, in all cases, to make allowance for the setting of the tide: and likewise, unless well acquainted, not to proceed but with the flood.

Between the West buoy of the Spaniard and the beacon of the Middle Ground there are not more than 12 or 13 feet of water at low ebbs. The most water in the Channel is on the North side, near the Gillman, which is steep-to. The Spaniard is flat. Vessels drawing more than 12 feet of water should anchor in this channel after four hours' ebb, with the East buoy of the Spaniard about S. by W., distant half a mile, in 16 to 18 feet low ebbs.

HORSE CHANNEL.—FROM *the* EAST BUOY *of the* SPANIARD (with staff and cone) to the HORSE CHANNEL the course and distance across the flats are S.S.E. ¼ E. 5¼ miles. The Last buoy, as already noticed, is black, with a staff and ball. The depth is from 10 to 14 feet, with several shoaler spots. Particular allowance must be made for the tide, which sets nearly across the beam. In running for the buoy of the Last you may bring the low West end of *Cleare wood* upon the East end of *Upper Hale grove*, as shown in the marks given for that buoy. In working you may stand to the westward, till St. Nicholas' church comes on with the Reculvers, and to the eastward until Sarr mill nearly touches the same. The most water will thus be found, being 9 to 11 feet at low ebbs. Great attention must be paid to the time of tide, and to the lead.

If requisite to anchor, before entering the Horse Channel, you may bring up in Horse-shoe Hole, between the South Knoll and Woolpack, in from 15 to 20 feet at low water, with St. Peter's church on the middle of Marsh Bay and the Reculvers, S. by W. ¼ W.; or with the Pan beacon open to the westward of the buoy of the South Knoll.

Those running down from the West buoy of the Last may steer for the buoy on the tail of the Horse (*red*), passing to the northward of it; then steer S.E. by E. ½ E.

From the Horse Channel you enter the channel called the GORE, on the S.W. of Margate Sands, and leave the *striped buoy* on the Gore Patch on the larboard hand.

Pursuing a course S.E. by E. you leave to the northward the *beacon* on the Hook of Margate Sand, and the two black buoys on the South side of the Margate Sand.

SOUTH CHANNEL.—The S.E. by E. course, with the North Down tower on the tip-end of the West cliff of Marsh Bay, is to be continued until Birchington mill, bearing S. by E., is on the Cliffend, and here you change the course to E. by S., with the Reculvers W. by N., which leads into and through the South Channel, until you are off *Longnose*, with Margate new church (near Fort Point) bearing W. by S. Distance on the E. by S. course, 6¼ miles.*

To clear the Point called Longnose, which lies off Foreness, keep Birchington seed mill nearly West, open of Ledge Point; or all St. Margaret's steeple (near the South Foreland) in sight above the land. When the North Foreland lighthouse bears S.S.W. ¼ W., you will be to the eastward of Longnose, which runs off N.E. two-thirds of a mile from Foreness, and has 5 fathoms close to it.

The usual leading mark for going to the southward of the *Cliffend Banks* is a small grove, appearing like a barn, kept open to the southward of the Reculver. In the channel are from 4 to 6 fathoms. With Birchington steeple S. by W., you will have passed the bank, and may stand toward Margate Sand into 5 or 4 fathoms, and toward the shore into the same depth until below Margate. Then stand toward the shore, until Birchington seed mill comes nearly on with Ledge Point, or into 6 and 5 fathoms, and into the same depth toward Margate Sand.

ANCHORAGES.—*In the Gore* you may anchor in 5 fathoms, with St. Peter's church midway between the house and barn in Westgate Bay, and with Monckton beacon on the middle of Upper Hale grove, S. ¼ W., in 4½ to 5½ fathoms. With a northerly wind you may anchor under Margate Sand, off Westgate Bay, with Margate old church on, or nearly on, Nayland Point, and Minster West mill on a barn in the bay, S. by W. ¼ W., where you will have 5 and 6 fathoms, good ground.

Near the Hook you may also anchor in about 5 fathoms, with Monckton beacon anywhere between the West side of Lower Hale grove and the middle of Upper Hale grove; and St. Peter's church, on with the house in Westgate Bay. In *Margate Roads* you may anchor with Margate old church on the pier head, bearing South, and Bishopton farm on the Reculvers, W. ¼ N., in 7 or 7½ fathoms. Another position is at 1 mile lower, with Nayland and Minster East mills in one; Foreness, S.S.E. ½ E. in 6½ or 7 fathoms. The last situation will serve with a southerly wind.

LONGNOSE stretches from Foreness two-thirds of a mile, and is a ledge of rocks that dries in many places at low ebbs, having a red buoy at its extremity.

TIDES.—*About and within the East buoy of Margate Sand* the first of the flood current sets S. by W. southerly; the middle of the stream sets West, and the last N.N.W. and N. by W. The first of the ebb sets N.E.; the middle, S.E. and S.E. by E.; and the last of it, South, and S. by E. But *between the East buoy and the shoal part of Margate Sand* the first of the flood sets due South; the middle, S.W.; and the last, N.N.W. and N. by W. The first of the ebb sets N.N.E.; the middle, E.S.E.; and the last, S. by E. and South.

In the Queen's Channel the tide flows at 12ʰ. Spring tides rise 15 feet, and neaps from 7 to 8 feet. The velocity of the first is about 2¼ knots, and of the latter only 1 knot. Off the Foreland the strength is considerably less.

At *Margate* it flows at 11ʰ 15', and at the *Reculver* at 11ʰ 30'; but the flood continues

---

* From the Gore you may pass to the northward of Cliffend Bank, with Bishopton farm, which stands on the first high land westward of the Reculvers, open a little to the northward of the same; this leads in a fairway between the beacon on the Hook of Margate Sand and Cliffend Bank; and when Birchington steeple bears S. by W., you will be to the eastward of it, and may proceed eastward as most convenient.

In working downward you may stand toward Margate Sand into 5 and 4 fathoms, toward the shore into the same depths, until below Margate, or at anchor in the road.

The thwart mark for the shoal water on Cliffend Bank is Monckton beacon well open to the eastward of Lower Hale grove.

to run until 12ʰ. Spring tides rise about 17 feet. In Margate Roads, and at the Hook of the Sand, they run with a velocity of about 2¼ knots, but near the shore the stream is weak. A great indraught sets into the *East Swale*, which influences the stream over the Flats. The flood here sets W. by S. The tides in the East Swale have been already noticed.

In the Five-fathom Channel it flows at 12ʰ; springs here rise 15 feet, and neaps about 9 feet.

SECTION III.

GENERAL DESCRIPTION OF THE SOUTHERN CHANNELS OF THE THAMES' MOUTH; WITH DIRECTIONS FOR SAILING FROM THE NORE TO THE DOWNS.

The CHANNELS, or PASSAGES, between the Nore and the North Foreland, are formed by several extensive sands, lying nearly in a parallel direction, and whose boundaries are marked out by numerous buoys and beacons, as represented on the charts.

The PRINCIPAL CHANNELS are those called the *Middle* or *Oaze Channel*, the *Knob Channel*, the *Prince's Channel*, the *Queen's Channel*, and the *South Channel*: besides which there are several inferior passages. The GREAT FLAT, which constitutes the basis of the shoals forming these channels, on the South side of the estuary or mouth of the Thames, commences at Sheerness, and extends from 20 to 23 miles to the East, and E.S.E. or S.E. by E. The western part of this flat is called the CANT, of which the northern edge extends 5 miles E.S.E. ½ E., in a line with the bar or Middle Ground of Sheerness, as described in page 5; and thence to the eastern extremity of the Shivering Sand, E. by S. 6 miles. Here it forms a swash at the back, or on the South side of the Shivering and Red Sands; shoals which have, to the southward, the GILLMAN, MIDDLE GROUND, SPANIARD, &c.

To the eastward of these, the bank spreads into the FLAT of the GIRDLER; the northern edge of which extends E. by N. 8 miles, to a passage between this shoal and the LONGSAND, called BULLOCK'S CHANNEL; farther West is THOMAS'S CHANNEL, which lies South and S.S.E. 3¼ miles in length between the Longsand and Girdler.

In the S.E. part the flat is divided by the PRINCE's and QUEEN'S CHANNELS, and terminates in the extremity of Margate Shoals, &c.

In the following description of, and directions for sailing through, the several channels, we commence with those called the *Knob* and *Prince's Channels*: including, in this section, the *Middle* or *Oaze*, *Thomas's*, and the *Queen's Channels*.

The first dangerous sand below the Nore is the Oaze, having only 9 feet on it in some parts at low water. But there is sufficient depth, on either side, for the largest ships. Hence the track from the Nore to the Knob Channel may be either to the North or the South of this sand; that is to say, a ship may pass either through the western part of the *Swin Channel*, leaving the buoy and lightvessel of the *Mouse* on the larboard hand, and the buoys of the Oaze on the starboard; or, through the MIDDLE CHANNEL or OAZE DEEP, leaving the three buoys of the Oaze on the larboard side, and the buoys of the Spile and Shivering on the starboard. The subject will be more readily comprehended by the description of buoys, &c. We commence with the track first mentioned, that on the North side of the Oaze Sand.

DESCRIPTION OF THE BUOYS AND BEACONS, AND THE SIDE UPON WHICH THEY ARE TO BE KEPT IN SAILING FROM THE NORE, THROUGH THE KNOB CHANNEL, TO THE NORTH FORELAND.

NORE LIGHTVESSEL, in 4 fathoms.

CANT BUOY.—On the edge of the Cant Sand, *white*, in 4 fathoms; starboard side.

WEST BUOY OF THE OAZE, large nun, *red*, with *staff and ball*; starboard side.

LIGHTVESSEL ON THE MOUSE, brilliant *fixed* light, in 4½ fathoms, at the S.W. end of the sand; port.

EAST BUOY OF THE OAZE, at the entrance of the Knob Channel, 8¼ miles E. ⅞ S. from the Nore light, large *black* nun, with *staff and ball;* on the starboard side.

BUOY OF THE NEW KNOB, *striped red and white*, in 3½ fathoms; on the port side.

BUOY OF THE KNOB, *red*, in 3¼ fathoms; on the port side.

SHIVERING SAND BUOY, *striped black and white*, with *white head, staff, and ball*, in 3½ fathoms; on the starboard side. Southward of the buoy there is anchorage in 7 to 9 fathoms. This spot is called the *First Deeps.*

EAST GILLMAN BUOY, *black and white in rings*, 1⅓ miles West of the Girdler lightvessel; on the starboard side.

PRINCE'S CHANNEL.

This important channel, between the Girdler and Shingles Sands on the North, and the Pan Sand and Tongue on the South, is now completely marked by its lightvessels, beacons, and buoys. From its easy access, and the openness of its channel, it is in every way preferable to the Queen's Channel. Its West and East entrances are marked by lightvessels, and its limits as follow :—

WEST GIRDLER BUOY, in 2½ fathoms, at the western extremity of the Sand, and half a mile northwards of the lightvessel, on the port hand.

The GIRDLER LIGHTVESSEL is moored in 3½ fathoms at low water, spring tides, and shows *one* bright *revolving light*, with the church spire, midway between George's Farm and Reculvers, S. ¼ E.; the West end of Clear wood, open to the eastward of St. Nicholas' eastern coastguard station, S. ¾ E.; Redding Street beacon, its apparent length open of Northdown Tower, S.E. ¼ S.

The channel between the Girdler lightvessel and the Shivering Sand buoy is clearly indicated by night by the Maplin light, which shows a *white light* over 8° of the circle, striking the Girdler light in the direction of S. ½ W., and the Shivering Sand buoy, S. by W. ¼ W.; you should tack as soon as this bright light is eclipsed either way.

A LIGHTVESSEL showing a *red revolving light* is moored on the North side of the channel, about midway between the Tongue and Girdler lights.—*Oct.* 1, 1856.

The *North side* of the Prince's Channel, in addition to the lightvessel, is marked by two standing iron beacons and buoys in the following order :—

The SOUTH GIRDLER BUOY, *red*, lies in 4 fathoms, about midway between the Girdler beacon and Girdler lightvessel.

The GIRDLER BEACON, placed on the *South Spit* of the South *Girdler Sand*, is distinguished by a triangle, the top of which is 45 feet above low water.

A spit of sand having extended itself from the Girdler Shoal in a S.E. direction, a buoy, coloured *red*, has been placed at the extremity thereof, in 3¾ fathoms.

The SHINGLES BUOY, *red*, lies in 4½ fathoms, about midway between the Shingles and Girdler beacons.

The SHINGLES BEACON, placed on the southern extremity of the dry sand called the *Shingles*, is distinguished by a top in the form of a diamond, which is 45 feet above low water mark.

The four buoys and beacons which denote the *South side* of this channel, and also the lightvessel placed at the East end of the Tongue Sand, which also marks the eastern entrance of the Prince's Channel, are marked and coloured as understated, viz. :—

EAST GILLMAN BUOY, *black and white in rings*, in 12 feet, on the starboard hand.

NORTH PAN SAND BUOY, *black*, lies in 5 fathoms at low water.

N.E. PAN SAND BUOY, *black*, in 7½ fathoms.

NORTH TONGUE BUOY, a *monster black buoy*, with staff and ball, in 6 fathoms.

N.E. TONGUE BUOY, *black*, in 4½ fathoms.

The TONGUE LIGHTVESSEL is moored in the eastern entrance of the Prince's Channel, in 10 fathoms. It shows *two* lights; one at the masthead, which is *white*, and the other at a lower elevation, and coloured *red*. It now lies with Minster East mill, on with the centre of the coastguard station in Westgate Bay, S. by W. ¼ W.; Margate old church the apparent width of its tower open to the eastward of the pier lighthouse; South Shingles beacon, N.W. ¼ N.; South Spit buoy, S.E. ¼ S. It is necessary to insist that vessels should always pass to the northward of this vessel.

The GIRDLER LIGHTVESSEL, described before, will indicate the western entrance of the channel; and from the South of this lightvessel a S.E. by E. ¾ E. course for 3¼ miles will bring you up to the North Tongue buoy; and from this an E.S.E. ½ E. course will lead midway between the N.E. Tongue buoy and Shingles beacon.

Half a mile S.S.E. of the Girdler lightvessel is a spot with 17 feet water, as shown on the chart, which the above course will lead near to; this can be passed to the southward,. or there is deeper water on the track given. No other directions are necessary; the channel is open throughout, and it is only necessary to tack on the first shoal cast, as the banks are steep-to. A small spit extends southward from the Shingles and Girdler beacons.—*September 11th*, 1846.

QUEEN'S CHANNEL.

This channel, to the southward of the Pan Sand and the Tongue, is buoyed as follows. The Girdler lightvessel is useful for making its western entrance. The buoys marking its limits are described as follow :—

BUOY ON THE WEST END OF THE PAN SAND; *chequered black and white*, with a *staff and ball*, in 2¼ fathoms, on the larboard side.

BUOY OF THE SOUTH KNOLL; *black*, in 2½ fathoms, on the starboard side.

PAN SAND BEACON; a standing *beacon*, on the port side, opposite to the South Knoll.

The PAN SAND is about 2 miles in length, and three-quarters of a mile in breadth; at the part to the northward of the beacon it is dry at low water spring tides. On the West end are from 3 to 6 feet; on the middle, 1 foot; and on the East end from 6 to 9 feet.

BUOY ON THE PAN PATCH, off the easternmost end of the Pan Sand; *chequered black and white*, in 2½ fathoms, to be left on the port side. The Patch, which extends hence toward the beacon, has only 9 feet on it at low water.

BUOY ON THE WEDGE, in the Queen's Channel, *black*, in 4 fathoms, on the starboard side, 2½ miles below the Pan Patch buoy. The buoy lies on the North side of the sand, which is about a quarter of a mile broad, and has on it but 1 foot of water at low spring ebbs. The extent of the shoal is about 1 mile E.S.E. and W.N.W.

WEST TONGUE BUOY, near the side of the former beacon, *black and white chequered*, on the port side.

NORTH SPIT BUOY OF MARGATE SAND; *black*, in 8½ fathoms, on the starboard side.

N.E. SPIT BUOY OF MARGATE SAND; a large *nun* buoy, *black and white in vertical* stripes, in 7¾ fathoms. It now lies with the high tower of Moro castle, its width open West of Neptune's tower, bearing S. ¼ W.; Powell's belfry, twice its width open West of the preventive station in Westgate bay, S.W. ¼ W.; North Foreland lighthouse, S. ½ W.; East buoy of Margate Sand, S. by E. southerly; North Spit buoy, W.N.W. —*July*, 1847.

EAST TONGUE BUOY, *chequered black and white*, in 4 fathoms, at the East end of the Tongue Sand; on the port hand.

EAST BUOY OF MARGATE SAND; *black*, with *staff* and *inverted cone*, in 4 fathoms on the starboard side. *Marks*—The cupola of Margate old church in a line with the chancel end of the new church; the high tower of Moro castle between the second and the third black cliffs to the westward of the South cliff at Kingsgate; a tree, which stands to the eastward of Minster East mill, just touching the North side of the Saltwater bathing house, which has a middle gable, at Nayland; the West end of Birchington wood on with the East cliff of Westgate Bay; and the North Foreland lighthouse bearing S. ⅓ W. a little westerly, distant 4¾ miles.

DIRECTIONS FOR SAILING FROM THE NORE, THROUGH THE KNOB, PRINCE'S, AND QUEEN'S CHANNELS, TO THE NORTH FORELAND.

KNOB, or KNOCK CHANNEL.—IN SAILING DOWN FROM THE THAMES MOUTH, or from athwart the Nore, to a fairway between the Oaze and Mouse for the Knob, or Knock Channel, with a westerly wind and a large ship, weigh at half ebb, and steer for the entrance of the Knob Channel, E. by S. 4½ miles, and E. ⅓ S. 4 miles, passing the buoys as before described. But observe throughout the navigation of these channels the tide is a beam tide, for which a particular allowance must be made, according to the wind and velocity of the stream. With the Mouse lightvessel about N.W., the East Oaze buoy S.W., and a depth of 6 or 7 fathoms, the Knob Channel is fairly open.

The entrance of the Knob Channel, between the Mouse and the East end of the Oaze, is 1½ miles wide, and has in it from 7 to 5½ fathoms of water, shoaling inward. Having advanced toward the Mouse buoy, you may steer S.E. toward the monster white buoy on the East end of the Oaze; you will then pass between that buoy and the new Knob, marked by a striped red and white buoy.

From the East buoy of the Oaze (large nun, black staff and ball), steer for the *beacon buoy* of the Shivering Sand, on a course S.E. ¾ S. 2 miles, allowing for wind and tide. Thus you will leave the red buoy of the Knob on the larboard, at two-thirds of that distance. In this course you will have 6 and 7 to 5 fathoms at low water. Between the buoys of the Knob and Shivering there is good anchorage in 6 and 7 fathoms.

From the Shivering Sand buoy, passing the West Girdler buoy and the Girdler lightvessel, the course with the flood is S.W. by S., with the ebb about S.S.W., distance nearly a mile. In this track will be found from 10 to 4 fathoms.. Between the Girdler light and Shivering buoy stand no nearer than in 7 or 6 fathoms on either side.

PRINCE'S CHANNEL.—The passage to the Prince's Channel from the Knob Channel lies between Shivering Sand buoy and the Girdler lightvessel. By day these two marks sufficiently point out the fairway; and by night, also, the revolving light of the Girdler is an excellent guide for turning either eastward or northward.

In addition to the guidance which the Girdler lightvessel affords by night, a bright light is shown in the direction of the fairway between it and the Shivering Sand buoy, from the Maplin pile lighthouse, below the principal red light. This light shows only over 8° of the circle, that is, in the direction between the Shivering Sand buoy and the Girdler lightvessel, or visible between the bearings of N. ½ E. and N. by E. ¼ E.; consequently, when you arrive in the fairway between the lightvessel and buoy, the course is toward or from this light, and tacking as soon as it becomes red on either side.

Having arrived to the southward of the lightvessel, a general E.S.E. course will carry you through the Prince's Channel. The channel is quite clear and open throughout, so that no directions are necessary. The buoys and beacons previously described point out the channel. The banks are steep-to; so that it is only necessary to tack upon the first shoal cast on either side.

QUEEN'S CHANNEL.—*The course and distance from half a mile beyond the Girdler lightvessel* to the chequered beacon buoy on the West end of the Pan Sand, across the FLATS, are S. by E. about 2 miles. With the wind to the southward of West, keep to windward of this course, especially with the ebb, which sets strongly to the E.N.E. In the track are 3½, 3, and 2½ fathoms, but to the westward is more shoal. Vessels drawing 16 or 17 feet should endeavour to cross between half flood and quarter ebb, as they draw more or less water.

At about a mile below, or to the eastward of the beacon buoy of the Pan Sand, the water in midchannel deepens from 2½ to 4½ fathoms, in the space called PAN SAND HOLE. Here is good anchorage, with the standing beacon bearing E. by N. to N.E. from three-quarters to half of a mile, and the black buoy on the South Knoll nearly S.E.

The course from off the West buoy of the Pan Sand, between it and the South Knoll, is S.E. by E. ¼ E. for about 2¼ miles, which will bring you abreast of the chequered buoy on the Pan Patch. In the track you will find from 2½ to 5 fathoms.

The course into the Queen's Channel, from the Pan Patch to between the buoys of the Wedge and the Tongue, is E.S.E. ¾ E. or E. by S., better than 2¼ miles. Here you will have, on the North side, the black monster buoy, and the chequered West Tongue buoy, and the black N.E. buoy of the Tongue; and, on the South, the red buoy on the Wedge. Proceeding hence E.S.E. ½ E., 5½ miles, you will clear the Queen's Channel, leaving the chequered East Tongue buoy and the Tongue lightvessel on the port, and the North Spit and N.E. buoys of Margate Sand on the starboard side.

The TONGUE, which forms the North side of this channel, is about one-third of a mile broad, and 3½ miles long, extending nearly E. by S. and W. by N., and is joined to the Pan Sand Ridge. On each end the depth is about 3½ fathoms; but in some parts there are only 2 and 3 feet at low water.

With a turning wind in this channel you may stand to the northward into 7 fathoms, and toward the Wedge to 8 or 9 fathoms. After passing the Wedge, stand toward the Tongue into 7 or 8 fathoms, and toward the North Spit of Margate Sand into 10 fathoms. In midchannel between the Tongue and the Wedge, and between the Tongue and North Spit, are 11 fathoms at low water.

From off the East buoy of Margate Sand (*black, with inverted cone*) to a fairway off the Foreland, the course and distance are S. by E. ¼ E. 6 miles, as hereafter directed.

In turning down the Queen's Channel, from the Pan Sand, you will find from 2½ to 3, 4, and 4½ fathoms, as low as the chequered buoy off the Pan Patch. You must pass on the North side of the South Knoll; but in steering from the West Pan Sand buoy you must avoid the Pan Sand Knoll, marked by a chequered black and white buoy: this must be left to the northward, and do not attempt to go between it and the West Pan Sand buoy. Below the Pan Patch the water deepens to 5, 6, 7, 8, and 9 fathoms. The upper part of the Wedge is steep, having 9 fathoms at a short distance; but, toward the lower end, vessels may stand in to 6 fathoms.

In coming down toward the North Spit buoy be cautious of standing to the southward into less than 10 or 9 fathoms, and to the northward into 8 or 7. In midchannel there is here from 11 to 12 fathoms.

From a mile below the buoy of the North Spit vessels may stand to Margate Sand to 5 or 4½ fathoms; and, to the northward, into 10 or 9 fathoms.

NORE TO THE KNOB CHANNEL, THROUGH THE MIDDLE OR OAZE CHANNEL.

OAZE DEEP, or MIDDLE CHANNEL.—This CHANNEL is that passage which lies between the sand called the *Oaze* on the North, and the *Spile*, the *Red Sand*, and *Shivering* on the South. It forms the most direct passage from the anchorage of the Nore to the Knob Channel, and is marked out by the following buoys:—

CANT BUOY, on the edge of the Cant; *white*, in 4 fathoms, on the starboard side.

WEST BUOY *of the* OAZE; *red*, monster, with *staff and ball*, in 3 fathoms, on the port side.

EAST BUOY of the SPILE; *striped red and white*, marked "East Spile," in 3½ fathoms, on the starboard side, nearly 3 miles S.E. by E. ¾ E. from the white buoy of the Cant.

MIDDLE OAZE.—Buoy, *chequered black and white*, in 3½ fathoms, on the southern edge of the sand, on the port side.

RED SAND BUOY; *red*, in 3¾ fathoms, on the starboard side.

EAST BUOY *of the* Oaze; large *black* nun, with staff and ball, in 3 fathoms, on the larboard side.

SHIVERING SAND BUOY; *striped black and white*, with head, staff, and ball, in 3¼ fathoms, on the starboard side.

DIRECTIONS.—The white buoy of the Cant, which marks the entrance of the Middle Channel, lies S.E. by E. ¼ E. 3¼ miles from the Nore Light. The course thence into the channel is E.S.E. 2 miles; from which the fairway through, to the midway between the buoys of the Knob and Shivering, lies E. by S. 5 miles.

It is recommended by the Trinity House that large ships do not stand nearer than to 8 fathoms on either side of the Channel. The entrance is only half a mile broad, but it widens to the eastward. From the Shivering Sand buoy you proceed for the Prince's or Queen's Channels, conformably to the preceding directions.

BULLOCK'S AND THOMAS'S CHANNELS.

BULLOCK'S CHANNEL divides the flat of the Girdler from the Long Sand, and runs in a parallel direction with Thomas's Channel to the N.W., from which it is separated by a bank of about a mile in width, having in some parts only 2 feet water. This newly formed channel is much more open than Thomas's Channel; at its north-western entrance it has 18 and 20 feet least water, and is there about one-third of a mile in width, but it soon increases to nearly a mile wide, with a depth of from 5 to 8 fathoms. The course in mid-channel through it is S.S.E. ½ E. and N.N.W. ½ W., length, 4 miles. Proceeding from the striped beacon buoy at the East end of the Shivering Sand the course

D

to its northern entrance is E. ½ N., and it is 6½ miles from it. Then bear round S.S.E. ¼ E., as before stated, and, having sailed about 3½ miles, the lightvessel near the East end of the Tongue will bear about S.S.W. 2½ miles off, when you will be clear of the sands, and can proceed as directed, for the Queen's Channel, &c. The S.W. entrance is much more open than that of Thomas's Channel, and may be found by its bearing and distance from the Tongue beacon buoy, as above given.

THOMAS'S CHANNEL, formerly called the SMUGGLER'S SWASH, is the channel at the S.W. end of the Long Sand. Its southern entrance lies N. by E. ¾ E. 3½ miles from the Tongue lightvessel, N. ¼ E. 5¾ miles from the East buoy of Margate Sand, and N. ¼ W. 11½ miles from the buoy of the Elbow, which lies to the E.S.E. of the North Foreland. From the entrance the channel lies in a curve N.N.W. and North, and has throughout from 8 to 6, 5, and 3 fathoms ; the middle part is not, however, more than one-third of a mile in breadth.

Those who attempt upon an emergency to pass through from the southward must be careful not to mistake for the channel a swash of the bank, which lies immediately on the West side of the entrance, and which has nearly the same depths of water.

From the North end of Thomas's Channel the course *upward*, through the Black Deeps or Sunk Channel, is W. ¼ S. 9 miles, to a fairway between the Knob and Shivering Sands. The depths, 10, 12, 9, 8, and 6 fathoms. Hence you may steer through the Oaze Channel, or for the West Swin. If the latter, the course will be N.W. ¼ N. 2½ miles, leaving the Knob buoy and the North or New Knob buoy on the East or starboard, and the East buoy of the Oaze on the West or larboard side.

DIRECTIONS FOR SAILING FROM THE NORTH FORELAND THROUGH THE QUEEN'S OR PRINCE'S CHANNELS, ETC., TO THE NORE.

In coming up with the Foreland, attend to the time of the tide and the strength of the wind, and make sail accordingly, so as to reach the Flats at the last quarter of flood, otherwise you would be obliged to anchor till the tide rises, according to your draught of water.

If there be little wind, make a proper allowance for the variable direction of the stream of tide near the East end of Margate Sand, which, as shown hereafter, has a tendency southward or toward the land during the first three hours of flood, and a tendency northward or from the land during the last three hours of the same.

The course from the North Foreland for the Queen's Channel (when the lighthouse bears N.W. by W. ½ W., about 3 miles distant, or about a mile outside the Elbow beacon buoy) is N.N.W. ½ W. 6½ miles to the East buoy of the Margate Sand ; the same course continued for 1½ miles further will clear the N.E. Spit buoy. The course through the Queen's Channel will then be open ; and then steer W.N.W. ½ W. for 6½ miles, which will bring you up to the Pan Patch buoy, one-third of a mile off to the N.E., and having the South Knoll buoy to the westward. On this course you will leave the North Spit buoy and the buoy on the Wedge on the port hand, and the nun beacon buoy and chequered buoy on the Tongue to starboard. From off the Pan Patch buoy the course through the Pan Sand Hole is N.W. by W. 2½ miles to the West Pan Sand buoy ; but this will take close to the 9 feet knoll, which is marked by a red and white chequered buoy, and it must be observed that you cannot pass within or to the northward of this buoy, therefore it must be left on the starboard hand. Hence you may proceed for the Knob Channel by reversing the courses, &c., given in the preceding directions.

Should you happen to be advanced in the Queen's Channel either too soon or too late for sailing over the Flats, it will then be safest, particularly for large ships, to come to an anchor. In moderate weather a vessel may anchor in any part of the channel. If it blows fresh from the southern quarter, anchor nearest the Margate Sand.

In turning from the East buoy of the Margate Sand to within a mile of the North Spit buoy, you stand to Margate Sand to 5 or 4½ fathoms ; to the northward to 9 and 10 fathoms ; and when you near the North Spit, until you come near the Wedge, stand to the southward into 10 and 9 fathoms, and to the northward into 8 and 7 fathoms ; in mid-channel you will have 11 and 12 fathoms. The West end of the Tongue is steep-to ; the West end of the Wedge has also 9 fathoms very near it ; but to the East end of each sand you may stand to 6 fathoms.

As you near the Pan Patch you will shoalen your water to 6 and 5 fathoms; and from the Pan Patch to the West Pan Sand buoy (*chequered, with a ball*) you will shoalen your water to 2½ fathoms: after passing the buoy you will increase it, for between the Shivering Sand and Girdler there are from 4 to 10 fathoms, and between the Shivering Sand and Knob from 5 to 8 fathoms; you may stand to the Knob to 8 fathoms, to the Oaze to 6 or 5 fathoms, and the Mouse to 6 fathoms; and from the Mouse to the Nore as noticed in the preceding directions for sailing downward.

If you intend to go through the Prince's Channel, now the most open and preferable, and from the spot before named, a mile East of the Elbow buoy, a N. by W. course for 9 miles will bring you to the eastward of the Tongue light vessel, when the Girdler light will be an excellent guide through the fairway. It should be remembered that a direct course cannot be made by night from off the Foreland for the Tongue lightvessel, on account of the Margate Sand, the eastern extreme of which is marked by the beacon buoy, before described; this left to port, the course is open to round the Tongue lightvessel; from which steer W.N.W. until within 3 miles of Girdler light vessel bearing N.W. by W.

SECTION IV.

MARGATE ROADS TO BEACHY HEAD, INCLUDING THE DOWNS.

FORENESS is the north-easternmost point of this part of the British coast. Ships bound outward from Margate Roads to the Downs must, in the first instance, be carefully kept clear of Longnose, a ledge of rocks stretching to the northward, two-thirds of a mile from it. This rock is uncovered in many parts at low ebbs. A *red* buoy was placed in April, 1823, off Foreness or Longnose Point, having the word *Longnose* on the head. The buoy lies in 24 feet at low water, spring ebbs, with the North Foreland lighthouse S. ¾ W. To clear this point, in sailing for the Gull Stream, keep Birchington church open of the East cliff of Margate, or Birchington seedmill open of Ledge Point, until the North Foreland lighthouse bears S.S.W. ¼ W.; a course thence S.S.E. ½ E., or according to the tide and the distance from the Foreland, will lead to the entrance of the Gull Stream, a good mark for which will be Foreness, kept a little open of Whiteness, or Neptune's Point, N.W. ½ N., until Ramsgate pier head bears W. ¾ S. The soundings are irregular, from 5 to 8 fathoms.

BROADSTAIRS.—The harbour of Broadstairs is formed by its wooden pier, about 100 yards in length, extending from the northern side of a cove. The entrance faces the S.W., but the harbour is much exposed to the sea, which is driven in by winds from the eastward. At spring tides there is about 16 feet of water at the pier-head, and 10 at neaps, but the harbour is dry at low water; and during spring tides nearly 100 yards outside the pier is left uncovered.

The NORTH FORELAND LIGHTHOUSE is an octagonal white tower, 70 feet high, built of flint, of which the lantern is 18½ feet above the level of high water; the light, brilliant and *fixed*, may be seen 6 leagues off.

The **GULL STREAM** is the principal channel from the Downs, and for vessels proceeding up or down Channel. It divides the Goodwin Sands from the Brake and the collection of chalky and detached shoals lying off Ramsgate, some of which extend on to the middle of its northern part. In approaching it from the northward there are several banks lying off the North Foreland, of which those that offer any danger to vessels, as well as those in the Gull Stream itself, are marked by buoys. We shall enumerate them, commencing from the North.

The ELBOW, a small shoal, on the western side; its least depth is in the middle, and is 3½ fathoms. Upon its outer extremity lies a *buoy, chequered black and white*, surmounted with a *staff and ball*, at the distance of 2¼ miles S.E. by E., from the North Foreland lighthouse.

Within the Elbow, almost immediately to the N.W., is a shoal of 3 or 4 fathoms, called the *Boiler*; and at half a mile W. by N. from the Elbow buoy is another, called the *Caldron*. Between these shoals is a depth of from 5 to 6 fathoms.

BROADSTAIRS KNOLL lies at about 1¼ miles from the North Foreland light-house, and a mile N.W. by W. from the buoy of the Elbow. This is a shoal between 1 and 2 cables' lengths in extent, with 2½ fathoms on it at low water. The marks for it are Broadstairs windmill, on with the chimney of the middlemost house on Crow Hill, bearing about W. ¼ N.; a small hut near the public house at Kingsgate, just open with the Ice House point, bearing about N.N.W. ¼ W. Within Broadstairs Knoll, at about one-quarter of a mile, are two patches, called the *Fox* and the *Goose*, of 2½ to 3½ fathoms. Small vessels pass between these and Broadstairs Knoll. There are several others to the southward upon the flat which extends from Ramsgate.

One of the latter is a ridge called the *Thistle*, on which a *black buoy* was laid in 1819, in 11 feet at low water, with the extremity of Broadstairs pier head 1 mile distant, on with the Albion hotel, Broadstairs. It is recommended that vessels of 9 feet draught of water and upwards do, at low tides, pass to the eastward of this buoy.

The GULL, a shoal having on one part only 17 feet at low water, lies 2¼ miles S.S.W. from the Elbow, on the same side of the Gull Stream. It stretches athwartwise, or S.E. and N.W., 1 mile, and ships passing through the Gull Stream cross over its eastern end in 4¾ fathoms. The shoalest part is distinguished by a *white buoy*, which lies on its N.E. side, with Jacob's Ladder on the West cliff at Ramsgate halfway between the two mills West of the West pier; the flagstaff of Dover castle on with that of Deal castle; and the North Foreland lighthouse, N. by W. ¼ W.

NORTH BAR.—Nearly parallel to the Gull, at the distance of three-quarters of a mile, is a narrow sand, of 4 fathoms, called the North Bar; 1 mile to the southward of which is another, called the Middle Bar. These lie nearly in the same direction as the Gull, and are similar in other respects.

On the North Bar a small knoll has grown up of 2 fathoms; upon this a *black buoy*, marked " North Bar," was placed in September, 1816.

The **BRAKE.**—The extensive bank called the BRAKE lies to the southward and westward of the sands above described. It is about 3 miles in length, and under half a mile wide, and runs in about a N.N.E. and S.S.W. direction, or North and South, *true*. The least depth on it is from 3 to 12 feet at low water, spring tides. It consists of sand to the depth of 4 or 5 feet and upwards, and forms a protection from the East to the anchorage in the Small Downs, as the Goodwin Sand shelters the whole of the Downs farther to the eastward.

Its eastern edge is marked by the following buoys :—On its N.E. part is a *red buoy*, which lies at the distance of 1¼ miles W. ¼ N. from the white buoy on the Gull. The marks for it are, St. Lawrence's church, on with the North cliff point of Ramsgate, N.W. by N.; and the North Foreland light, N. by E. northerly. From this buoy the sand extends to a *black mast buoy*, with round head, which lies on its southern extremity, about 4½ miles.

THE SOUTH BRAKE BUOY denotes the southern extremity of the Brake. It is, as stated, a *mast buoy*, painted *black* with a *round head*, and lies in 4½ fathoms water, with Waldershare monument, in line with a barn midway between the two windmills next South of Sandown castle, W. ¾ S.; North Foreland lighthouse, in line with the preventive station house on Broadstairs East cliff, N.N.E.; Middle Brake buoy, N.N.E. ½ E.; South Sand Head lightvessel, S. by W. ¼ W. Vessels when nearing this buoy from the Gull Stream should not bring it to bear to the southward of S.W., and should never attempt to cross the sand to the northward of it.

On the eastern edge of the *Brake Sand*, at nearly midway between the North and South Brake buoys, is a *chequered red and white buoy*.

GOODWIN SANDS.—These well known sandbanks have been divested of much of their danger since the present excellent system of lighting and buoyage has been completed. They can now be approached fearlessly, should the weather permit, as their limits are now well marked by different lightvessels and buoys. The first means adopted for pointing out their situation was the establishment of the North Foreland lighthouse. To this succeeded those on the South Foreland, which, being brought in one, lead clear of the South extremity. Besides these shore lights, off its North end is moored the Goodwin lightvessel; towards the middle of its inner face lies the Gull

Stream lightship, and the South Sand Head is indicated by a third. Of the several standing marks that have been erected on the sand, not one now remains. On its outer or eastern face there are now four large and conspicuous buoys. These, with the other buoys lying round it, will be described in their order.

THE NORTH SAND is of an irregular semicircular shape; the northern or outer edge forming the curve, and the southern the base. The bank is thence divided into two divisions, each tapering to the southward. That on the East is the SOUTH SAND, or CALLIPER; that on the West, the BUNT and FORK. The northern part of each division is dry in many places long before low water.

THE SOUTH SAND and FORK form the deep inlet now called TRINITY SWASH, or BAY, from which there is an outlet to the N.E.; near the latter is stationed the light-vessel called the *Gull Stream Light*.

The GOODWIN or NORTH SAND HEAD LIGHTVESSEL is principally intended for the use of vessels from the northward, and exhibits *three brilliant lights* on separate masts, at 35 and 23 feet above the level of the sea; the mainmast being the highest. A red ball is hoisted on each mast by day, and a gong is sounded in foggy and snowy weather.

The lightvessel lies N.E., nearly 2 miles from the nearest part of the North Sand Head of the Goodwin, in 10 fathoms, with the North Foreland lighthouse N.W. ¾ N. 6¼ miles; Ramsgate pier lighthouse, N.W. by W. ¼ W. 6¼ miles; and the South Foreland high light, S.W. by W. ¼ W. 13¼ miles. The following are the official directions given.

1st. The grand intention of the Goodwin light being to keep the vessels to the eastward of the Goodwin, the masters of all ships and vessels, in coming from the North Sea toward the Strait of Dover, must be careful not to bring the Goodwin light to bear more southerly than S.S.W. by compass; but, on the contrary, they should always keep the light rather to the westward than to the southward or eastward of that bearing, while they are to the northward of her; and they will be sure then to pass far enough to the eastward of her, and every part of the Goodwin, by steering a S. by W. course after they pass her.

2ndly. The masters of all vessels coming from the Strait of Dover toward the North Sea must be very careful not to shape a northerly course, until the Goodwin light bears N. by E. by compass; but, on the contrary, they should always keep the light rather to the northward of that bearing than to the eastward of it, while they are to the southward of her; and they will then be sure to pass far enough to the eastward of her, and every part of the Goodwin. And,

3rdly. Should any ship or vessel, coming from the North Sea toward Dover Strait, be forced by unavoidable necessity, on account of wind or tide, or otherwise, and the master, through choice, gives up his intention of proceeding to the southward, at the back of the Goodwin, or to the eastward thereof, he has it in his power, by a single bearing of the Goodwin light, to anchor under the North Sand Head, in 6 or 7 fathoms of water, clean ground, and ride there as safely as the lightvessel does; in order to which he must keep to the northward of the light, and, when it bears about South of him, half a mile or so distant, he may anchor. Or, should he prefer getting in to the westward of the Goodwin, so as to have the Gull Stream open, he may run in to the northward of the Goodwin upon a N.W. course, till he judges he has run about 2½ or 3 miles within, or to the N.W. of the light, and anchor in 7 or 8 fathoms, with the light bearing S.E.

Of the *buoys* which mark the most projecting parts of the Goodwin, the northernmost is that on the *Northern Goodwin*, which has extended to the northward, and a KNOLL, of 9 feet at low water, has been formed, lying much in the way of vessels passing into or out of the Gull Stream. Near the western edge of this knoll the *buoy* has been laid down in 4 fathoms: it is striped *red and white*, and lies with the following marks:—St. Peter's church tower, on with the highest windmill at Broadstairs, bearing N.W. ¼ N.; North Foreland lighthouse, N.N.W. ¼ W.; Gull buoy, N.W.

The GULL STREAM LIGHTVESSEL, already mentioned, is moored off that part of the Goodwin called the Trinity Swash. It is painted *red*, with the word GULL on each side, and shows two brilliant fixed lights on separate masts.

It is now moored in 8½ fathoms at low water spring tides, with the following marks and compass bearings, viz.:—Ramsgate church tower, in line with the middle of the

Albion hotel at that place, N. ¾ W.; Upper Deal windmill, its length on the outer end of Deal pier, S.W. by W. ½ W.; Middle Brake buoy, N.N.W. ¾ W.; Goodwin light-vessel, E. by N. ¼ N.; South Sand Head lightvessel, S.S.W.; South Foreland high lighthouse, S.W. ¼ W.

SOUTH SAND HEAD LIGHTVESSEL.—On the 25th of February, 1832, a vessel was stationed near the *South Sand Head of the Goodwin*, having a single lantern, exhibiting *one brilliant fixed light*. The vessel is moored in 13 fathoms, with the South side of a conspicuous gap, on the high land westward of Dover Lines, on with the extreme point of the South Foreland, bearing West; South Foreland upper lighthouse, W. ⅛ N. An experimental floating beacon painted *red*, with ball at the top, was moored in September, 1851, at a short distance from the lightvessel.

WRECKS ON THE GOODWIN, &c.—By order of the Honorable Corporation of Trinity House, 8th November, 1832, in cases of shipwreck on the Goodwin Sands, the following directions are to be carried into effect on board the *Goodwin, Gull Stream, and South Sand Head lightvessels* :—

If a vessel is on shore to the northward, a *white rocket* is to be discharged in a *northerly* direction, fired at an angle of 45 degrees, as shown in the figure annexed.

. If to the southward, a *red rocket* is to be fired in a southerly direction, at an angle of 45 degrees.

If to the *eastward*, a *blue rocket* is to be fired in a perpendicular direction.

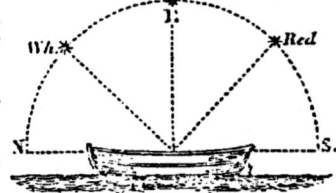

The *eastern side of the Goodwin Sands* is effectually marked by four large and con-spicuous nun beacon buoys; one off the North Sand Head, a second at the South side of the entrance to the Swatchway, a third at the North end of the South Calliper, and a fourth at the South end of the same.

The first of these, coloured *red*, *bearing a staff with a triangular top*, has been placed off the N.E. part of the sands, in 11 fathoms at low water spring tides, with St. Lawrence church, on with the Royal hotel at Ramsgate, N.W.; South Foreland high lighthouse, its length on with the cliff northward of St. Margaret's Bay, S.W. by W. ¾ W.; North Foreland lighthouse, N. by W. ¾ W.; and the North Sand Head or Goodwin lightvessel, N.N.E. ½ E.

The buoy near the Swatchway is a nun buoy of large size, painted *black*, marked "Swatchway," and surmounted by a staff having a diamond top, on the South side of the projection of the sand near to where the safety beacon stood. It lies in 15 fathoms water, with upper Deal church just open to the right of Deal castle, W. by N.; Gull lightvessel, N.W.; Goodwin lightvessel, N.N.E. ¼ E.; North Foreland lighthouse, N. by W.

The *South Calliper buoy*, which follows this, was placed in lieu of the beacon, which was destroyed in October, 1847. It is a *large nun buoy*, surmounted by a staff and cage, and painted *black* and *white*, in horizontal stripes, moored in 13 fathoms at low water spring tides, with Waldershare monument, in line with the centre of the low cliff North of Kingsdown, W. by N. ¼ N.; Thanet mill, midway between Ramsgate church and the obelisk on the pier, N. by W. ¼ W.; South Sand Head lightvessel, W. by S.; and the Goodwin lightvessel, N.E. by N.

The *South-east Goodwin buoy*, first moored in June, 1847, was placed in its present situation in May, 1848. It is a large nun buoy, painted *black*, with *staff and globe*. It was moored into 8½ fathoms at low water spring tides, and now lies with St. Lawrence church, its breadth open West of Ramsgate mill, N. ¼ W.; Shakspeare's cliff, just open of the South Foreland, W. ½ S.; South Sand Head lightvessel, W. ¾ S.; and the South Calliper buoy, N.E. by E. ½ E

Note.—Masters of vessels, pilots, and others, are cautioned to give this and the other buoys on the S.E. side of the Goodwin Sand, when sailing from one to the other, or from them to the North and South Sand Head lightvessels, a berth of not less than one-half mile in passing them, on account of the tide, which sets with great strength to the N.W. towards and over the sand.

The part called the *Bunt Head* lies to the S. by W. of the Gull Stream lightvessel, with St. Lawrence's mill on with the North cliff of Ramsgate, and is steep. An elbow has grown up on this sand, which projects considerably beyond the line of the site of the Fork buoy and the Gull lightvessel, which portion of the sand continues to increase in a W.S.W. direction, so that it has been found necessary to remove the buoy four times since first being placed. This *buoy* is coloured *black and white, in circular stripes*, and marked "Bunt Head." It now lies with St. George's church, Ramsgate, in line with the East pier head, N. ¼ E.; Waldershare tower on with the spire of a new chapel at Deal; Gull Stream lightvessel, N.E. by N.; South Brake buoy, N.W. ¾ W. The recent extension of the Bunt Head renders the navigable channel very narrow.

The sand stretches hence nearly South about a mile, and its extremity is called the FORK. Previous to the extension of the Bunt Head, the extremity of this spit was marked by a chequered buoy; but this having been rendered unnecessary by the extension of the Bunt Head, it was removed 15th September, 1849.

DIRECTIONS FOR THE GULL STREAM, &c.—SMALL VESSELS off Foreness, from the spot whence this spot bears S.W. ½ S., and the North Foreland lighthouse S. by W., may steer S.S.E. about 2⅓ miles, or until the lighthouse bears W. by S. A course thence S.S.W. ¼ W. 8½ miles will lead directly to a berth between the South Brake buoy and the Bunt Head buoy, when the Downs will be open.

The course here described leads between Broadstairs Knoll on the larboard, and the Fox and Goose on the starboard side. Thence over two shoal patches of 2½ and 2 fathoms, and to the eastward of the North buoy of the Brake, which will be left close on the starboard hand, and which, therefore, serves as a guide in the course. (*Directions for running into Ramsgate harbour from the North buoy of the Brake are given hereafter.*)

LARGE SHIPS must leave the buoy of the Elbow and that of the Gull on the starboard hand, and thence proceed through the Gull Stream. From abreast the buoy of the Elbow to that of the Gull the course and distance are S.S.W. ½ W. 2½ miles, until the South Foreland high lighthouse, bearing S.W. ½ W., comes on the middle of Old Stairs bay, which is the leading mark through the Gull Stream. The turning mark is, the lighthouse from cliff to cliff of Old Stairs bay. This mark will carry you clear through to the anchorage in the Downs, the marks for which are shown hereafter.*

The mark for the Gull Stream is not good, as the objects are so distant, and it is to be observed that it will lead up to the Gull lightvessel in its present position. A good substitute for it will be the Gull lightvessel and South Foreland high light in one, bearing S.W. ¼ W., which will lead well outside the Gull. This course may be carried up to the lightvessel, when, giving it a berth to the eastward, you may proceed as before directed.

In sailing through in thick weather, approach no nearer to the Brake than in 6 fathoms, nor to the Goodwin than in 9 or 10 fathoms. Along the Brake the soundings are more regular than toward the Bunt Head, the latter being steep-to. The narrowest part of the channel between the Brake and Goodwin is about 1¼ miles wide. In this channel are several spots of 5 and 6 fathoms.

In coming from sea, &c., ships must not bring the North Sand Head (or Goodwin) light to the eastward of S.E. until the Gull Stream light bears S.W. ¼ S., and the North Foreland light, N.N.W. ⅓ W. They will then have the Gull Stream open; and by steering S.W. ⅓ W. until they bring the Gull light N.E. by E., they may then steer W.S.W. for an inshore berth in the Downs, or keep on a S.W. ⅓ W. course for a man of-war's roadstead.

* In hazy weather, when the leading mark to sail through the Gull Stream cannot be seen, there is no good mark for keeping to the eastward of the shoals off the North Foreland; in this case the best direction that can be given to large ships is, to observe the approximating angle, viz.; take, with a sextant, the altitude of the North Foreland lighthouse, from the base to the very top of the lantern; for if this angle be less than 10′ of a degree you will be at a sufficient distance without the Elbow and other shoals; but if the angle be greater, you will not be sufficiently to the eastward.

This angle of altitude is only to be taken when just abreast of the shoals, and must be observed in the same way as that taken by one vessel when in chase of another, to ascertain, by the alteration of altitude of the chase, whether she gains or loses.

Leading mark through the Gull Stream.   a. The South Foreland lighthouses.   b. c. The two sides of Old Stairs Bay.   c. Old Parker's Cap.

Particular care and attention must be observed in taking the above bearings, and in the steerage of ships, as the angles are small and the channel narrow, both in sailing for the Downs in the night, and also in being unavoidably driven, or in sailing, through the Gull to the northward.   The Gull lightvessel must at all times be passed to the westward.

Should you be off the North Foreland in the evening or night, and be bound for the Downs, with a southerly wind, you ought to be off the North Sand Head when the stream begins to run to the southward, and may then steer out for the back of the Goodwin, S.S.E., until you come to the lightvessel off the North Sand Head ; or, should the latter be gone, until you get into 18 fathoms of water.*   The North Foreland lighthouse N.W. by N. will carry you clear of the North Sand Head.   Keep the lead going, and approach no nearer than in 7 fathoms.   From the depth of 18 fathoms you may alter your course to S.S.W., until past the Swash, and thence to the South Sand Head to S.W. ¼ W.

In sailing along the East side of the Goodwin, after passing to the South of the Swash and the Callipers, do not approach nearer to the sand than in 14 fathoms ; the large buoys will show its edge.   Folkestone high land or church tower open of Shakspeare cliff is the mark for sailing in, clear of the South Sand Head.   Or you may steer in for the land more to the southward, by keeping the two lighthouses on the South Foreland in one, bearing W. by N., until the water shoalens toward the Foreland to 14 or 12 fathoms, whence you proceed to the N.N.E. for the anchorage.   The lighthouses exhibit most excellent brilliant *fixed* lights, which may be seen at more than 8 leagues off.

DOWNS.—The Downs, or roadstead, strictly so called, is a tract opposite the town of Deal, extending from off the southern part of that town to the South buoy of the Brake.   The ground is generally good, and sheltered in a considerable degree by the Goodwin Sands.†

Off the town there is, however, a sand called *Deal Bank*, which must be avoided.   It lies about half a mile from shore, and has only 17 feet least water over it.   For the South end the mark is Deal church on with the King's buildings at the South end of the town ; and, for the North end, Deal lowest mill on with the boat house to the northward of Deal. Ships should not approach nearer to it than 7 or 6½ fathoms.

The depth of water on the northern and southern parts of this bank having so considerably increased as to render the buoys at those stations no longer necessary, these buoys have accordingly been taken away, and in lieu thereof, one red buoy, marked " *Deal Bank*," has been placed upon a projecting part of that sand, and in 6 fathoms at low water spring tides.

In working between the Bunt Head and Fork, tack in 8 fathoms on the Goodwin, and in 7 on the Brake.   Between the Fork and South Sand Head, when you have the old wall which stands to the northward of Kingsdown on with Ringswold church, the Goodwin is steep-to ; therefore tack in deep water, or 14 fathoms.

On standing toward the Fork or Bunt Head in the daytime, tack before the high lighthouse touches old Parker's Cap.

For anchoring in the Downs with a large ship the marks are, the South Foreland high light on the middle of Old Stairs Bay ; or the Hopeland, within the South Foreland,

* St. Peter's church tower a little open to the right of Broadstairs mill is a mark for sailing to the northward of the North Sand Head.   In the night stand no nearer than to have the North Foreland light N.W. by N.

† The new and commodious landing pier at Deal extends about 300 feet from the shore at Beach street, close to the Royal Hotel.

For the convenience of vessels watering at Deal, a company have laid on pipes to the end of the pier, so that ships' boats may now lay at the end of the pier at all times of the tide, except dead low water spring tide, and fill their casks without any risk.—*Oct.*, 1842.

S.W. ¼ W.; and Upper Deal mill on with Deal castle, in from 7 to 9 fathoms; the ground here being good. To moor, lay the best bower so as to have an open hawse with a southerly or inshore wind.

Should, in the night, the wind blow hard from S.S.E., or South, so that you part from your anchors, bring, if possible, the South Foreland light to bear S.W. ¼ W., and steer N.E. ½ E., which will carry you through the Gull Stream, between the Brake and Goodwin. In going through, keep the lead going, and approach no nearer the Goodwin than 9 fathoms, nor to the Brake than 6 fathoms of water. When the North Foreland lighthouse bears N.W. by N., an East or E.S.E. course will carry you clear of the North Sand Head. On the flat, off the Foreland, are but 6 and 7 fathoms; but with a depth of 18 or 20 fathoms you will be clear of all the sands.

In sailing to the southward, from the Downs, the common mark is Upper Deal mill a ship's length open to the southward of Walmer castle; but a better mark is Walmer castle, its breadth to the left of Upper Deal church tower, bearing N. by W. ¼ W., which will lead clear of the South end of the sand in 12 or 14 fathoms.* Another direction is Upper Deal mill halfway between Walmer castle and the first chalk cliff.

SMALL DOWNS.—The small Downs is the track which lies between the South end of the Brake and the shore, extending about 2 miles from Sandown castle toward Ramsgate. The ground affords good anchorage in from 4 to 5 fathoms, decreasing to 3 and 2½ fathoms. The best marks for anchoring are the *Bullock*, a small sand hill which stands about 2 miles to the North of Sandown castle when appearing between the two churches of Sandwich; or Deal mill and Sandown castle in a line; or St. Margaret's church on the small windmill to the North of Deal, which is the best place in all the Downs for small vessels.

RAMSGATE.—RAMSGATE HARBOUR consists of an inner and outer basin, formed by substantial stone piers, extending 1,310 feet into the sea, and encloses an area of 42 acres. The inner basin is used as a wet dock for vessels to load or unload cargoes, &c., and contains a dry dock, where vessels of 300 or 400 tons burthen can be repaired, &c. The entrance to the outer harbour is 200 feet in width, and opens to the S.W.

The average rise of spring tides is from 15 to 16 feet at the pier heads, and of neap tides 10 feet, giving in the entrance 19 feet at high water of spring tides, and 16 of neaps.

The bottom outside consists of chalk rock, with not more than 6 feet of water at some distance from the harbour's mouth at low water spring tides.

From the Small Downs vessels may proceed to Ramsgate by the following directions, which are those lately published by the Harbour Trust:—

It being of importance that ships should not run for Ramsgate harbour when it is low water, the following rules must be observed:—A red globe will be hoisted upon a mast on the West cliff near Jacob's Ladder, in the day time, when there is a depth of 10 feet of water between the pier heads; and, in the night, a *red* light in the lighthouse upon the West pier will be lighted when there is the same water; and they will respectively be continued until the water falls to 10 feet; when there is less than 10 feet, it is a green light.

APPEARANCE OF RAMSGATE.

A. *The Lighthouse.*   B. *The Committee Room and Clock.*   CC. *The Pier.*

The *lighthouse*, which is on the West pier, shows a *red* or *green light*, as above, at 37 feet above high water spring tides; but when there is less than 10 feet water, this light is changed to a *green* light. A second *green* light on the West cliff, when in line with

* A TIME BALL is shown at the Royal Navy Yard; it is raised half-mast high at 12ʰ 55ʹ p.m. *nearly*, and raised to the top at 12ʰ 57ʹ p.m. nearly. It is dropped by the galvanic current from the Greenwich Observatory *exactly* at 1ʰ p.m., Greenwich mean time. If it is accidentally deranged, it will be lowered gradually, and again raised to be dropped by hand at 2ʰ p.m.; but the accuracy of the time cannot be guaranteed within two seconds.

that on the pier, shows the direction of the Old Cudd Channel. When there are 10 feet and upwards in the harbour, the usual *red* light on the pier and the *green* light on the West cliff constitute the leading lights for the entrance.

It is high water, on the full and change, in the harbour, at 11ʰ 20′. At 9ʰ 20′ a.m. the tide begins to set to the N.E., and it so continues five hours and twenty-five minutes. On the moon's quarters it is high water at 4ʰ 20′.

At about one hour after the 10 feet signal is made, there will be 16 feet of water with spring tides, between the pier heads ; two hours after, or at high water, about 20 feet.

With neap tides, one hour after the 10 feet signal is made, there will be 12 feet; two hours after, or at high water, 15 feet.

These are the average depths, but they are much affected at times by the wind; southerly winds *decrease*, and northerly winds *increase*, the depths of water.

Before the harbour there are numerous shoals, which at low water have very little depth on them ; there are channels between them, but they are narrow, and require care. The QUERN SHOAL lies to the North of the Brake Sand ; it is of chalk, and has a depth of only 6 feet on it at low water. It has a *white* buoy on it.

The DYKE SHOAL is to the northward of the Quern, and the two together front Ramsgate harbour ; upon its South end is a *black* buoy, which, with that on the Quern, shows the Nine-feet Channel, called Old Cudd, the entrance to Ramsgate, as hereafter described.

Between the South end of the Quern and the Brake is the Cliffsend Channel, which is the part where the sandy bottom begins, it being all chalk to the northward. To the southward the chalk commences off Deal, and extends across the South part of the Goodwin, so that the part comprehended between these points, which forms the Downs and Small Downs, is a tract of sand, of which the sandy shore of the Sandwich Flats on the West and the Goodwin to the East are the limits. The chalk, however, extends down the Gull Stream nearly to the lightvessel.

Should a vessel break adrift in the Downs, it would be probably with a southerly gale, which sends the heaviest sea into it, and with the flood tide. This, therefore, would be the tide which would carry a ship into Ramsgate harbour; but as the tide runs in the direction of the *flood* until *half ebb* there would not be water all that time, therefore this should be borne in mind on such an emergency.

Winds from the N.N.W. and North send a nasty sea into this northern part of the channel, from the great fetch the waves have from the North Sea, and it sometimes causes vessels to drive with winds from that quarter.

The channel within the Brake Sand, leading from the Small Downs between its southern part and the shore, becomes gradually shoaler as you approach its northern end, there being 4 to 5 fathoms at its South part, decreasing to 11 or 12 feet at low water at its northern entrance. Nine feet is the lowest water in the entrance, but 11 feet is the average, so that this passage is closed against ships drawing above this during the period of low water, a strong argument against the formation of a harbour at the back of the Brake. A vessel drawing 18 feet can pass through, an hour before or after high water of ordinary tides, but not at neaps, with 17 feet from two hours before to two hours after. From the South Brake buoy direct inshore to Sandown castle the depths are from 7 to 8 fathoms, and farther North 6½ to 3 fathoms.

TO SAIL IN, *from off Sandown castle,* steer about halfway between the shore and the Brake, keeping St. Lawrence's church about a ship's length open to the eastward of West Cliff lodge, a white house, which stands on the cliff between Pegwell White cliff and Ramsgate, bearing N. ¾ E. by compass, for about 4 miles, until you bring Wood-nesbury or Wensbury church (in the country) on with St. Clement's church, in Sandwich, which is the southernmost of two churches in that town ; you are then as far as the *Rattler Shoal,* or near the spot where a white buoy is placed, and will have the obelisk on with the West pier head ; keeping these in one will lead you up to a red buoy, which lies W.S.W. from the lighthouse, three-quarters of a mile, in 6½ feet at low water; pass close on the outside of this buoy, and steer directly for the West pier head, taking care to keep within the transporting black buoy, placed just without the entrance of the harbour.

In approaching the harbour, if the tide sets to the eastward, keep a good sail on the ship, and steer close to the West pier head (you cannot be too close) ; and if you cannot conveniently make fast to one of the buoys within the harbour, throw all your sails aback, and let go your anchor ; or, if you have no anchors, run to the East bank directly toward the pier-house ; you will then be under the direction of the harbourmasters, who will order you a proper berth.

N.B.—The best time to enter Ramsgate harbour (if the vessel does not draw too much water) is two hours before high water, or when the tide begins to set to the N.E. without the pier heads.*

DIRECTIONS FOR SAILING *toward the harbour in the* NIGHT, which is only to be attempted by vessels of burthen in cases of extreme necessity.

All captains of ships in the Downs, in bad weather, should know their exact situation before dark, by intersected bearings of Sandown castle and the Halfway houses ; and consequently their bearings and distance from the white buoy within the Rattler, already noticed. They should also keep a good lookout for and note the time when the 10 feet water signal is made.

If vessels part their anchors, or are obliged to cut from them, they must steer by their bearings (obtained before night) such course as will bring them to the white buoy, when the light on the West pier head will bear N.E. by E. by compass, the only guide in the night ; keeping the light on these bearings will bring you up to the West pier head, when you must enter in the manner before directed.

N.B.—If the tide be running to the eastward, you must take particular care not to let the light get to the northward of N.E. by N. till you almost touch the pier head, or the tide will certainly set you to the eastward, past the entrance. It is hoped that no vessel will cut or run for Ramsgate harbour in the night time, unless in case of real distress, lest by so doing she runs into greater danger with a view to avoid only a temporary gale, which perseverance and good ground tackle might have enabled her to ride out, at least till daylight. But the safest way, in the night, is to run out of the Gull Stream, by bringing the South Foreland high light to bear S.W. ¼ W. by compass, till you come abreast of the Gull Stream light, keeping her on the starboard side ; then steer N.E. ¼ N. until you bring the Goodwin floating light to bear about S.E., in 7 or 8 fathoms of water. You may then anchor, or bring to for the night.

LIGHTHOUSE, or OLD CUDD CHANNEL.—This is a narrow channel, which lies to the northward of the Brake, and having in its shoalest part only 9 feet of water. Being bounded by several dangerous shoals, it should be attempted only by those who are well acquainted, or in case of great emergency. In sailing in, you leave the North buoy of the Brake to the southward, or on the larboard hand, and thence pass between the buoys marking the channel between the shoals called the *Quern* and *Dyke*, on some parts of which there is only 1 foot at low water. The northernmost of these buoys is *black*, and lies in 7 feet water, on the S.W. extreme of the *Dyke Spit*. The southern buoy is *white*, in a similar depth, and marks the N.E. edge of the *Quern*. The width of the channel between these buoys is less than a cable's length. The mark to sail through is Pugin tower, a remarkable new brick building (to the westward of the town) just open to the left of the pier, bearing N.W. by W.

In the night time, the direction of Old Cudd Channel is shown, as before stated, by the red or green light on the pier head, in one with a green light on the West cliff.

With the North Foreland lighthouse directly on the North cliff of Broadstairs, you will be to the N.E. of the Quern. The thwart mark for the South end of this sand is St. Lawrence's mill on the North cliff of Ramsgate. With the top of St. Peter's church a handspike's length above the land, you will be clear of the Dyke.

S.W. of Ramsgate is an extensive bay, filled with sand banks, called the *Sandwich Flats*, through which the river Stour runs with a tortuous course. This is called Sandwich Haven. The southern point of the mouth of the river is called Shellness ; and between this and Sandown castle, to the North of Deal, is a spot where the last of the shingle is found, which coming from the westward along the shore causes so much trouble, expense, and detriment to all the harbours on the S.E. coast. This spot is known by the name of the *Shingle End*.

* It is to be observed that at this time the water has risen on a spring tide 12 feet, and on a neap tide 10 feet perpendicular ; and there is at the pier head 6 feet at low water on full and change, and 8 feet water at neap tides.

The town of DEAL is 6 miles S.S.W. of Ramsgate; and at Walmer castle, 1½ miles farther on, the chalk cliffs again appear. The South Foreland is 5½ miles from Deal.

The SOUTH FORELAND LIGHTHOUSES, occupying the summit of the bold headland, serve to mark the South end of the Goodwin Sands, bearing W. by S., and E. by N., *true*, from each other, or W. by N. northerly, by compass, from seaward. The high lighthouse was re-erected in 1841; and was characterized by the American Commissioners, in 1846, as "beyond comparison the finest and most complete lighthouse they had seen in Europe." The low lighthouse was rebuilt in 1846.

The lights are both *fixed;* the high light at 372 feet, the low light at 275 feet, above high water. The light from the high lighthouse is not visible to the northward of the line of bearing of W. by S. southerly. This arrangement is to avert the danger of the rocky patches off Copt Point, East of Folkestone. Masters of vessels drawing more than 14 feet water should adhere to the old rule, which requires that the *lower* light shall be kept in sight when approaching the shore; and masters and pilots of all vessels *not* bound to Folkestone harbour are now instructed to *stand off* immediately the *high* light disappears.

ELECTRIC TELEGRAPH.—The SUBMARINE CABLE of the ELECTRIC TELEGRAPH, extending from the South Foreland to Belgium, lies in an E. by S. direction (by compass), with the South Foreland lighthouses in line, bearing W. by N., until without the stream of the Goodwin Sand, passing about 1 mile to the southward of the South Sand Head lightvessel, after which it takes a general E.S.E. direction across to the Flemish Banks. It is desirable that vessels should not anchor with this mark or bearing on, lest, by so doing, they damage the electric cable, or lose their own anchors. (*January* 28, 1853.)

The ELECTRIC TELEGRAPH between the same point and France also requires caution. In order to prevent mischief occurring to it, it is desirable that vessels should not anchor off the South Foreland when the high lighthouse bears between North and N.W., and within the distance of 3 or 4 miles from the shore; nor, if beyond that distance, when it bears N.W. by N., on which bearing it will appear in one with a dark patch on the cliff. And as respects the opposite or southern side of the channel, it is equally desirable that vessels should not anchor when the two conspicuous windmills of *Coquelles*, which stand on the high ground between Calais and the village of Sangatte, bear between S. by E., and S.E. by S. (*December* 23, 1851.)

DOVER, a good tide harbour, is situate W. ¾ S., 3 miles from the South Foreland. Its entrance, which is formed by two piers, is narrow. The channel is in a N.N.W. direction.

The *Harbour of Refuge*, commenced in 1848, is to enclose an area of about 520 acres, under the superintendence of Messrs. Walker and Burges. The works begin from Cheeseman's Head, 500 yards West of the present West pier head. The breakwater will extend out in a general S.E. direction for 600 yards, and E. by S. 800 yards farther; then an entrance 700 feet wide; then extending 1,200 yards E. by N., turning to the shore N. by E. 1,200 yards, reaching it at three-fourths of a mile East of the Marine parade. During the progress of the works, a *blue light* is shown from their extremity to point out the danger of approaching too near.

The present HARBOUR of DOVER consists of an outer and an inner basin, with a backwater which opens into the latter, called the *Pent*. The outer harbour, recently enlarged, contains an area of 12½ acres; the inner basin, 6¼ acres; and the Pent, 11½ acres. A wet dock of 1½ acres opens into the western side of the outer harbour, which again communicates with a graving or repairing dock.

The entrance between the pier heads (which are formed partly of stone and brickwork, faced with wooden piles) is 110 feet in width, and opens to the S.S.E.

The average rise of spring tides, as shown on the mark board at the North pier, is 17 feet 3 inches; and of neap tides, from 12 to 13 feet; but the depth at high water in the harbour at spring tides is only 17 to 18 feet, and in the basin 16 to 17 feet, and about 3 feet less during the neaps. The harbour is, therefore, left dry at low water.

TIDE SIGNALS and LIGHTS.—Since January 1, 1852, the following tidal signals were substituted for those previously in use. The depths are those shown by the index or tide guage on the North pier:—

With from 7 to 10 feet water. By day, a red flag with a black ball under at the customary staff on the South pier. *By night,* a small low *red* light on the North pier, and a similar light on the outer extremity of the South pier.

With from 10 to 13 feet. By day, a red flag on the South pier. *By night,* the *lights* now in use, viz., two large *red* lights on the signal staffs of the South pier, and the above mentioned small low *red* light on the North pier.

With 13 feet and upwards. By day, a red flag with a black ball over on the staff on the South pier. *By night,* the lights as above.

A *brilliant green light,* projecting its rays towards the harbour's mouth, will be exhibited throughout the night, by the clock tower in the inner part of the harbour, and will show midway between the piers.

No signal to ships in general will be made between 7 feet at ebb and 7 feet at flood, by the index board on the North pier; and whenever at other times the harbour is inaccessible to vessels, the flag (if in the day) will be pulled down, and (if at night) the light or lights on the South pier will be extinguished; and only upon the former being rehoisted, or the latter relighted, can the harbour be entered.

Caution is the more necessary in standing into Dover during a gale, as there is a counter-current, not more than 2 cables' lengths in breadth, which sets directly athwart the harbour's mouth, from the last quarter of flood till the end of the first quarter ebb.

To sail in from the westward, run close to the stone jetty, which lies to the West of the pier head, then toward the castle, until you can see the gates of the basin, when it becomes requisite to haul round quickly for the harbour. Observe, however, that it is not safe to enter without a pilot.

The marks for anchorage in Dover Road are St. James's church in the valley, which has a flat steeple, bearing about N.N.W., and the South Foreland nearly E.N.E., or the white way, to the N.W. of the castle, directly over the hill, or between the hill and St. James's church. You may anchor wherever agreeable, in from 7 to 14 fathoms.[*]

To the westward of Dover the chalk cliffs again form the coast; the cliffs at that town lying at the back of the principal street. Shakspeare or Hay cliff is three-quarters of a mile West of the town. It is much reduced from its original height, but is still an object of admiration. It is now pierced by a double tunnel, through which the South Eastern Railway enters the town of Dover, the station being just to the West of the harbour, on the beach. Emerging from this tunnel the stupendous works are carried westward, sometimes through cuttings at the base of the cliffs, and sometimes open to the sea, the passing trains being visible from the offing. Near Folkestone, after passing through several tunnels, it takes a more inland course towards the metropolis, and the chalk cliffs themselves terminate at a short distance East of the harbour, where they are replaced by lower ones of greenish sandy stone.

FOLKESTONE lies 5½ miles W. ¼ S. from Dover. This place has a small harbour, frequently filled with fishing boats, which are protected by a strong battery on the right. Athwart of Folkestone, in 12 or 14 fathoms, there is indifferent anchoring ground; near this place, and to the westward of it, are several dangerous ledges of rocks, by which numerous ships have been taken up, some extending half a mile from shore. You will avoid them by keeping the South Foreland open of Dover cliff, or not approaching nearer than in 12 fathoms. A *red light* on the larboard side of the entrance to Folkestone indicates when there is a depth of 10 feet or more water. There is anchorage off Folkestone with lighthouse on with eastern houses of town, bearing nearly North.

---

[*] SIGNALS.—The agents to Lloyd's at Deal, Dover, and many other places, have signal posts to communicate with shipping; and the information is regularly transmitted to that establishment.

The distinction between Dover cliff and the South Foreland (so as to know whether to the eastward or westward of Dover in thick weather, when nothing else can be seen,) is, that the cliffs to the westward are white and smooth surfaced, with small dark patches of grass; while those to the eastward are marked with horizontal strata of flint.

Most excellent holding ground is found with St. James's church tower on with Old Park in the valley, and the South Foreland lights open in from 10 to 14 fathoms; this is for large ships. Small vessels usually anchor in the bay, where the ground is compact sand, and in some parts chalk, here and there covered with "ross," or worm casts.

The harbour, entirely artificial, is formed by rubble stone piers, and encloses an area of 14 acres.

The rise of spring tides averages about 18 to 20 feet, and neap tides from 12 to 14 feet.

The harbour has recently been improved by the South Eastern Railway Company, who have removed the shingle, and have cleared it so as to have a depth in it of 18 feet at high water. Should the bar increase at any time, it will be removed, so as to preserve this depth; and works are now in progress to considerably increase this depth for steam vessels.

A branch from the railway enters the harbour at the N.W. side, and by means of which, goods, &c., will be rapidly transmitted to the metropolis and the intermediate places. At the western end of the harbour is an extensive hotel, &c., which has been lately erected.

MILL POINT is the first projection westward of Folkestone, and like Copt Point, to the eastward of it, is fronted by rocky ledges extending from 1½ to 3 cables' lengths off them. Hythe church, open of the stone wall in front of Shorncliffe battery, leads to the S.W. of them.

At 1½ miles westward of Folkestone is the pleasant watering place of Sandgate, off which is good anchorage with the wind to northward of E. by N.; the best position is with the pier clock at Folkestone just clear of Mill Point, in 6 to 8 fathoms.

HYTHE is 4 miles West of Folkestone. The water is shoal for 2 miles off the town, and large ships should go about when the South Foreland high lighthouse is shut in by Shakspeare cliff. To the westward of Hythe is the extensive plain of Romney Marsh, of which Dungeness is the South extreme. The *Newcome, Swallow,* and *Roar Banks* lie in the bay between Hythe and Dungeness. The Roar is a narrow sandy ridge of 9 to 12 feet water, parallel with the shore, at 1½ miles from it. The *Swallow Bank* lies in the East Road; it has a shoal spot of 18 feet, which is cleared to eastward by Beachborough summerhouse in one with Hythe church. The *Newcome* is near to the point, and has a *black buoy* close outside of it in 16 feet water.

DUNGENESS lies 20 miles W.S.W. ½ W. from the South Foreland, and 13 miles S.W. by W. ¾ W. from Folkestone. Upon it stands an excellent lighthouse and buildings connected therewith, painted red. It shows a brilliant fixed light at 92 feet.

Dungeness forms a remarkable shingle point, projecting in a S.S.E. direction 4 miles beyond the fair line of the coast, affording shelter in the East bay from North round westerly to East, or for nineteen points of the compass. If there is any southing of East in the wind, there is no shelter in either bay.

The quality of bottom in both bays is fine sand over clay and mud, and excellent holding ground throughout.

The rise of tide at Dungeness is 22 feet on springs, and 13 on neaps, being the largest rise along this coast. The tide stream, both on ebb and flood, sets past the Ness, and fairly through the bay, along the 7 fathom ridge, at the rate of 2½ miles an hour on springs, and 1½ miles on neaps, gradually decreasing to half this strength as you approach the shore into the 3 fathoms edge. It is also stated that the tide sets fair from the point to the South Foreland, and that there is an eddy tide off the Ness, setting S.E. towards the coast of France, beginning about 5 miles off.

The EAST BAY affords good shelter to vessels of all classes, in from 4 to 12 fathoms, upon good holding ground, with the wind between N. by E. and S.W. The best position is with Lydd church just open North of No. 2 battery, and the lighthouse bearing S.W. by W. ¼ W., in 7 fathoms water.

In the WEST BAY the only bank is STEPHENSON'S or CHAPEL BANK, of 20 feet, which lies nearly due West, 3½ miles from the lighthouse. Shakspeare cliff open to the southward of the lighthouse, or Fairlight mill in sight to the westward of Fairlight church, will carry you well to the southward of the bank; and the tower of New Romney church, open to the westward of Lydd smock mill, leads considerably to the westward of it.

RYE.—The entrance of Rye harbour lies W.N.W. 7 miles from Dungeness lighthouse. The town itself lies 2 miles North of the low water line. The harbour has constantly to contend with the shifting beach, which, coming from the westward, has totally altered, at different periods, the form and position of the harbour.

The average rise of spring tides here is about 17 feet, and during neap tides from 9 to 12 feet at the pier head, whilst the lift in the bay is 22 feet. At low water the harbour is left dry.

The entrance to the channel leading to the town is shown by several buoys, the outermost, about one-fourth of a mile within low water mark, a *black* one, to the West, and one *chequered black and white*, to the East, the channel lying between them. Above these is another black buoy to port, and two white buoys to starboard, above which the passage up is shown by the *lights in one*.

The *two tide lights* are shown from the Camber, North of the entrance, while there are 10 feet water on the bar. When in one they bear N. by W., and lead over the sand in front of the harbour. On the shingle beach to the westward of the martello tower two thwart lights are shown from the time the tide begins to flow, till there is only water for a boat to go out; they are only visible from the S.E., and in one *lead up* the channel to the Dolphin, when the harbour lights come in one, and lead up the channel. By day, *tide signals* are made from the telegraph at the mouth of the harbour.

It is required that vessels in the night time lie off abreast of the harbour, and not too far to the westward, as the martello tower is an obstruction, and may prevent the pilots on the outlook from seeing the vessel's lights. It is necessary to show a good light by night, and the usual signal by day.

The BOULDER BANK, nearly 3 miles in length and three-quarters of a mile broad, with 11 and 12 feet over it, and 3 and 4 fathoms around. It lies at the distance of about three-quarters of a mile from the coast, between Rye Harbour and Fairlight. The S.W. end lies with Morris cliff (which is to the southward of Hastings church), W. by N., and Rye tower on with an alehouse near the beach, N.E. ¼ N. Fairlight mill, open to the westward of the semaphore, leads to the S.W. of the bank; and Playden steeple, in one with the turret of Rye church, leads considerably to the S.E. of it.

HADDOCK CLIFF, and the high land of *Fairlight* or *Fairleigh*, lie nearly 6 miles to the westward of the old harbour of Rye, and 11¾ miles W. by N. from Dungeness.

Between Fairlight Down and Beachy Head the strand is composed of coarse shingle, studded here and there with small rocky heads, particularly in the vicinity of Hastings and Cliff's-end Point. The mill on Fairlight Down is 600 feet above the level of the sea.

The pleasant coast westward of Fairlight presents, in succession, the town of Hastings, (the first of the cinque ports), and the villages of Bexhill, Pevensey, Eastbourne, &c.

HASTINGS is seated at the foot of a range of hills, which slope gradually down to the sea beach, along which the principal part of the town is built. The new watering place of *St. Leonard's* is just to the westward of the town of Hastings, and is much resorted to in the season.

The principal maritime importance of Hastings is its fishery, which employs a considerable number of boats, the chief produce of which is forwarded to London by railway. For the service of these fishermen, *two lights* are shown at Hastings: the upper light, *bright*, from the town; and the lower, *red*, on the beach, 508 feet apart. These lights brought in one N.N.E. direct the boats in running on shore. They are shown from March 25th to September 29th.

Between Pevensey and Eastbourne is *Langley* or *Pevensey Point*, a slight projection of the coast, 5 miles from Beachy Head lighthouse. The coast is here lined with martello towers, generally one-quarter of a mile apart. This point separates the bays of Pevensey from Eastbourne on the South; and off the coast between it and Beachy Head is a cluster of shoals extending 6 miles in a S.W. direction, the outermost with 4 fathoms water.

The SOUTHERN HEAD or HORSE is the farthest out, and lies S.E. by E. ½ E. 8¼ miles from Beachy Head lighthouse, and Pevensey church bearing N. by W. from it. There is 4 fathoms on its shoalest part. Between this and Langley Point are several patches of 5 fathoms.

The HORSE of WILLINGDON lies within the former, and has 18 feet on one spot. It is more than half a mile long, and, with the exception of the above patch, has 21 to 27 feet on it. From the 18 feet spot the lighthouse bears W.N.W.; Eastbourne church and Southbourne new church in one, N.W., and Pevensey church North.

ELPHICK'S TREE, with 27 feet, lies three-quarters of a mile N.W. of the Horse of Willingdon.

KINSMAN'S NAB, with 3½ to 5 fathoms, is 1 mile E. by S. of the Horse of Willingdon.

ROYAL SOVEREIGN SHOAL, by far the most formidable of this group, has only 10 feet water on it, and, being 6½ miles from the point, it is very dangerous. It bears E.S.E., just 8 miles from the lighthouse; S.S.E. ¼ E. 4½ miles from Langley Point; and S.E. by S. 2 miles from the Horse of Willingdon. A large *nun buoy*, painted *black*, with staff and ball, is moored to the South of it.

RATTAN SHOAL consists of two or three spots of 5 fathoms, surrounded by the depth of 6 and 7½ fathoms, lying to the N.N.E. a mile to a mile and a half from the Royal Sovereign shoal spot.

HOLYWELL BANK, or SANDACRE.—This bank lies against the East side of Beachy Head, the outer edge being three-quarters of a mile off the shore. It has only 12 or 15 feet water at nearly this distance, and therefore prevents access to Eastbourne Bay too close with the point.

The *flood tide* sets off strong from Beachy Head to the S.E. offing, with no great in-draught to Eastbourne Bay.

Seaford cliff, kept in sight to the southward of the pitch of Beachy Head, will lead at least 2 miles to the southward of the Royal Sovereign shoals. Beachy Head light, kept open of the Eastbourne cliff, also leads outside all the shoals.

BEACHY HEAD.—At about 6 leagues W. ¼ S. from the pitch of Haddock Cliff, and 9½ leagues W. ¼ N. from Dungeness, is BEACHY HEAD, a high and steep white chalk cliff, with its telegraph and watchhouse, to the westward of which are the SEVEN CLIFFS, the most remarkable land on this coast.

About 2½ miles to the N.E. of Beachy Head is EASTBOURNE, or *Beach Town*; to the S.E. of this place vessels may stop a tide, in 7 or 8 fathoms. Hereabout the bottom is rocky to nearly a mile from shore; but farther off there is fine sand ground.

LIGHTHOUSE.—On a spot called *Belle Tout*, being the summit of the second cliff to the westward of Beachy Head, is a *lighthouse* of the first class, which was completed in September, 1828, and exhibits a powerful *revolving* light. This light burns at an elevation of about 285 feet above the level of the sea, and exhibits its greatest brilliancy once in every 2 minutes. It may be seen, in clear weather, between 6 and 7 leagues off.

Ships sailing from the eastward will open the light when bearing N.W. ¾ W. westerly; and, whether going up or down Channel, when to the eastward of Beachy Head, and within 3 leagues of it, by keeping the light open, will pass to the southward of all the shoals in its vicinity.

DIRECTIONS FOR THE STRAIT OF DOVER.

The direct course from the Downs, outward, past the South Foreland, is S.W. ¾ S., about 2 leagues; depths, 9 to 15 fathoms; and thence to Dungeness W.S.W. ½ W., 20 miles; observing to allow for tides, &c. To turn out with a West or S.W. wind you should weigh at high water slack, or when the N.E. stream has ceased to run; and cast in shore, so as to have the first of the tide, which sets out from shore very strongly. Observe to stand no nearer to the sand opposite to Deal than in 6 or 7 fathoms; nor between Walmer castle and the cliff than in 8 or 9 fathoms. In passing the Foreland, give it a sufficient berth, as there are 10 fathoms near the pitch of the land. To the Goodwin, when off Deal, stand no nearer than in 10 fathoms; when Deal mill is between Deal and Walmer castle, no nearer than in 12; and when the mill is on with Walmer castle, no nearer than in 14 fathoms; always observing not to shoalen toward the Goodwin, this sand being steep-to on both sides. In the daytime you may see on its edge the rippling of the tide.

When you have the church and land of Folkestone open of Dover pier, you may then steer for Dungeness.

WORKING.—*In working down between Dover and Dungeness*, while you are to the East of Folkestone, you may stand to the shore to 12 and 11, and off, toward the Varne, to 16 fathoms, beyond which the strength of the tide is lost. Toward the rocks near Folkestone, before mentioned, stand no nearer than in 14 or 13 fathoms, and off, no farther than in 18 fathoms. Between Hythe and Dungeness you may stand in to 11 fathoms, and off, to 20 and 22 fathoms.

When beating up or down channel, in thick weather, between the South Foreland and Dungeness, do not go into less water, when standing in, than 14 fathoms, which will keep you to the southward of the rocks off Folkestone and the banks near Dungeness.

Between half flood and half ebb you may stand freely off, as there is not less than 20 feet on the outer banks.

ANCHORAGES.—*If requisite to come to an anchor*, to the eastward of Dungeness, you may haul up into 8 or 9 fathoms, with Dungeness light S.W. by W., and Romney tower N.W. by W., where you will have, above the Swallow Bank, fine sand and mud mixed with clay. Or, if more agreeable, you may proceed to anchor between Dunge beach and the Swallow Bank, by sailing in on the North side of that sand, with the tower of Lydd church on with a beacon upon the coast, bearing W. by N. This will lead in between that sand and the edge of the Roar. To the southward of the entrance you may anchor as convenient, in from 5 to 7 fathoms.

Ships from the westward, to anchor within the same bank, may pass Dungeness as most convenient, until Romney smock mill comes on with the great stone upon the South side of Romney Bight, bearing N. ¼ W. Steer in with this mark, until Dungeness light bears S.W. ¼ W.; you may then haul up toward the bank, and anchor in what depth you please, in from 5 to 7 fathoms. Small vessels may proceed farther in, to 3½ and 4 fathoms.

With the wind between N. by E. and W. by S. the eastern bay of Dungeness affords good shelter to vessels of every class, in from 4 to 12 fathoms, good ground. The best spot is in 7 fathoms, with Lydd church open to the northward of Lydd N.E. mill, and the lighthouse S.W. by W. ¼ W.

In WEST ROAD, to the westward of Dungeness, between Dungeness shoal and the shore, is a depth of from 8 to 3 fathoms. In 5 fathoms there is here good anchorage, and out of the strength of the stream of tide. To sail in, bring Lydd church N.E., and keep it in that direction until the lighthouse on the Ness bears E. by S.; you may then anchor, or proceed toward the lighthouse until Lydd tower bears N.E. by N. The depth is from 5 to 6 fathoms, with fine ground.

The West Road is a good stopping place during N.E. winds, and preferable to the Road of Dover. *Marks for the best ground*, in about 6 fathoms: New Romney church tower in one with Lydd church; the mill on Fairlight Down in one with, or open to the westward of Fairlight church; and Dungeness lighthouse E. ¼ S. Small vessels may run farther in toward the beach, only guarding against a sudden shift of wind.

To run out to the eastward, from the West Road, keep the lighthouse E. by S. until Lydd tower bears N. by E. Then haul round the end of Dungeness shoal, and steer out S.E. by E. until the water deepens to 12 fathoms.

With Dungeness lighthouse E. ½ N., distant from 5 to 9 miles, vessels may stop a tide in any part, there being 7 and 8 fathoms of water, with fine clear ground.

If bound to the westward from the eastern bay of Dungeness, bring the lighthouse to bear North; then steer W.S.W. until you have 13 or 14 fathoms; you may then shape a course for Beachy Head, or down Channel.

In working down Channel ships stand toward Dungeness to 16 fathoms, and from it to 18 or 19 fathoms.

Between Dungeness and Fairlight ships may stand in to 9 fathoms; and, to the westward of Dungeness Shoal, smaller ships may stand in to 6 and 5 fathoms (the soundings being gradual), and off to 24 fathoms. Between Fairlight and Beachy Head it is not prudent to stand in nearer than 18 fathoms. In the night no ship should stand in to less than that depth, unless her previous situation be well ascertained.

TIDES IN THE DOWNS AND BETWEEN THE FORELANDS, ETC.

At the North Foreland it is high water, on the full and change, at 11ʰ 16′, and the tide rises about 10 feet; at Ramsgate, as already noticed, it flows at 11ʰ 20′; at Deal, nearly at the same time. At Ramsgate spring tides rise above 15½ feet, and neaps 10 feet. At the South Foreland it flows at 11ʰ 5′. The stream in the Downs, however, continues to run until 2ʰ 30′, and the flood runs nearly for 6½ hours. Stream in the Downs to N.E. from two hours before high water until four hours after it. Strong N.E. winds sometimes keep back the tide more than an hour, and southerly winds the contrary. At Dover the time is 10ʰ 50′. At Folkestone, 10ʰ 45′. Here springs rise 15 feet, and neaps 9 feet. At Dungeness springs rise 22 to 24 feet, neaps 13 to 15 feet on the Ridge, and at Hastings, springs 22, neaps 14 feet.

To the E.S.E., about 3 miles from the North Foreland, during the first half flood upon the shore, the stream sets S.S.W., and soon after it is slack water; after which it sets West, N.N.W., and N.W., until half ebb. So that the ebb tide, out of Margate Roads,' runs three hours to the eastward before the tide of ebb runs to the southward through the Downs: from this reason, if a ship be in Margate Roads, with a wind at S.W., sail should not be made to beat and go round the Foreland until half ebb, when the tide will be going to windward through the Gull Stream. Spring tides run about 1½ miles in an hour; neaps about half a mile. When low water slack begins off the Foreland in a gale of wind, the tide frequently sets in all points of the compass.

At *Ramsgate* the flowing tide very seldom continues more than five hours, and sometimes scarcely so much. It is nearly the same at Dover.

SECTION V.

THE STRAIT OF DOVER, AND THE COASTS OF FRANCE AND BELGIUM, BETWEEN BOULOGNE AND OSTEND.

SHOALS IN THE STRAIT OF DOVER.

The **VARNE**, called by the seamen of Boulogne and Calais the *Rouge Banc*, is the northernmost of a group of banks which, lying nearly midway between the French and English coast, divides the Strait of Dover into two channels.

The Varne lies in an E.N.E. and W.S.W. direction, being nearly parallel with the northern part of the Ridge, from which it is divided by a 20 fathom channel 2 miles wide. It is about 5 miles long, and rather less than half a mile wide, and its principal portion has less than 4½ fathoms on it. About the middle of it is a part about 1½ miles in length, on the summit of which there is but 9 feet of water at spring tides.

The bank is very steep, and its abrupt ascent from a depth of 14 and 20 fathoms renders it a formidable danger. It occasions strong eddies, and, with bad weather, a furious sea. It ought to be carefully avoided.

At the hamlet of Paddlesworth, in Kent, is a conspicuous and compact clump of fir trees. The marks for the centre and shoalest part of the Varne are this clump twice its breadth open to the eastward of Folkestone church, and the guard house on Cape Blanc-nez S.E. ¾ E., exactly over the top of the chalk cliff beneath it. The fir trees N.N.W. ¾ W., in one with the central of three martello towers standing to the eastward of Folkestone, will lead to the eastward of the Varne; and Lympne windmill, N.N.W., just in sight to the westward of Lympne church, leads to the westward of it. The mill on Fairlight Down, one-third nearer to Lydd church than to Dungeness lighthouse, leads between the Varne and the Kentish shore.

The **RIDGE**, or LE COLBART, as it is called by the French, is an extremely dangerous sandbank, lying South of the Varne, nearly in midway between the two coasts, abreast of Cape Gris-nez and Dungeness. Its S.W. end, in 3 fathoms, lies exactly half-way between, and on the line joining Dungeness lighthouse and the entrance to Boulogne. It is about half a mile broad, and 9 miles long, its direction N.E. ¼ E. and S.W. ¼ W. The North part of it is 9 miles N.W. ¾ N. from Gris-nez light, and 12 miles S.S.W. from the South Foreland lights.

The Ridge, or Colbart, is very steep, and rising at once from the depths of 14 and 15 fathoms it occasions strong eddies. The sea is always heavy on it, and vessels ought not to cross it under any circumstances.

You pass through the space between the Boulogne Middle and the Ridge, by keeping the summit of Mont Couple on the centre of the first deep valley which is seen to the South of Cape Gris-nez, bearing East, or by keeping the summit of Mont Lambert a little open to the right of the belfry on the Haute Ville of Boulogne S.E. ¼ E.

The **BOULOGNE MIDDLE**, so called by Captain White, is named the *Ridins* by M. Beautemps Beaupré. In 1835 the shoal consisted of three or four patches of sand (least depth 22 feet), irregularly disposed on a rocky (*chalky*) bottom, of a depth varying from 8 to 13 fathoms. It is not dangerous, except from the heavy sea it sometimes occasions.

The WESTERN VERGOYER, known to the French fishermen as the *Bassurelle*, was first shown on our charts, by Captain White, in 1832. It is a bank of sand about 6 miles long from E.N.E. to W.S.W., and nearly 2 miles broad. Its highest part is towards its N.E. end, and on it are seven or eight small patches, with 24 feet least water on them.

The **VERGOYER** is a bank of sand about 14 miles in length, its North part being 10 miles, and its South part 17 miles from the French coast. It is not dangerous in fine weather, except in its northern part, where there is a bank of about a mile in diameter, on which, in 1835, there was only 12 feet water in one spot, gradually increasing to 27 and 40 feet North and South of it.

THE COAST OF FRANCE.

BOULOGNE.—The harbour of Boulogne occupies the entrance of the valley of the Liane, a small river. The sea forms before the entrance a beach of sand, which uncovers at low water, to the extent of half a mile out, the highest part of which remains dry for a long time at each tide, and is driven toward the shore by the wind, where it increases, by little and little, the downs against which the N.W. jetty is built. The same beach extends to the North of the jetties, and the eddies which they occasion draw the sand into the North part of the entrance of the valley, so that the shore advances to the West. It is in the middle of this part that, by means of two strong wooden jetties, the entrance to the harbour is opened.

The town of Boulogne, lying on the East side of the harbour, is built in the form of an amphitheatre, at the bottom and on the side of a small valley, enclosed between two high hills. The chief buildings which are visible from sea are the belfry tower and the colonnade of the new cathedral of the Haute Ville, and the spire of the church of the Basse Ville, the flag of the Marine Baths, and a mill placed halfway up to the S.E. of this flag.

The channel leading to the port is comprised between two jetties of unequal length. It is four-tenths of a mile long, and 220 feet wide, and runs to the N.W. by N.

It is high water (establishment of the port) on the days of the new and full moon, at 11ʰ 26′ at night, and the rise is from 18 to 24 feet. With strong winds from S.S.W. to W.N.W. the sea rises one or two feet higher, and with those from S.E. to E.N.E., nearly a foot less than the ordinary tides.

The sea being very heavy at the entrance of Boulogne, when it blows hard from the S.S.W. by W. to N.N.W., it is as well to be certain, before running for the harbour, that there is water enough to enter without the risk of touching.

The time during which the channel is practicable is shown by means of two fixed lights (visible 9 miles), placed perpendicularly, one above the other, on the outside of a small tower on the N.W. jetty head, and by a *red* light (visible one mile), placed on a wooden stage, placed on the head of the N.E. jetty. The upper light on the N.W. jetty and the *red* light on the N.E. jetty are lit when there is about 9½ feet water on the ground before the jetty head, and the lower light on the N.W. jetty at the moment of high water. They are all three extinguished when the water falls to 9½ feet.

By day, the state of the tide is signalled by a red flag, hoisted over the small light-tower on the N.W. jetty. It is shown as soon as there is 12¼ feet in the channel, and lowered when it falls to the same depth. The harbour masters and assistants are always on the jetty heads while the entrance is practicable.

The most favourable winds for entering Boulogne are those from S.S.W. round by N. to N.E., but strong winds from the N.E. are dangerous to enter the port with, on account of the violent gusts which come from the high lands to the North of the town.

Every vessel which, being near Boulogne, finds the sea too heavy to enter the harbour, should bear up immediately for Calais; for, when Boulogne harbour is inaccessible from the heavy sea, that of Calais is practicable ; and reciprocally.

The entrance of Boulogne is N.W. by W. from the summit of Mont Lambert, and W. by S. from the column of the Grande Armée. The summit of Mont Lambert is the highest point around Boulogne, and is 1,802 feet above low water. The top of the statue on the column is 1,469 feet above the same level.

The coast between Cape Gris-nez and Boulogne forms a slight curve to the East. This port is 8¼ miles from the cape, and the entrance is nearly *true* South from it.

CAPE GRIS-NEZ is one of the most remarkable points of the northern coast of France. The coast here makes a sharp turn in its direction, and its height (165 English feet) allows it to be seen, in clear weather, at 14 or 15 miles off. The peaked rocky cliff in which it terminates, as well as those which surround it to the East and South, are of a dark gray colour, assuming a purplish tinge when they are illumined by the sun's rays.

The LIGHTHOUSE is established at a quarter of a mile South of the extremity of the cape. The LIGHT, revolving in half a minute, is from a tower 46 feet high, and the light (of the first order) at 193 feet, consequently visible 22 miles off. It will be distinguished from the new Calais light by the difference in its character. Gris-nez light being eclipsed every 30 seconds; while Calais, a steady light, shows a brighter flash every 4 minutes.

CAPE BLANC-NEZ lies about 6 miles E.N.E. ¼ E. from Cape Griz-nez, and owes its name to the high chalk cliff which terminates it. Between the capes the coast forms a slight curve, in the bottom of which is the village of *Wissant*, inhabited by some fishermen.

From the prominent headland which Cape Gris-nez makes, and the great change in the direction of the coast at this point, there is, during the flood, an eddy which extends a long distance to the N.E., and a counter-current along the coast from near Wissant towards the S.W. It is probably to this eddy that the formation of the deposits of sand and broken shells called the *Banc à la Ligne* is owing. This bank fills up the bend in the coast, and extends 4 miles to the E.N.E. of the cape, its outer edge being 2 miles from the shore. Its highest part uncovers at times, and towards its N.E. end are numerous ridges or *ridens* of sand, on which there is 4 to 9 feet water. These are called the *Barrière.*

A line of rocky ground, partly covered with sand, contiguous to the coast, extends East and West, from Wissant nearly to the village of *Sangatte*, and 2 miles outside Cape Blanc-nez. The shoalest part forms two flats, separated from each other, and dangerous to all vessels. That to the West is called the *Quenocs*, and has 7 feet least water upon it. It is 1½ miles, N. by W., from the guardhouse of Cape Blanc-nez, and 2½ miles W.N.W. of the steeple of Sangatte. The second is nearer the land, and is called the *Rouge-Riden.* Its shoalest part has 7 feet over it, and lies N. ¼ E. 1 mile from the guardhouse on Cape Blanc-nez.

You will keep half a mile North of the East shoal of the Rouge-Riden, by bringing the steeple of Sangatte, bearing S.E. ½ S., between the two mills of Coquelles, 2 miles inland, and occupying the highest ground. The entrance of Calais is 4 miles East of Sangatte.

The RIDEN de CALAIS, a bank 4 miles long, extends between Sangatte and Calais, and forms the North side of the anchorage called Calais Roads. It is not dangerous, except to large vessels.

CALAIS lies 11½ miles E.N.E. ½ E. from Cape Gris-nez; S.E. ¼ S., 22½ miles from Dover; and S.E. ¾ S., 20½ miles from the South Foreland.

The *entrance to the harbour* is about 260 feet wide, and opens to the N. by W. ¼ W. It runs between two parallel wooden jetties of equal length.

The tides rise as follow:—Springs, 19 and 20 feet for weak tides; mean, 22 feet; and 23 to 24 ft. 3 in. at equinoctial spring tides. At neaps the ordinary rise is 16 and 17 feet. The time of high water occurs at 11ʰ 30′ a.m., or 11ʰ 49′ p.m., reckoning from corrected noon. It is to be remarked that the tides rise higher in the harbour with strong winds from W.N.W. to S.W. than they do with those from E.N.E. to S.E. Thus, with gales from the S.W., which render navigation of the Channel so dangerous, the port of Calais can

Calais Cliff, &c., with the town bearing about S.E. by S. [S.E. by E. true.]

smaller, at spring tides, vessels drawing 18 and 19 feet water; but with winds from the eastward the sea rises less, and then at neap tides not above 10 feet can be admitted.

Fort Rouge is to the West of, and near to, the old head of the western jetty. It is built of wood, and on one of its highest buildings they signalize, during the day, that the channel is practicable, by hoisting a large red flag. This flag remains hoisted while there are 12¼ feet in the channel. At night the same is indicated by a bright light shown from Fort Rouge at 33 feet. This light is shown while there is 8½ feet water in the channel, but is not exhibited if the weather will not allow vessels to enter.

When the sea is heavy at the entrance the pilots cannot get out to vessels; but to remedy this as far as possible, there is established, on the old head of the East jetty, at 800 feet from the end of the open pile work, a mast with a moveable yard, on which a balloon will be hoisted (when the flag is up at Fort Rouge, showing that the entrance is practicable), and signals made to vessels entering. If they are in the right direction, the mast is kept vertical; if otherwise, the mast with the ball is inclined in the direction they ought to steer.

In foggy weather the proximity of the jetties is signalized by tolling a large bell.

CALAIS ROAD.—This anchorage is comprised between the Riden de Calais and the strand West of the harbour. Towards the bank the depth is from 10 to 14 fathoms, and 7 and 9 fathoms at half a mile off the shore. The bottom is of sand, with broken shells; but according to the pilots, beneath this there is good holding ground, which the anchors of large ships penetrate, so that such ships anchoring on the South slope of the Riden will ride out a N.W. gale. The bottom is much inferior nearer the land. The road is sheltered by the land from S.W. to E.S.E., but is entirely open to the rest of the horizon.

CALAIS LIGHTHOUSE.—Till the year 1848 the lighthouse was in the centre of the town, but on October 15th, 1848, a beautiful new tower was completed in one of the angles of the fortifications at the N.E. side of the town. The tower is octagonal, 167 feet high, and of elegant form. The light is brilliant and fixed, but varied every four minutes by a bright flash, preceded and followed by short eclipses, but which are not total within 12 miles. Being elevated 190 feet above the sea, it may be seen 21 miles off.

On the *western jetty* a *red* light is shown at 16 feet, visible 2 miles off.

On *Fort Rouge*, to the right of the entrance, a *bright tide light* is shown at 33 feet. This, as above stated, is shown while there is 8½ feet water, and only during weather that the harbour is accessible.

The entrance of Gravelines harbour is 10 miles, E. ½ N., from the entrance to Calais. The coast between them is low and sandy.

GRAVELINES is a small port for fishermen and coasters, the chief trade of which is in the export of fruit and provisions to England. The harbour is in the N.W. part of the town, at the mouth of the River Aa, the freshes of which, in the wet seasons, clear the harbour and entrances of the accumulations made during the dry season.

In weak spring tides the harbour can only admit 11¾ feet draught, and this only during five or six days of the time of the highest tides.

The channel, which is 2 miles long, is in the same direction with the harbour, and is in a straight line towards the N. by W. ¼ W. It consists of two distinct parts, the one on the strand, and the other on the land between Fort Philippe and Gravelines. A beacon marks the West entrance to the channel. The surface of the rocks at the end of this jetty is 17½ feet above low water spring tides.

The eastern jetty is very carefully preserved, but not lengthened; its extremity is marked by a large wooden beacon, capped with a wooden lantern, surmounted by a vane.

The tides rise here from 6 to 20 feet at springs, and 2 to 4 at neap tides. The establishment of the port, or high water, is at 12^h (midnight).

The time during which the entrance is practicable is shown during the day by a red flag hoisted on a mast, at the commencement of the western jetty, and remains so while there is sufficient water for the fishing vessels.

Just behind the flagstaff, on the same side of the entrance, are two small posts, on which are hoisted two small fixed lights, visible about 5 miles off, which, brought in one, lead into the harbour. One of these is shown from sunset, the other is hoisted while there is 6 feet water in the channel. These two small lights are maintained by the fishermen, and consequently only shown while their boats are in sight. They are likely to be mistaken by strangers for the lights in the houses.

GRAVELINES LIGHTHOUSE was chiefly established to point out the position of this dangerous coast by bearings with those of Calais and Dunkirk. The tower is 101½ feet high above the lowest tides, and is a Doric column of clear red colour. The light, first shown on May 1, 1843, is a *fixed* light, of the third order, at 95 feet above high water. It stands 175 yards from the shore, in the West part of Port Philippe, and 65 yards from the eastern side of the channel.

The distance between the harbour entrances of Gravelines and Dunkirk is nearly 10¼ miles, and the intervening coast, with some inflexions, runs E. by N. and W. by S., *true*. The low plain which lies at the back of the shore extends further than the eye can reach. The only objects seen on it are the clumps of large trees which surround the villages and farms, some steeples rising above these, and some windmills.

DUNKIRK.—This is a military and commercial port, and is the principal French port on the North Sea. In a commercial view it is very important, and particularly for the number of vessels employed in the cod fishery.

The maritime establishments at Dunkirk (*Dunkerque*) consist of an entrance channel above a mile long, ending in a dry harbour, at the end of which is a floating basin and an inner harbour, which last also dries at every tide. The floating basin and the surrounding buildings belong to the government.

The entrance of Dunkirk runs to N. by W. ¼ W., is 1 1/10 miles in length, and 76 yards wide. The channel is comprised partly between the quay of the citadel and the extension of the town quay to the Cunette sluice, and partly between wooden pilework. The entrance channel to Dunkirk does not dry but within 2 cables' lengths of the harbour; beyond this the channel formed by the watercourses varies from 1 to 8 feet in depth.

With winds from the western quarter vessels drawing 15 or 16 feet may lie beneaped on the deposits in the channel for three or four days, or on the banks in the harbour for four or five days; but with winds from the East they will only lie there one or two days at most. The tide rises at 150 yards from the end of the West jetty, from 16 to 19½ at ordinary, and 21 feet at equinoctial spring tides. At strong neap tides the rise is 16 feet, but sometimes only 13¾ feet.

It is high water (establishment of the port) at 12ʰ 13′.

On the terrace of a small and elegant building, lying at 100 yards S.E. of the new lighthouse, there is a flagstaff, by which signals are made of the state of the tide when rising or falling.

A small fixed light of 6 miles range, at 23 feet above high water, is shown throughout the night, on the head of the western jetty, to show its position.

The channel is also indicated by the new light of Heuguenar, which was first shown on Jan. 1, 1845. This *fixed* light is upon the Heuguenar tower, 2,400 yards S. by E. ¼ E. (S. 39° E. *true*) from the entrance. The tower formerly showed the high light now removed to the new lighthouse, hereafter described. This light, specially intended to show the channel between the jetties from the entrance to the town, sends a bright ray in that direction. To the right or left of this, the light is not visible in ordinary weather to the distance of 5 or 6 miles, but in an angular space of 10° or 12°. But its range in the direction of the channel, S. by E. ¼ E., will extend to 12 or 15 miles, so that it is often seen before the light upon the western jetty.

DUNKIRK NEW LIGHT.—A light formerly established on the top of the Heuguenar (or Leuguenaerd) tower, not being sufficiently high, a new and handsome brick tower, in the form of a great column, has been erected between the western jetty and the ruins of Fort Risban. This new tower is 180 feet high, on which is a revolving light of the first order, eclipsed every minute, and visible in clear weather 24 miles off. The light is 193¼ feet above the high water mark. It is nearly half a mile S. by E. ¼ E. from the end of the West jetty, and 1,700 yards N. ¼ W. of the tower of Dunkirk, which is 20 feet lower than the lighthouse. The eclipses of this light will not be total within 12 or 15 miles. The light being continuous will serve to keep the situation of the light in view. The flashes will be seen beyond the limits of the dangers, and reach the South side of another group of banks, surveyed by Captain Hewett, R.N. The tower is conspicuous by day, and was first illuminated on May 1st, 1843, at the same time as the Gravelines light.

ROAD OF DUNKIRK.—The road is comprehended between the exterior limit of the shoals off the coast, on which there is less than 4½ fathoms, and a bank of but little depth, which joins the coast at 11 miles East of Dunkirk, before Broer's Duyn. The space proper for anchorage is about 6 miles long from West to East, and 4 or 5 cables' lengths broad. The portions of the bank which bound the road to the North are named in order, Snouw, Braeck Bank, Hil's Bank, and Traepegeer. Their arrangement will be seen on the chart.

It is composed of two deeper parts, where the ground is very good holding, divided from each other by a bar of sand, 3 cables' lengths wide. There is 7 and 8 fathoms on the sandy bar, but the holding ground is bad. The middle of the bar is N.N.W. of Dunkirk new lighthouse. The western fosse, when the depth is 8 and 9 fathoms, is good holding, and begins N.E. of Mardick Tower, and extends to the sandy bottom. The second fosse commences when the tower of Heuguenar is in one with the new lighthouse, and extends to the Passe de Zuydcoote. The depth varies from 8 to 11 fathoms, and the bottom good, particularly before the town of Dunkirk. It is in this part of the road that large vessels anchor; comprised between the bearings of the Heuguenar tower touching the East side of the new lighthouse, and the same tower in one with Dunkirk tower. It is sheltered by the Braeck and Hil's Banks from the sea during N.W. and N.E. breezes.

The channels to Dunkirk Roads were re-buoyed in 1855. All buoys and beacons painted *red* to be left to starboard, and those painted *black* are to be left to port, by vessels entering the roads from sea: and buoys painted with alternate red and black horizontal bands may be passed on either side. Warping buoys are painted white. Beacons and turrets are painted white, and each mark has the name of the shoal it indicates, and a number, showing its numerical order from seaward; the even numbers on the red buoys to starboard, and the odd numbers on the black buoys to port.

Vessels leaving Dunkirk Road by the Zuydcoote entrance will find, after passing it, in the western part of Nieuport Road, excellent holding ground in 5½, 7, and 9 fathoms water.

THE FLEMISH BANKS.

The banks which render the northern coasts of France so dangerous occupy a considerable area in the southern part of the North Sea. They extend 15 miles off shore on the meridian of Calais, and to 42 miles off on the meridians of Dunkirk and Nieuport. Collectively, these banks and those hereafter described, northward of the Belgian shores, are known by the name of the FLEMISH BANKS, and they may be divided into two groups:—the first of those near the shore, some of which have been previously noticed, and are always known by the name of the DUNKIRK BANKS, and the second of those lying out of sight of land or the range of the lighthouses, the eastern position and depth of which were imperfectly known till the survey by the lamented Captain Hewett.

All these banks converge towards the Strait of Dover, and are formed of fine grey and black sand. They are considerably raised above the general depth, and usually very steep toward the land, and slope gradually towards the offing. Their highest parts, to which the French pilots give the name of *Pollaerts* (or *Polders*), are dangerous to vessels of all classes. They occasion very heavy and cross seas, and in hard weather they break.

These ridges lie on an immense bank of sand, gravel, and broken shells, which lies against the shores of France, Belgium, and Holland, the soundings on which are less than 18 fathoms. A similar bank is attached to the English coast, and between them is a channel of greater depth than 18 fathoms.

The DUNKIRK BANKS are eleven in number. Commencing with the outermost, their names, according to the French sailors, are:—The *Sandettié*, the *Out-Ruytingen*, the *In-Ruytingen*, the *Bergues Bank*, the *Dyck*, the N.E. part of which is called the *Clif d'Islande*, the *Smal Bank*, and that which bounds Dunkirk Road, which, as previously shown, is composed of several parts, bearing the names *Snouw*, *Braeck*, *Hil's*, and *Traepegeer Banks*.

The other banks, to the North and N.E. of the former, are named, proceeding from North to East, the *Fairy Bank*, the *North Hinder*, the *West Hinder*, the *East Hinder*, *Bligh* or *Blyth Bank*, and *Thornton's Ridge*.

The SANDETTIE (in Flemish *Zand-detic, little sand or bank*) is called *Ourting* by the French sailors. It is the first bank met with in coming from the N.W., and bounds the deepest channel to the South. It is 12 miles long N.E. ¼ E. and S.W.¼ W. (true); its breadth varies from 4 to 9 cables' lengths, and it is so steep-to on its South and S.E. sides that at less than a half cable's length from its southern edge there are 18 and 20 fathoms water. The slope is much more gradual to the N.W., and may easily be avoided by the lead.

There are two spots on the bank which are certainly dangerous to pass in bad weather. The northern one, on which there is 19 feet least water, lies 18 miles N.N.W. ½ W. from Dunkirk light, and 17½ miles N.E. ½ N. from Calais light. The southern patch, on which are only 18 feet least water, is 3½ miles W.S.W. from the former one; and besides these there are several patches on which are from 19 to 22 feet water; but on all the rest the depth varies from 27 to 40 feet. The Sandettié, rising suddenly from the bottom, causes strong ripplings, which make a very heavy sea in blowing weather; at such times the sea breaks on the shoaler spots.

The OUT-RUYTINGEN, the second of the Dunkirk Banks, lies nearly in the middle of the space between the Sandettié and the coast of France. It begins at 7 miles off shore on the meridian of Calais, extending in a curve to the East and E.N.E., being 16 miles long, and terminating at 12 miles off shore, when the spires of Bergues are in one with the tower and light of Dunkirk bearing S. ¾ E. The western part of this bank is that formerly called by the Calais sailors the *Dyck*. The Out-Ruytingen is nearly perpendicular toward the land, and slopes gradually to the North. The parts which have less than 5 fathoms water form two banks or "*pollaerts*," 2½ miles apart, with 26 to 41 feet, so that any vessel for Gravelines or Calais can pass it. The West bank, called erroneously the Dyck, is 3½ miles long, and half a mile broad. Its shoalest part in 1836 was 9 feet, and lies with the steeple of St. Pierre les Calais in one with the mill of Furnes bearing S. by W. The eastern patch is 9 miles, and half a mile broad. The least depth, which varies, is about 11 feet; the rest is from 16 to 20 feet. There are considerable ripplings on this bank, and it breaks on the shoalest patches, and there is a very heavy sea on its edges in hard weather. Small vessels should avoid crossing it in bad weather, as the sea rises on it without notice.

The IN-RUYTINGEN is 8 miles long within the depths of 8 fathoms, from W.S.W. to E.N.E., and is 3 miles broad from S.S.E. to N.N.W.; it is in the form of a triangle, and is 2½ miles from the East part of the Out-Ruytingen. Its West end is 9½ miles N. by W. ½ W., and its N.E. end 12½ miles N.N.E. from Dunkirk light. The irregularity of the depth on this bank always causes a bad sea on it. In 1836 the patches with less than 24 feet on it were two in number, separated from each other by a depth of 5 and 6 fathoms. The western patch occupied the middle of the bank, and was 2 miles long, North and South, and 1½ miles broad. On its summit there was but 8 feet water, which spot lay with Dunkirk lighthouse in the middle of the space between Cassel and the spires of Bergues. On the eastern patch the least depth was 13 feet, and it was about 1½ miles in length.

The BERGUES BANK was so named by M. Beaupré, and is a prolongation of the N.E. point of the Out-Ruytingen, and lies 1 mile North of the eastern flat of the In-Ruytingen. In 1802, when it was first defined, it had 5 fathoms water on it; but in 1836 there was but 21½ feet on a spot bearing N. by E. ¼ E. 13 miles from Dunkirk light. Its shoalest part is about 3½ miles in length.

The DYCK is the largest of the Dunkirks, and commences at 4½ miles N.E. of Calais light, and trends for 18 miles parallel to the shore, as far as the meridian of Dunkirk; it thence runs to E.N.E., and reaches 13 miles farther off. The western part of this great bank, as far as the meridian of Gravelines, is called the WEST DYCK or ORTEIL; the central part, between the meridians of Gravelines and Grande Synthe, is the DYCK, properly so called, and its eastern part is generally called CLIF D'ISLANDE. These three banks form a narrow and continuous ridge, the *pollaerts* of which are separated by depths of less than 6 fathoms.

The N.E. part of the *Clif d'Islande*, on which there are only 16 to 22 feet water, and around which the sea is always very heavy, is a formidable danger; the more so as it rises suddenly from a depth of 12 to 17 fathoms, and is thus difficult to avoid by the lead, and being so far from the land, unless the weather be very clear, you cannot make out the remarkable points of the coast.

The IN-RATEL is properly only a branch of the Middle Dyck. It is about 7 miles in length, and about a mile broad. It is steep-to on all sides; its East end, on which are 16 to 17 feet water, terminates suddenly in a depth of 6 to 7 fathoms at 6 miles N.N.E. $\frac{1}{2}$ E. of Dunkirk light. The pollaert of the In-Ratel is 2 miles long, and 5$\frac{1}{4}$ cables' lengths broad. It has only 1 foot of water at low water on its highest point, which lies with the spires of Bergues touching the East side of the tower of Dunkirk, and is 5$\frac{1}{4}$ miles N. $\frac{3}{4}$ W. of Dunkirk light.

The OUT-RATEL is an isolated bank to the S.E. of the East Dyck, and parallel to it, at 2$\frac{1}{2}$ miles distant. Its name, which means "rattle," perhaps is derived from the noise of the heavy sea which is almost always found on it. The S.W. point of the bank is terminated by a dangerous patch of 7$\frac{1}{4}$ feet least water. You will keep to the northward of the dangerous parts of the banks between the Clif d'Islande and the Middelkirk Bank, on the westernmost of the Ostend banks, in not keeping to the South of Ostend light bearing S.E. $\frac{3}{4}$ E.

The GRAVELINES SHOAL, which was discovered in 1836, is a small spot of 21 feet, about a mile across, and 2 miles from the West end of the Breedt Bank, and is 3$\frac{3}{4}$ miles N. by E. $\frac{3}{4}$ E. from Gravelines light. The pilots and fishermen of Gravelines called it the *Franc Banc.*

The BREEDT BANK and the EAST BREEDT BANK are connected with the In-Ratel by depths of 18 to 31 feet; as their names indicate, they are the largest of the Dunkirk Banks. The West end of the Breedt Bank, where the dangerous part begins, is 3 miles off shore to the North of the high shores of the point of Gravelines, and 4$\frac{3}{4}$ miles N.E. $\frac{1}{4}$ E. from Gravelines light. There are three dangerous patches on this bank. The middle of the westernmost is 3$\frac{1}{2}$ miles off shore to N. $\frac{1}{4}$ E. of Mardyck steeple, and has only 3 feet least water on it. The middle patch is 2 miles in diameter, and its highest part uncovers 5 feet at low water springs. This particularly dangerous spot is 3 miles N. $\frac{1}{4}$ E. of Dunkirk light, and from it the great tower of Dunkirk is seen between Cassel and the spires of Bergues, but rather nearer the former. The third patch is 3$\frac{1}{2}$ miles long, and one-third of a mile wide; on its West part there is but 6$\frac{1}{2}$ feet water, and 9 and 10 on the rest.

The *East Breedt Bank* is connected with the Breedt Bank by a narrow shoal of 5 miles in extent, on which are from 26$\frac{1}{2}$ to 37 feet water. It lies E. by N. and W. by S., and is about 6 miles in length. Its S.W. point is 14$\frac{1}{2}$ miles N.E. by E. $\frac{1}{2}$ E. from Dunkirk light; 10 miles N.E. $\frac{3}{4}$ N. from Furnes, and 11 miles W.N.W. of Ostend light. Its East end terminates in some shoal spots of 25 feet. The least depth on the East Breedt Bank is 15 feet.

The SMAL BANK. The West point of this bank, which is 2$\frac{1}{4}$ miles from the Dunkirk lighthouse, and with it bearing in one with the tower of Dunkirk, is connected with the Breedt Bank by depths of 15 to 22 feet. From this it extends 6 miles East, and then 8$\frac{1}{4}$ miles E.N.E. The dangerous part of this bank, formed by spots with less than 10 feet water, is of considerable extent. The southern edge of this bank bounds the *West Deep* to the North. It is steep, and requires care in tacking. The Smal Bank is connected with the Nieuport Bank by a narrow bar of 17 to 23 feet water. The West point of the Nieuport Bank, which has 15 to 16 feet water, lies with the tower of Furnes on with the East part of Broer's Duyn, bearing S. $\frac{1}{2}$ W. Between the East point of the pollaert of the Smal Bank and the N.E. part of the same bank, are several isolated shoal spots of 11 to 16 feet water, which may be avoided by the direction previously given for quitting Dunkirk Roads by the Zuydcoote entrance.

The *Snouw, Braeck Bank, Hil's Bank,* and the *Traepegeer,* have been previously noticed.

The FAIRY BANK, a high sandy ridge, lies on the eastern edge of the deep water channel. On its South end the 8 fathoms water lies 18 miles N.N.E. $\frac{3}{4}$ E. from the new light at Dunkirk, and from this the bank extends N.E. $\frac{1}{2}$ E. for 10 miles: its breadth not exceeding 8 cables' lengths. The Fairy Bank has two patches or pollaerts; one, 2$\frac{1}{2}$ miles long, on which there are not less than 24 feet water; and the second, at the North extreme of the bank, and which is very small, has 30 feet water. The new light at Dunkirk may be seen, in clear weather, from the South parts of the Fairy Bank, and also from the West Hinder.

The NORTH HINDER is an extremely dangerous sandbank, and may be considered as a prolongation of the Fairy Bank. It is 7 miles long, 5 or 6 cables' lengths broad, and lies N.E. and S.W. It has but one spot or narrow pollaert, about 2 miles long, and with 26 to 30 feet water. This shoal spot is about the middle of the bank; the rest of the soundings on it vary from 6 to 8 fathoms. The North point of the North Hinder is in lat. 51° 42′ N., lon. 2° 35′ E., and is 24½ miles S.E. by E. ¼ E. from the Galloper light. Vessels should on no account pass to the eastward of the line joining this and the Fairy Bank.

The WEST HINDER is to the South of the former, and to the East of the Fairy Bank. It is a sandbank 15 miles long, and three-quarters of a mile broad. The pollaert of the West Hinder occupies almost its entire length, forming a sort of continuous crest, on which there is nearly throughout a depth of 17 and 18 feet water, but in no part more than 30 feet. The only passage practicable for large vessels bound to Flushing or Antwerp, and intending to enter by the Inner Wielingen, is between the Out-Ruytingen, the Bergues Bank, and the Clif d'Islande on one side, and the Fairy Bank and the West Hinder on the other.

The EAST HINDER lies to the East of the West and North Hinders, and is a sandbank of 11¼ miles in length, by 6 or 7 cables' lengths broad, lying N.E. and S.W. The East and North Hinders are separated by a channel 4 miles broad, with 17 to 22 fathoms water, but it ought to be avoided by large vessels.

BLIGH BANK is parallel to the East Hinder, and 3 miles to the eastward of it. It is of sand, and extends 10 miles N.E. and S.W. The Bligh (or Blyth Bank) has but one pollaert, a mile in length, on which is a depth of 29 and 30 feet water. On other parts the soundings are very irregular, from 32 to 53 feet. The irregularity of the bottom, both on the bank and around it, renders it quite impossible at this distance from the land.

THORNTON'S RIDGE is a bank of sand, which rises from a depth of 13 to 17 fathoms at 15 miles from the Belgian shores, and beyond the range of the lights. It is 13 miles long, and 1½ miles broad, lying East and West. The West point of Thornton's Ridge is 3 miles S.E. of the South end of the Bligh Bank, but North of this they diverge. The interval between these is the best, or least dangerous, channel for large ships quitting the road or harbour of Dunkirk when bound northward, and when with S.W. winds it is decided to pass between the banks.

THE COAST OF BELGIUM.

Between Calais and Dunkirk there is a high land up in the country, called *Mont Cassel*: in clear weather this land may be seen from sea, and serves to distinguish this part of the coast from all others in the vicinity; but the fortresses about the town, and the steeples of Bergues, about 4 miles within, on the South, will certainly prevent mistake. At 3 miles eastward of Dunkirk is the church of *Leffrinkoucke*, with a spire; beyond this is that of *Zuydcoote*, with a square steeple. Six miles and a half eastward of Zuydcoote is *Furnes*, with two spires of different heights; and near this is *Wulpen*, with one only.

About 11 miles East from Dunkirk is the *Broer's Duyn* [*Brother's Down*], a long, white sandhill, which may be known by its appearing higher than any of the adjacent sandhills, and by Furnes steeples, standing up in the country, and bearing nearly South. The BOUNDARY between FRANCE and BELGIUM is 7 miles East of Dunkirk.

NIEUPORT.—This place lies 4 miles eastward of the Broer's Duyn, and 15 miles to the East of Dunkirk; it has a small lighthouse, with a castle, and several steeples and mills, which appear from sea like a fleet of ships; but the great church steeple, which is square, with a turret on its top, appears large, and more conspicuous than the rest.

A *tide light*, for the use of the coasters, was established here in 1825, and is kept lighted only when such vessels may pass the bar, or from half flood to half ebb. The light, being 32 feet above the sea, may be seen at 6 miles off, on approaching from the West, in the direction of S.S.E., and to those from the eastward in the direction of S.S.W. On entering the port the light must be brought to bear S. 18° E. The harbour is now fit for small vessels only, which have to lie dry on hard sand; the channel, in which is a beacon at its entrance, is 1¾ miles long, very narrow, unsheltered on the western side, and with strong winds cannot be attempted without risk of danger.

OSTEND lies 9 miles E. by N. from Nieuport; and appears, when at a distance, like an island: it has a church with a large spire steeple, a town house with a large square tower on it; a conspicuous lighthouse; and three windmills. Two of the mills may be seen very plainly, one at each end of the town; but the third seems to stand in the middle of the town, and therefore cannot be so easily discerned.

Ostend, as it appears from the pier head.

The LIGHTHOUSE is 72 feet high, and stands in the N.E. corner of the town, near the end of the western jetty; its lantern shows a bright fixed light at about 87 feet above the sea: it is regularly lighted, and may be seen 4 leagues off.

Besides this principal light, the following are shown:—

On the head of the *western* pier or jetty, facing the entrance, a *green* light is shown at 23 feet, and visible at 4 or 5 miles off.

On the head of the *eastern* pier, a *red tide* light at a similar elevation.

A bright tide light at 50 fathoms, inside of the end of the eastern pier.

A bright tide light on the end of the sea wall, on the downs East of the town, and near Fort Imperial.

These lights, as now established, were first shown January 21st, 1849, and must be attended to as follows:—

1. The *green* light on the western pier is intended merely to indicate the position of the pier head, and is shown throughout the night.

2. The entrance of the harbour must not be attempted unless the *red* light of the eastern pier is also shown.

3. When both of these lights are shown, they signify that there is more than $8\frac{1}{4}$ feet water between the pier heads, and less than $14\frac{1}{2}$ feet.

4. As soon as there are $14\frac{1}{2}$ feet water between the pier heads the *red* light will be extinguished, and the usual tide lights, one near Fort Imperial, East of the town, as above, and the other on the end of the sea wall, will be shown.

5. These tide lights will in their turn be extinguished when the tide has again fallen to $14\frac{1}{2}$ feet water, at which time the *red* light on the eastern pier will be relighted, and kept burning till the water falls to $8\frac{1}{4}$ feet, when it will also be extinguished.

In bad weather, when there can be no communication with the pier heads, these arrangements must, of course, be interrupted; and all vessels are cautioned not to attempt the harbour when the tide lights are not displayed.

It must be observed that the tide still sets to the eastward two hours after high water in the harbour.

We have already noticed that Ostend lies 9 miles E. by N. from Nieuport. From the road of Nieuport the course and distance to Ostend, within the Strom Bank and the bank along shore, are East, 9 miles. The depths are 5, 6, 4, and $3\frac{1}{2}$ to 3 fathoms.

Vessels bound in for Ostend Outer or Great Road may enter between the Middelkirk and Ostend banks (lying as already described), with the steeples of Furnes and Oost Dunkirk in a line, bearing S.W. $\frac{1}{2}$ S. until Ostend lighthouse bears S.E. The last mark leads into the road, where you may anchor with the great steeple of Ostend S.E., and Nieuport steeple just within a large sandhill, nearly S.W., in $5\frac{1}{2}$ or 6 fathoms, about $2\frac{1}{2}$ miles from shore.

There is also good riding more to the eastward, within *Ostend Bank*, on clay ground, in 6 fathoms, with the body of Ostend S. by E.; Middelkirk, S.W.; and Blankenburg, E. by S.

To sail from the OUTER to the INNER ROAD, small vessels cross the Strom Bank, with the town house of Ostend bearing S.E., but must wait until half flood.

There is generally a pilot vessel lying at sea, with a blue flag hoisted, in order to put pilots on board of those ships which want them: and at tide time flags are hoisted on shore at the following periods, namely, a *small blue flag* when 14 feet of water is on the bar; a *large blue flag* when 17 feet; and a *red flag* when 24 feet.

SECTION VI.

THE SWIN AND KING'S CHANNEL, FROM THE NORE TO THE EAST END OF THE GUNFLEET.

1.—GENERAL DESCRIPTION.

The PASSAGES of the WEST SWIN and of the EAST SWIN, or KING'S CHANNEL, lie between flats and ridges of sand, the extremities of which are clearly pointed out by buoys, beacons, &c.; the nearest lands being low and flat, and the objects on them not clearly distinguishable, unless in the fairest weather.

The **WEST SWIN** is bounded on its northern and western sides by the *Maplin Sand* and *Whitaker Spit;* and on its southern and eastern sides by the *Oaze Sand* and *Flat of the Barrows,* on the latter of which lie the shoals called the *Mouse,* with the *West* and the *East Barrow.* Off the northern side of this flat extends the sand called the *Swin Middle,* or *Heaps,* the western end of which, distinguished by a *lightvessel,* bounds the N.E. side of the West Swin Channel.

The **EAST SWIN**, or KING'S CHANNEL, is bounded on the northern side by the *Gunfleet Sand;* on its southern side by the *Swin Middle,* or *Heaps,* and the *Sunk Sand.*

Of the Shoals above mentioned, the following is a general description.

OAZE SAND, &c.—To the E.S.E. ¼ E., at the distance of 4¼ miles from the Nore lightvessel, lies the western end of a sand called the *Oaze,* which extends from a monster red beacon buoy on that end to a monster black beacon buoy on its eastern end, East 4 miles. The southern side of the shoalest spot (6 feet) is marked by a chequered black and white buoy, midway between the former two.

The MAPLIN is that great flat of sand which stretches off from Shoeburyness, and to the eastward of the Isle of Foulness. It covers at about 1½ hours of flood. Upon its edges are three black buoys, called *West* or *Shoeburyness, Middle,* and *East Shoebury Buoys;* a black buoy, the *Blacktail Spit;* a beacon named the *Blacktail;* a buoy, painted black, called *Foulness Spit,* or the *Maplin Buoy;* and a lighthouse with fixed red light, off which is a *black buoy.* There is also a beacon on the N.E. spit, called that of the *Whitaker,* which appellation is also given to a swashway at the back, or North side of the sand.

Off the Ridge, or North side of the Maplin Sand, lies the sand called the BUXEY, which is covered at about 3¼ hours' flood, and forms the North side of the Whitaker Swash. This sand has a buoy at each end, and an iron beacon on its northern edge, and is about 5 miles in length.

LIGHTVESSEL, &c.—In the month of July, 1838, two lightvessels were moored, the one upon the *Flat of the Mouse Sand,* from which a *brilliant* fixed light is exhibited from sunset to sunrise throughout the year; and the other off the Maplin Sand, near the Sheers beacon, which has been replaced by a lighthouse.

The MAPLIN LIGHTHOUSE, which is constructed of iron, upon screw piles, stands at one-quarter of a mile West from the site of the Sheers beacon, as shown in page 46 hereafter, with the Swin Middle lightvessel N.E. ¾ E. 4½ miles, and the Whitaker beacon N.E. ¼ E. 5 miles. The light is distinguished from that of the Mouse by being of a *red* colour. There is also a bright light shown over 8° of the circle, to point out the channel between the Shivering Sand buoy and the Girdler lightvessel, and it is masked over the Maplin Sand.

The GUNFLEET is that extensive sand which lies to the eastward of the Buxey. The whole extent of this sand from the *Spitway,* or Swash, between it and the Buxey, is 12¼ miles. It trends from a black buoy, marking the entrance of the Swash, nearly E. ¼ N. 8 miles, to the pile lighthouse which stands on its elbow or hook, outside of which is a black buoy, called the Gunfleet Spit; and thence to a buoy called the Middle buoy, painted black and white in circular bands, E. by N. ¼ N. 2½ miles; and from this to a black beacon buoy, upon its eastern extremity, N.E. by E. 2¼ miles. Midway between the Spitway and lighthouse is a buoy, *red and white striped,* which is noticed hereafter. A considerable extent of this sand, at the back of the Middle buoy, is called the *East Knock,* and is not covered till about 2¼ hours' flood: to the westward of this there are other patches, dry at low spring tides; and near the West extremity of it is the *West Knock*, covered only from about 2 hours' flood.

The MOUSE is now considered as merely the extremity of the WEST BARROW, the first dangerous shoal on the South side of the WEST SWIN. It has a black buoy on its western end, at a short distance eastward from the light vessel.

The WEST BARROW is a sand covered at about 2¼ hours' flood. It extends in an E. by N. and East direction, nearly 4½ miles from the Mouse buoy, and is three-quarters of a mile in breadth. On its northern edge or elbow is a chequered black and white spiral buoy (*Oct.* 1848) 2½ miles E.N.E. ¼ E. from the Mouse lightvessel. From the N.E. part of this shoal the western edge of the Flat of the Barrows extends nearly N.E. 4¼ miles to its northern edge, which forms the South side of a channel between it and the Swin Middle, called the *Middle Deeps.*

SWIN MIDDLE, or HEAPS.—This sand lies in a curve, at about 1 mile to the northward of the Flat of the Barrows, already noticed. It is marked by a *lightvessel* on the western end; a *black and white chequered buoy* on the hook or elbow; a *striped black and white* buoy on the N.E. projection, called the N.E. Middle; and a large *black nun buoy*, with a *staff and ball*, on the eastern end. The bearing and distance between the West end and hook are E. by N. ¼ N. 2½ miles; and from the hook to the East end they are E. by S. 3 miles. The breadth of the sand is one-third of a mile; and between it and the Barrow Flat the channel, or *Middle Deep*, has 8, 9, 6, 5, and 7 fathoms.

The LIGHTVESSEL on the S.W. end has one mast, and shows *one brilliant revolving light*, elevated 36 feet above the sea; it lies in 4 fathoms, with the Maplin light bearing S.W. ¾ W. 4½ miles; the Whitaker beacon, N. ¼ E. three-quarters of a mile; and the Hook of the Middle buoy, E. by N. ¼ N.

The BARROW KNOLL, or EAST BARROW HEAD, lies at the distance of 1¼ miles from the lightvessel on the S.W. end of the Swin Middle. It is nearly 1 mile in extent, and is covered at about 1¼ hours of the flood.

The FLAT OF THE BARROWS, from the Mouse buoy, on its western point, to its eastern extremity, at E. by N. ½ N., is 13¼ miles in length. Its depths are variable, from 4 fathoms to 1; but several parts are dry at low water. The greatest breadth is about 3¼ miles.

The SUNK is an extensive bank which separates the Barrow Deep from the Black Deep, or Sunk Channel. From the Sunk Head buoy (chequered red and white), which marks its N.E. extremity, to the bank called Knock John, at its S.W. end, the distance is 18 miles, and its general breadth is about 1½ miles. Throughout its length, which runs generally parallel to the direction of the channels, there are extensive patches nearly awash at low water, while others are left quite dry. The northernmost, called the Great Sunk, is 3 miles from the Sunk Head buoy. The Little Sunk is 2½ miles farther to the S.W.; and between them is a narrow swatchway through the sand of 2½ to 6 fathoms. The westernmost patch is called Knock John; the western extremity of the part which dries on it is 5¼ miles due East from the East Oaze buoy.

Between the Knock John and the East Oaze buoy are the two shoals called the Knob and the New Knob, the South sides of each of which are buoyed, the former with a red buoy, and the latter with a striped red and white buoy, called the North Knob. Between these and the East Oaze buoy is the Knob or Knock Channel.

At about 1¼ miles N.N.E. from the eastern extremity of the Sunk is placed a lightvessel, described hereafter, which is of the greatest importance to the safe navigating of the King's Channel.

2.—DESCRIPTION OF THE BUOYS AND BEACONS, THE SIDE UPON WHICH THEY ARE TO BE KEPT IN SAILING FROM THE NORE EASTWARD.

THE three MAPLIN BUOYS beyond Shoebury, *black*, marked *West Shoebury, Middle*, and *East Shoebury*, and lying on the edge of the sand, have been before alluded to, p. 5. The *West Shoebury* or *Shoeburyness* buoy is nearly 2 miles N.W. by W. ¾ W. from the Middle Shoebury buoy.

MIDDLE SHOEBURY BUOY lies in 3 fathoms, with the Nore lightvessel S.S.W., on the port side.

EAST SHOEBURY BUOY lies in 6 fathoms, with Middle Shoebury buoy, W. by N. ¼ N.; Nore lightvessel W. by S. ½ S., on the port side.

BLACKTAIL SPIT BUOY.—A *black spiral buoy*, surmounted by a *staff* and *square cage*, has been placed at the spit of the Blacktail Sand, in 3¼ fathoms, within a cable's length of the dry sand; East Shoebury buoy, West; Mouse lightvessel, E. by S.; Nore lightvessel, W. ¼ S., on the port side.

CANT BUOY.—On the edge of the Cant Sand; *white*, in 4 fathoms, on the starboard side.

BUOY on the WEST END of the OAZE.—Large *red* spiral buoy, with *staff and ball*, in 3 fathoms, starboard.

BLACKTAIL SPIT.—The spit of the Blacktail Sand being steep-to, and an important turning point in navigating the western part of the Swin Channel, the Maplin light has been masked, and not visible to the northward of the line of the Blacktail Spit, the S.E. Maplin, and Maplin buoys, with the object of more effectually enabling vessels to avoid grounding on the Spit of the Blacktail Sand in the night time, when the buoy may not be readily seen.

The LIGHTVESSEL on the *Flat of the Mouse*, westward of the buoy; described in page 44.

S.E. MAPLIN BUOY.—A *black buoy*, marked S.E. Maplin, has been placed in 4 fathoms, midway between the Blacktail Spit and Maplin buoys, on the port side.

MAPLIN, or FOULNESS SPIT BUOY, *black*, in 2¾ fathoms, larboard.

WEST BARROWS, ELBOW BUOY.—A large spiral buoy, *chequered black and white*, in 6¼ fathoms, on the starboard side; at 2½ miles from the buoy of the Mouse, on the starboard side. At 3 ships' lengths to the northward of the buoy are 10 fathoms of water, and the dry edge of the eastern spit of the sand bears S.S.E. a little more than a cable's length from it.

MAPLIN LIGHTHOUSE, erected on screw piles, in 1840, at a quarter of a mile West from the former site of the Sheers beacon; 2¼ miles E.N.E. from the chequered buoy on the Maplin; and 1¾ miles N.N.E. ¼ E. from the white buoy of the West Barrows. The structure is painted red, and shows a fixed *red* light at 45 feet above high water. In addition to this red light, shown in all directions, there is a *white* light shown over 8° of the circle, to point out the channel between the Girdler lightvessel and the Shivering Sand buoy, as shown hereafter.

MAPLIN SPIT BUOY, *black*.—In 2¾ fathoms, at rather more than 1 cable's length from the lighthouse, on the port side. No vessel must attempt to pass between the buoy and the lighthouse.

NORTH-EAST MAPLIN BUOY.—A *black* buoy, on a projecting part of the sand, due N.E. of the lighthouse, at six-tenths of a mile distant from it, in 2¾ fathoms at low water, on the port hand.

EAST BARROW SPIRAL BUOY.—Black and white in circular stripes, in 6 fathoms, on the starboard side.

LIGHTVESSEL of the SWIN MIDDLE.—With one revolving light, on the starboard side, lying on the western extremity of the sand, as shown in page 45

WHITAKER BEACON, in 4 feet, on the Whitaker Spit, larboard, with the Maplin lighthouse S.W. 5 miles. At 160 fathoms outside of it is a depth of 3 fathoms at low water.

WHITAKER BUOY, *red*, on the Whitaker Flat, larboard; Whitaker Beacon, W. by S. ¾ S., distant 1⅝ miles.

The BUXEY is an extensive sand which dries at about 3¼ hours' flood, forming a continuation of the great flat of the Gunfleet, from which it is partly separated by the Spitway to the Colne, &c., described below. There is a channel between it and the Whitaker, and also to the westward, between it and the Ray Sand, both leading to Burnham, &c. Its limits are now marked by the beacons and buoys following:—

The beacon, formed of iron, and distinguished by a *cross*, is placed on the N.W. part of the sand, which is dry at low water, spring tides, with Tillingham Preventive Station Staff, W. by S.; West Buxey buoy, S.W. ¼ S.; Maplin lighthouse, S. ¼ W. The *black* buoy on the North side, marked "North Buxey," is laid in 4 fathoms at low water, with

Buxey beacon, S.W. by W. ½ W. The *black* buoy on the South side, marked "South Buxey," is laid in 2½ fathoms at low water, with Brightlingsea church just open to the eastward of two remarkable round-topped trees, at the West end of Brightlingsea wood, N. ¾ E.; Whitaker buoy, E. by S. ½ S.

There is also a *black* buoy, marked "*West Buxey*," upon the western point of the sand, where the channel of the river divides into the two arms which encircle the Buxey Sand.

SWIN SPITWAY BUOY.—*Black*, in 3 fathoms, on the larboard side.*

The NORTH HOOK MIDDLE BUOY.—*Chequered black and white*, in 4½ fathoms, starboard.

NORTH-EAST MIDDLE BUOY, coloured *black* and *white* in stripes, near the extremity of the N.E. projection of the sand, in 4½ fathoms, starboard.

BUOY *of the* HEAPS.—*A nun buoy* of large dimensions, painted *black*, with a *staff and ball*, 3 fathoms, starboard. *Marks.*—The Naze tower, N.N.E. ¾ E.; Great Holland church, N. by E.; and the Sunk lightvessel, E. by N., 9¼ miles distant.

S.W. GUNFLEET BUOY.—This buoy is *striped red and white*, marked *S.W. Gunfleet*, and lies in 3½ fathoms, on the port side.

GUNFLEET LIGHTHOUSE, a structure on screw piles, showing a *revolving light* coloured *red*, the flashes succeeding each other at intervals of 30 seconds, was completed in May, 1856.

GUNFLEET SPIT BUOY, *black*, in 4½ fathoms, larboard, placed on the South extremity of a projecting spit of sand which has grown up to the *eastward* of the present *Gunfleet Lighthouse.*

MIDDLE GUNFLEET BUOY, *black and white, in circular bands*, lies midway between the Gunfleet lighthouse and the N.E. Gunfleet buoy; port side.

SUNK LIGHTVESSEL, at about 1¼ miles N.N.E. from the eastern end of the Sunk, in 10 fathoms, starboard. *Marks.*—Gunfleet lighthouse, W.N.W. 4½ miles; the Naze tower, N.N.W. ½ W.; Harwich high light, N. by W. The vessel exhibits *one brilliant fixed light*, at 30 feet above the sea, which may be seen at 3 leagues off.

A BUOY, chequered red and white, has been laid upon the *Sunk Sand Head*, with the Gunfleet beacon N.W. by W. ½ W., and the Naze tower N.N.W.

N.E. END *of the* GUNFLEET, a *black* beacon buoy, with a staff and ball, laid down in 1826, in 4 fathoms, larboard side. *Marks.*—The Naze tower and Walton hall (a white building farther inland) on with each other, bearing N.W. ½ N.; Harwich lights, nearly N. by W.; and the Sunk light, S. ½ E.

Naze tower and Walton hall in one.
(*The top of the tower is 138 feet above the level of high water.*)

* SPITWAY to the COLNE, &c.—At seven-eighths of a mile N. by W. ¼ W. from the Swin buoy is the Wallet Spitway buoy, *red, with staff and ball*. This now lies in 4 fathoms, with a white cottage between St. Osyth and the beach, in a line with the chancel of St. Osyth's church, North; the Naze tower, half the length of the tower on the Cork Land, N.E. by E. ¼ E.; Eagle buoy, N.W. ¾ W.

The course through the Spitway is N.W. ¼ W. 2½ miles, leaving both buoys on the larboard hand; then bear N.N.W. for 1 mile, and thence to the entrance of Maldon river, N.W. At the latter, two buoys were placed in 1816. The southern one, *striped black and white*, off the East end of the Knoll, in 2 fathoms; the other, *black*, on the S.E. end of the Eagle, in the same depth, at half a mile from it, bearing North. The channel way, or entrance, is between these buoys.

A red buoy has since been placed on Colne Bar Head, in 3 fathoms, bearing from the Eagle buoy N.W. by N., and from the Knoll buoy N. by W. ½ W.

From the Spitway, as above mentioned, the course to and over the bar, between the Eagle and Knoll, is N.W., which will lead to a berth off the red buoy on the Colne Bar Head; and leaving this buoy on the East or starboard hand, the course into the Colne, in the best water, will be North; or, up to the West Mersey, N.W. ¼ W.

3.—DIRECTIONS FOR SAILING FROM THE NORE, THROUGH THE SWIN AND KING'S CHANNEL.

THE direct course and distance from half a mile North of the Nore light to half a mile South of the Blacktail Spit are E. ¼ S. 5¼ miles, and thence to a fairway between the lightvessel of the Mouse on the starboard, and the Maplin buoy on the larboard, the course and distance will be E. ½ N. 3 miles.

Allowance, in these courses, must be made for the tide, noting that the ebb sets to the S.E. and E., and caution must be observed in approaching the Maplin on the North side. But observe, when between the Nore and Blacktail Hole, that in turning you do not stand far to the northward of the Warp, until you are nearly as low to the Blacktail as the Maplin Sand is steep-to.

Hollyhill trees, commonly called the Kettlebottom trees, which stand above Chatham, are a very useful mark in sailing to the West Swin. They are distinguished by the letter *b* in the view annexed, wherein *e* represents the point of Sheerness; *c*, the left hand end of the Blue Town; *a*, Chatham valley; and *d*, the Isle of Grain.

Sheerness. *Isle of Grain.*

This mark leads just clear of the West end of the Oaze; Hollyhill trees (*b*) being about their apparent length on upon the left hand end of the Blue Town (*c*); or Chatham valley (*a*), nearly on with the left hand end of the Blue Town, leads just clear of the West end of the Oaze.

The right hand end of Hollyhill trees (*b*), as shown in the following view, on with the left hand end of Grain Isle wood (*c*), or Chatham valley (*a*) a little more than twice the apparent length of Hollyhill trees, open to the left of Grain Isle wood, leads just clear of the Knock Spit.

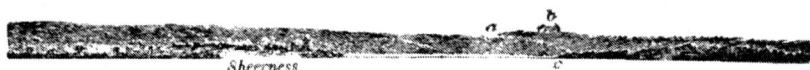
Sheerness.

From the depth of 6 and 7 fathoms northward of the Nore light there are 8 and 7 to 10 fathoms off the Blacktail, and thence from 8 to 10 fathoms to the Maplin or Foulness Spit buoy, where the depth increases.

When as low as the Blacktail, should the wind or tide prevent your going through the Swin, you may come to an anchor in *Blacktail Hole*, in 8 or 9 fathoms at low water; the Nore light bearing W. ¼ S. 5½ miles.

From the mid-channel, between the lightvessel of the Mouse and the Maplin buoy, to a proper berth without the *Maplin light*, the course and distance are E.N.E. ⅛ E. 3½ miles; and from off the lighthouse to the mid-channel, between the lightvessel of the Swin beacon and the Whitaker beacon, N.E. ½ N. 4⅓ miles. Due allowance, however, to be made for the tide, which sets strongly; the flood in a *true* S.W. direction.

Between the Maplin light and that of the Middle there is an excellent roadstead in every part, for ships in general, with 6 or 8 fathoms everywhere, from the lighthouse to within 1 mile above the floating light of the Middle.

It is to be observed that vessels, working down in this part, should stand toward the Maplin Sand, into only 4 or 5 fathoms, putting about when in 8 or 9 fathoms to the southward, in order to avoid the Barrow Flat. Be careful, also, of not getting to the southward of the Middle; as the tide sets with great strength between it and the Barrows, through the *Middle Deeps*.*

The CHANNEL *between the* WHITAKER *and the lightvessel on the West end of the* MIDDLE is narrower than has been hitherto described; it being, with a depth of 6 and 7 fathoms, about a mile in breadth. The course and distance from off the lightvessel to the *Elbow*, or chequered buoy on the Hook, are E.N.E. ⅛ E. 2¾ miles; and thence to the Gunfleet Lighthouse, E. by N. 8 miles.

* The *Middle Deeps* form a channel 6 miles in length, and have throughout from 8 to 7, 6, and 5 fathoms.

Between the nun beacon buoy on the East end of the Heaps and the S.W. Gunfleet buoy is the Middle Ground, mentioned below. In the night you may easily know when you are to the northward of this bank by finding a sticky bottom, while to the southward of it you have sandy ground.

At the distance of two miles below the Spitway, it is not safe to approach nearer to the Gunfleet than in 7 fathoms; when you should put about. Be cautious, likewise, of standing too near the Heaps. Hereabouts the striped red and white buoy on the Gunfleet may be seen, and will be found useful. It lies about 4 miles E. ¼ N. from the buoy of the Swin Spitway.

The floating light lying N.N.E. from the East end of the Sunk is an excellent guide for the rest of this channel, especially in the night. It may be approached with the greatest safety, when bearing East, or E. by N., to 11, 10, or 9 fathoms.

Should you arrive at the beacon buoy of the Gunfleet Head at low water, with the wind from the N.E., it may be best to run in, to the back of that sand, through Goldmer's Gat, into the Wallet, where you may come to an anchor, as hereafter described, in 6 or 7 fathoms, with Walton Hall, a remarkable house upon the Naze, *described on page* 47, a sail's breadth open to the westward of the Naze tower.

TIDES IN THE SWIN AND KING'S CHANNEL.

The flood tide sets upward through the King's Channel and Swin, into the Thames, nearly in the direction of the several shoals which have been described. The flood in the first two hours sets with great velocity between the Long Sand and Sunk. The ebb in a contrary direction, according to its strength and that of the wind. Through the Swin and King's Channel the tide sets with considerable strength, especially in the West Swin, between the Mouse and the Maplin. It also sets strongly through between the Middle or Heaps of the Barrow Flats.

The ebb sets strongly and diagonally across the Mouse and West Barrows. In proceeding downward, be careful that the ebb does not set you aground between the Mouse and the West Barrows. Indeed it is of consequence to be attentive to the tides in every part of this navigation.

The flood tide sets W.S.W., and ebb E.N.E.; and in a great degree runs in an oblique direction over all the sands and shoals between the N.E. part of the Shipwash and the Gunfleet.

On the days of full and change, it is high water in the King's Channel at 12ʰ, and the highest tide rises about 16 feet: neaps, 10 feet. At the Nore it is high water at 12ʰ 30′, and the rise is 14 feet. Allowance must, in all cases, be made for the wind: as, with an easterly wind, the tide flows sooner; and with an opposite one, the contrary.

In the channel on the West of the red buoy on the West end of the Oaze, in that between the West Barrow and Maplin, in that between the lightvessel of the Middle and the buoy of the Whitaker, and in the West Spitway, the stream turns, or alters its direction, at 12ʰ 20′; at about halfway between the East end of the Gunfleet and Harwich Naze, at 12ʰ 10′; and at about 2 miles S.S.W. from the same end of the Gunfleet, at 12ʰ.

In the inlets, or rivers, the tide flows and rises as follows:—Burnham River and Kay, Maldon River, entrance, and Colchester River, at 12ʰ; rise, 14 feet. At Maldon Kay an hour later, and there the rise is only 6¼ feet.

SECTION VII.

KING'S CHANNEL AND SHIPWAY TO ORFORDNESS, AND HARWICH HARBOUR.

KING'S CHANNEL TO ORFORDNESS.

1.—DESCRIPTION OF THE SHOALS, BUOYS, BEACONS, ETC.

The SUNK SAND is narrow and steep-to on both sides, extending about E.N.E. and W.S.W. (*or rather more easterly*); a considerable portion, as already shown, is dry at low ebbs. The lightvessel, noticed on page 47, is placed at 1¼ miles N.N.E. from the East end of this sand : it exhibits a brilliant light in the night, and a red ball at the mast-head during the day ; in foggy weather a gong is struck six times in every 10 minutes.

In working between the Sunk and the Gunfleet, stand no nearer to the Sunk than with the light bearing E. by N. The black nun beacon buoy on the East end of the Heaps bears from the light W. by S. 9¼ miles.

The WEST ROCKS form an extensive and dangerous range, of which the eastern part lies 2½ miles N.E. ½ E., or rather more easterly, from the N.E. buoy of the Gunfleet. Some parts are nearly dry at low water ; but the soundings in other parts vary from 1 to 4 fathoms. The range is 2 miles in breadth, in a line N.E. by E. and S.W. by W., and extends outward 5½ miles from the Naze.

The East spit of these rocks is distinguished by a buoy, striped *black* and *white*, with the words WEST ROCKS thereon. It lies in 3¾ fathoms, with the Gunfleet beacon buoy S.W. by W. ½ W. 2⁷⁄₁₀ miles ; and the Sunk light, S.S.W. 5 miles.

The CORK SAND and LEDGE.—Nearly N. ¼ W. 3¼ miles from the East spit of the West rocks lies the eastern part of the Cork Sand, a considerable part of which is dry at low water. From this, to the reef called the Cork Ledge, the bearing and distance are N.W. by N. 1 mile.

LIGHTVESSEL off the CORK LEDGE, with a brilliant *revolving* light every half minute, lies in 4½ fathoms, with Walton martello tower, just open North of the East martello tower, N.W. ¾ N. ; Harwich High lighthouse, N.W. ¾ W.

The CORK KNOT is a rocky shoal, of 19 or 20 feet, lying 1½ miles East from the Cork Ledge, to which it appears to be connected. Its outer extremity lies N. by E. 4 miles from the buoy on the East spit of the West rocks.

The ROUGH or RUFF.—This is a reef of 2 and 3 fathoms, extending 2 miles N.N.W. and S.S.E. Its S.W. side is distinguished by a *red* buoy, which lies in 3½ fathoms. The shoalest spot (2 fathoms) on the Rough is North of the Rough buoy.

The UPPER or WEST ROUGH.—This is a rocky shoal, similar to the Rough, which has on its shoalest part 2¾ fathoms. It lies 1½ miles W.S.W. of the Rough.

The SHIPWASH is a very narrow ridge of sand, forming the S.E. side of the SHIPWAY, and extending about N.E. and S.W. 8 miles. Some parts of it dry in low ebbs, and it is steep-to on both sides. This is a dangerous bank, as ships coming in from sea have not sufficient warning by the lead, in approaching it.

A *spiral beacon buoy*, of large dimensions, has been moored at a short distance from the S.W. end of the sand. It is coloured *black* and *white*, in *horizontal stripes*, and surmounted by a black ball ; from it the Sunk light bears S.W. by W. 8 miles ; the beacon buoy on the Gunfleet, W. by S. 7¼ miles ; the buoy on the Rough (*red*), N.W. ½ W. 3¼ miles ; the chequered buoy on the Bawdsey sand, N. ¼ W. 5 miles.

A buoy, coloured *black* and *white*, in *horizontal stripes*, has been placed in 8½ fathoms, at low water, spring tides, on the N.W. side of the Shipwash Sand, about midway between the floating lightvessel at the N.E. end, and the large beacon buoy at the S.W. end of the Shipwash.

LIGHTVESSEL.—At the N.E. end of the Shipwash a lightvessel, with fixed light, similar to that of the Swin Middle (described in page 45), in 9 fathoms water, nearly half a mile N.N.E. from the extremity of the sand, with Aldborough church nearly N. by E. and Orford high light N. by W. ; Bawdsey church, half the apparent length of its tower to the East of the second martello tower on the cliff, W. by N. northerly.

A S.W. course from the lightvessel, having due regard to the tides, will carry a vessel clear of the sand. The object of this vessel particularly is, to enable ships of great draught of water to proceed with safety through the channel between Bawdsey Sand and the Shipwash, instead of going into Hosley Bay. In sailing along the Shipwash, care must be taken to give an allowance in the course for the set of the tide, the flood setting about W.S.W., and the ebb E.N.E., which thwart this sand about two points.

BAWDSEY SAND, forming the N.W. side of the SHIPWAY, is about 4 miles in length, and three-quarters in breadth near the S.W. end. The soundings are very irregular upon the shoal ; 12 feet is the least water on it, which is near the S.W. part of the shoal, at which end *a white and black chequered buoy* is placed in 6 fathoms.

The N.E. end of Bawdsey Sand, called the *Baldhead,* or *Bawdhead,* lies with Orford high light N.N.E. 4 miles. It is distinguished by a *black buoy,* lying in 5 fathoms.

This sand now extends more to the N.E. than formerly; and Orford low light with Aldborough mill in a line, bearing N.N.E. ¾ E., leads over the N.E. part in 3½ fathoms.

The SLEDWAY is the channel between the S.W. end of the Bawdsey Sand and the Rough.

The KETTLEBOTTOM is a shoal of serpentine shape, extending nearly 2 miles N.N.E. ¼ E. from the S.E. or chequered buoy on Bawdsey Sand. It lies within, or to the northward of, the South part of Bawdsey Sand, and its least depth is about 2 fathoms, with uneven and irregular soundings.

The CUTLER, which lies off Bawdsey Cliff, is a rocky shoal, with uneven soundings. The lights of Orfordness in one lead over its outer edge in 2 fathoms. In consequence, a *black buoy* is placed on its southern extremity, which lies in 4½ fathoms, with Orfordness low light a little open to the southward of the high light.

BAWDSEY or WOODBRIDGE HAVEN, an inlet similar to the estuary of the Orwell, is entered between Bawdsey Cliff and Felixstow. On the S.W. point are some beacons to point out the channels across the bar; and a small nun buoy, coloured *red,* and marked " W*E* HAVEN," has been placed in 3 fathoms off the entrance.

The WHITING is the narrow bank forming the southern side of the channel way of Hosley Bay. Its N.E. end lies not a mile distant from the beach, with Orford church bearing N. ¼ W. The shoal extends thence S.W. by W. ¼ W. 3 miles. The lighthouses on Orfordness in one lead close upon the inner edge of this sand: therefore, in working through Hosley Bay, the lower or easternmost light must be kept in sight to the northward of the high light.

The extremities of the Whiting are now marked out by *three red buoys.* The first buoy is on the S.W. end, and lies in 3¾ fathoms. The second buoy is on the *Hook* or innermost edge of the sand, in 3 fathoms, 2½ miles from the S.W. buoy, and lies with Orfordness lighthouses in one, bearing N.E. by E. The third buoy, with a *staff and ball,* is on the N.E. end, within the distance of a mile from the beach, with Orford church bearing N. by W., and the high light N.E. ¼ N.

FLAGSTONE.—Between the southern part of the Whiting and the entrance of Orford Haven there is a rocky tract, of 1¼ miles, called the *Flagstone.* It lies half a mile from the Whiting, and parallel thereto. The least depth on it is 5 fathoms.

SHOALS without ORFORDNESS.—The SHOALS at Orfordness and its vicinity to the northward are, the *Ridge, Aldborough Napes,* and *Sizewell Bank.*

The RIDGE is a sand forming a long oval, and there is, *at present,* a swash of 4 and 5 fathoms to the S.W. of it. There is now one *black buoy* on the outer edge of its shoalest spot of 12 feet.

ALDBOROUGH NAPES, a shoal of 2½ and 3 fathoms at low water, extends nearly N.E. and S.W., from the depth of 5 fathoms at each end, 2½ miles.

Upon the eastern edge of the shoal lies a *mast buoy,* painted *black,* in 5 fathoms at common spring ebbs, and at about 1½ cables' lengths to the eastward of that part where the sea breaks the highest in easterly gales. The sand is here about 350 fathoms broad; viz., from 5 fathoms on the eastern edge to 5 fathoms on the western. It is steep-to on each side; and, at a distance of about 1 cable's length, in the direction of E.S.E. from the buoy, there are 10 fathoms; and, at a distance of about 2 cables, 14 fathoms.

SIZEWELL BANK, to the E.N.E. of Thorpness.—This bank, like many others, has within a few years considerably increased, and it now, in fact, forms a shelf, three-quarters of a mile broad, from the South part of Aldborough town to the distance of nearly 6 miles to the N.E. The depths on it vary from 4 to 2½ fathoms; but on its shoalest part, at 1¼ miles from Sizewell, are only 10 feet at low water. This spot lies with Thorpness W.S.W. ½ W. 1¾ miles, and Dunwich church N. by E. 4¼ miles.

A *buoy* painted *black* and *white* in *circles,* marked " *Sizewell Bank,*" has been laid on the S.E. edge of this shoal, in 5 fathoms. Orford castle, open to the southward of Aldborough town, or bearing S.W. by W. ¾ W., leads clear of the bank.

THE MARK FOR COMING IN FROM SEA, from the northward between Aldborough Napes and the Sizewell Bank, is Orfordness lights in one, bearing S.W. by W. ¼ W., which will lead in a fairway between the Napes and the shore to the westward. But observe that these lights in one will lead within the *Ridge*, whence you may sail out between that shoal and the coast, with Aldborough church about N.N.E. Or rather you may run along, eastward of the Ridge, with Aldborough church bearing N.N.W. until Bawdsey Cliff is open of the point of Orfordness: then steer 1½ miles, S.W. by W. until Bawdsey church comes well open to the left of Orfordness. Hence you round into Hosley Bay, &c.

The LIGHTHOUSES *of Orfordness* are built of stone, and are, respectively, 83 and 55 feet in height from the base. In 1852 the towers were painted *red* to make them more conspicuous in the daytime: the buildings round them are painted *white*: the lights are brilliant and fixed; those of the high tower may be seen, in clear weather, more than 7 leagues off.

ELECTRIC TELEGRAPH.—The submarine cables of the Electric Telegraph from Orfordness to Holland lay in a direction E.S.E. from the Orfordness high lighthouse, with the lighthouse, on with Gedgrave high trees, bearing W.N.W.; and it is desirable that vessels should not anchor with those marks or bearings on, lest, by so doing, they damage the electric cable, or lose their own anchors.—(*June* 7, 1853.) In February, 1854, some buoys, marked with the words "Electric Telegraph," were laid down in the line of its direction. It is desirable that vessels should not anchor within a quarter of a mile northward or southward of the line of these buoys.

Off Aldborough you may anchor in good ground, with an off-shore wind, in 6 or 7 fathoms, with Orfordness high light S.W. by W., and Aldborough church N.W.

Should you be coming in from sea from the southward, for Orfordness, in the night, with the wind scant to the southward, you may when within, or to the westward of the Gabbards, bring the low light as far to the North as N. by W., which will lead clear of the N.E. end of the Shipwash. Should the wind be to the northward, be cautious of not bringing the light farther to the westward than W. by N., until within Aldborough Napes.

If, in coming in, you should make the high light N. by W. ½ W., you may, without danger, if to the northward and a scant wind, bring it West; and if to the southward, N.W. by N.

2.—DIRECTIONS FOR SAILING FROM THE KING'S CHANNEL TO ORFORDNESS, ETC.

The SHIPWAY.—Vessels bound outward to the N.E. from the KING'S CHANNEL may either pass directly from off the Gunfleet buoy to Orfordness, through the SHIPWAY, between the Shipwash and Bawdsey Sand; or, hauling round to the northward of the Rough, pursue their course thence to Orfordness, through Hosley Bay.

In the first case, having arrived at the spot whence the N.E. beacon buoy of the Gunfleet bears West, and the Sunk light S.S.W. ¾ W., you have to keep an exact N.E. course for 16 miles; which will lead to a berth 2 miles S.E. by E. of Orfordness low light. On this N.E. course, at 1½ miles, the *black and white buoy* on the spit of the West rocks will be distant about a mile on the larboard hand; at 4 miles you will be nearly midway between the *red buoy* of the Rough, on the larboard, and the striped monster beacon on the S.W. end of the Shipwash on the starboard hand; at 8 miles you will have the *chequered buoy* on the Bawdsey Sand on the larboard (1½ miles distant); and thence, passing the *black buoy* on the *Baldhead* or N.E. end of Bawdsey Sands, at 13 miles, you will be abreast of the *lightvessel* off the N.E end of the Shipwash; and may then shape a course to avoid the Napes, &c., as shown hereafter.

Throughout this navigation the depths vary from 11 to 8, 6, 7, 9, and 8 fathoms. You must be cautious in approaching the shoals, as they are steep-to; and observe to make sufficient allowance for the tide, which sets as shown in the description of the Shipwash, page 50.

HOSLEY or HOLLESLEY BAY, &c.—*From the Gunfleet beacon buoy* the course and distance in a fairway, for Hosley Bay, are N.E. by E. ¼ E. 3 miles; and hence, from off the East spit buoy of the West rocks, a N.E. course for 3 miles will lead clear of the Rough. The Sunk light from this part will bear nearly S.W. ¼ S., and the anchorage in Hosley Bay, N. by E. 6¼ miles.

In passing the Rough, known by its red buoy, you will have Bawdsey church and the beacon in a line, bearing N. 3° W., and may run in for the buoy of the Cutler (*black*) in this direction, or rather with the church open to the right of the beacon. From off the buoy of the Cutler to the anchorage in Hosley Bay the course is N.E. ¼ N. 3 miles.

Observe in all cases to allow for tide, whether flood or ebb; the former setting W.S.W. and the latter E.N.E. In the track between the Gunfleet, West Rocks, and Rough, are from 6 to 9, and thence to 6 and 5 fathoms at low ebbs. •

In turning to windward, approach no nearer to the West rocks than till Alderton church comes on with Bawdsey church on the rising part of the cliff; nor to the West end of the Shipwash than till Bawdsey church comes on with the N.E. end of the long wood to the eastward of Bawdsey Cliff. Or, to the West rocks stand no nearer than 5 fathoms, nor to the Shipwash than 7 fathoms.

When past the Rough stand no nearer to Bawdsey Sand and the Kettlebottom than till the tree to the northward of Orford church comes nearly to the West side of that church; nor to the Cork Sand or Knot than till Harwich steeple comes on with the East martello tower, standing a mile to the N.W. of Landguard Fort. In the night, approach no nearer than 5 fathoms; or to the Cutler than 5¼ fathoms. Hence, in working into Hosley Bay, stand off to 6, and in toward shore to 4 fathoms.

The best anchorage in the southern part of Hosley Bay is with Hosley church N. by W. ¼ W. In the northern part you may anchor between the Hook buoy of the Whiting and the N.E. end of the Middle Ground, in 6 or 7 fathoms, good ground.

ORFORDNESS.—*From the southern anchorage in Hosley Bay* the course to *Orfordness* is between the Middle Ground on the larboard, and the three white buoys of the Whiting on the starboard side. These clearly mark out the channel. From the anchorage in 6 fathoms, by steering N.E. by E. 2 miles, you will have the leading mark on, which is the lower or easternmost lighthouse kept open to the northward of the high light.

Close inshore there is a *contra* tide, caused by the point above the Ness. This counter tide runs down during the flood with as much velocity as the tide in the channel runs up. Some ships, by getting into this eddy, have missed stays with a turning wind, and run on shore.

In the fairway, between Orfordness and the Whiting, are from 8 to 9 fathoms, and in the narrowest part 6 to 8 fathoms. Should the buoy be gone, open the black mill to the eastward of the church, and you will have passed the sand.

If bound out to sea from Hosley Bay, you may, after passing the N.E. buoy of the Whiting, steer S.E. by E., or East; and if bound to the northward, keep alongshore, observing not to shut Bawdsey Cliff in with the point of Orford beach until Dunwich Cliff be open of Thorpness.

ORFORDNESS to SEA.—The mark leading clear of the Ridge is Bawdsey Cliff, bearing W.S.W. ¾ W., kept well open of Orford beach, until Aldborough church bears N.N.W., when you will be about halfway between the black buoy on the Ridge and the S.W. end of Aldborough Napes. From the last spot a course N.E. ¾ N. leads clear of the Sizewell Bank, &c. To clear the S.W. end of Aldborough Napes, the mark is Orford castle a sail's breadth open to the southward of the church, and bearing W. by N.

3.—HOSLEY OR HOLLESLEY BAY TO HARWICH.

DESCRIPTION AND DIRECTIONS.

HOSLEY BAY *to* HARWICH.—Between Hosley Bay and Harwich harbour are several dangers not yet described. These are the *Platters*, the *Andrews*, *Ridge*, *Pye Sand*, *Hallidays*, *Altars*, &c.

These shoals are so nearly together that it is scarcely possible to give an adequate description of them; we are therefore under the necessity of referring the reader to the chart of the harbour,* in which the whole will be found, with the several marks.

The first shoal in sailing from Hosley Bay is the *Cutler*, which lies off the middle of Bawdsey Cliff, and is sometimes nearly uncovered at low ebbs.

* The New Survey of the Coasts of Essex and Suffolk, from the Western Spitway to Orford Haven, including the harbour and environs of Harwich, with the rivers of Ipswich, Woodbridge, &c., on a very large scale, improved from Captain Washington's Survey, lately published by Mr. Laurie.

The *course* from the lower part of Hosley Bay to abreast of this shoal is S.W. by W or S.W., according to the tide, keeping while within the Whiting (or until Orford haven bears N.N.W.) Orfordness lower or easternmost light open to the northward or left of the high light, and when above the Whiting, the low light open to the southward of the high light, until Harwich church appears nearly in the middle between Felixstow Cliff and Landguard fort. Observe to stand no nearer to the Cutler than into 4 fathoms. When above the shoal, Ramsholt church will appear open to the westward of Bawdsey Cliff; with this mark, should the wind be from the N.W., you may haul in toward the land.

The upper lighthouse of Harwich, bearing W.N.W. ½ W., leads clear of the Cutler in 4½ fathoms.

In running from Hollesley Bay to Harwich by night bring Orfordness low light open to the left or northward of the high one, keeping it so till up to the S.W. end of the Whiting; then steer S.W., opening the low light on the opposite side of the high one; and when the Cork Ledge revolving light bears W. ¼ S., steer for it; after passing it, keep it bearing E. ½ S. till the Harwich lights are in one (N.W. by N.); run in with them on till the body of Landguard fort bears N. by E., then haul to S.W. a couple of cables' lengths, and anchor; or if bound into the harbour from the last position, open Harwich high light its own breadth to the left of the low one, and proceed as hereafter described.

FELIXSTOW ROAD and the PITCHING GROUND.—The anchoring ground called *Felixstow* or *Felstow Road* lies between the extensive ledges and bank which stretch from Felstow or Bull's Cliff on the North side, and the Cork rocks or reefs on the South side. These last are now marked by a light vessel with a revolving light.

The PITCHING GROUND lies within Felstow Road to the westward, being bounded toward Landguard Point by the shoals called the *Platters* and *Andrews*, and at the West end by that called the *Ridge*. Its depths are 5 and 6 fathoms, and the bottom of muddy sand. Cross marks for anchoring are Beach tower between the two Walton mills, or just East of Walton village (high).

The ROLLING GROUND lies within the Pitching Ground, and off Landguard Fort; on its South side are the Holiday or Halliday Flats; the depth in it is from 2½ to 6 fathoms. Cross mark for anchoring is Landguard Fort buildings shut on Trimlies wood, N.N.E.

The PLATTERS lie to the E.S.E. of Landguard Point, and extend nearly a mile from shore. There is fully a fathom over it. The marks leading clear of the outer part are Orford church and castle a sail's breadth open of Bawdsey Cliff.

The ANDREWS, a shoal nearly dry, lies within the Platters, and stretches from off Landguard Fort three-quarters of a mile to the S. by E.

The RIDGE, which lies to the southward of the Andrews, on the opposite side of the channel to HARWICH, is a rocky bank nearly a mile in length from S.E. to N.W., and in the middle part nearly half a mile broad. Its shoalest part has about 8 feet over it at low ebbs. This part lies with Erwarton steeple N.N.W. ½ W. well on with Harwich Beacon cliff. From the S.E. end Landguard Point bears N. ¼ W.

HARWICH.—The town of Harwich, which had declined much from its former prosperity, occupies the extremity of a peninsula composed of clay. Previous to the introduction of steam navigation, when this port was the principal outlet for the traffic towards Germany and the North of Europe, Harwich was thriving, its harbour busy and of excellent accommodation, and easy of access. The change consequent upon altering the mode of communication with the North Sea continental ports, coupled with other circumstances arising about the same time, caused the prosperity of the place to be much damped, and in a series of years the harbour, from neglect and want of proper control, was so much changed in its character that it no longer had the advantages it once possessed.

The railroad system having again altered the character of the internal communication of the kingdom, Harwich might again assume its former importance, and it doubtless will do so, from its natural advantages being placed on a proper basis by the skilful adaptation of artificial means to combat the effects of tide and current, which have hitherto so much deteriorated it.

The present lighthouses at Harwich, which are represented in the margin, were first lighted on the 31st of March, 1818. The highest is of grey brick, 60 feet high above the level of high water ; the lower is white, and 27 feet only. They exhibit *brilliant fixed lights*, and bear from each other N.W. by N., and were at first used as a leading mark, when in one, for the fairway into the harbour ; but since the great increase in length of the spit off Landguard Fort, they now *lead on to the Point*, and are consequently not used, except to point out the fairway between the Andrews and Ridge buoys into the Rolling Ground. There is also a *lower light* in the high tower, as hereafter shown.

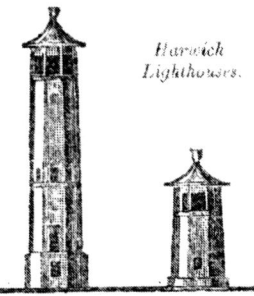

Harwich Lighthouses.

The *Beacon Cliff*, or *Blackman's Head*, southward of the town, has receded upwards of 500 feet in a direct line from the sea within these forty years ; off it are the dangerous Cliff-foot rocks, described hereafter. Upon the destruction of this cliff the whole fortunes of the harbour appear to have turned. It is composed of clay, in which are masses of septaria, or cement stone, the procuring of which latter, aided by the action of the sea, which washed up to it, has caused the great diminution in its extent before mentioned.

The BREAKWATER was completed in July, 1849. It extends 1,521 feet in length, in an E.S.E. (*true*) direction from the Beacon cliff. It is 45 feet broad at the base, and 10 feet on the top. At its outer extremity is a cage beacon elevated on a mast.

LANDGUARD FORT, on the opposite side of the entrance, is situated on a tongue of low land, which from the current sweeping down over the Felixstow Ledge was rapidly extending in a W.S.W. direction from the fort, and making great alterations in the channels leading into the harbour, as before-stated. There are *lights* now shown from the fort to lead round the shoals off Landguard Point, as hereafter shown.

At the distance of nearly a mile E.N.E. from Landguard Fort is a martello tower, on the eastern beach ; and at 1¹⁄₁₅ miles N.E. of the fort is Walton martello tower, lying on the shore opposite to the entrance of the river Stour ; and to the N.N.W. of it is Fagborough cliff, 66 feet high, lying opposite to the entrance to the harbour.

Shotley Point is the extremity of the land, dividing the Orwell from the Stour. On its S.E. face are two martello towers. The shoal water extends for three-quarters of a mile from the rising ground, in a S.E. direction, the outer part of which is called the Horse Bank.

The depth of water within the harbour is from 4 to 6 fathoms, at low water spring tides ; the bottom is clean, and the holding ground good. Spring tides rise 11½ feet ; they never exceed 2 knots, and run fairly through the channels, except at the entrance, where the ebb sets across the banks.

ENTRANCE OF THE HARBOUR.—The approach to Harwich is well indicated by the Cork lightvessel, with a *revolving* light, described on page 50.

The edges of the shoals forming the Pitching Ground, or outer entrance of Harwich harbour, are now distinctly marked by four buoys, which were first laid down in 1826. On the North side are two *black* buoys, upon the edges of the Platters and Andrews ; and on the South side a chequered red and white, and a white one upon the Ridge. The two inner buoys (*black* and *white*) are only four-tenths of a mile asunder, and lie a little without the bar which separates the Pitching from the Rolling Ground.

Between the Rolling Ground and Harwich are the following shoals, viz.: the Cliff-foot, Altar, Cod, and Guard ; and these shoals, with those formerly called the Glutton, Bone, and Gristle, divided the entrance into two principal channels.

The *Cliff-foot Rocks* form the western side of the entrance to the harbour ; they lie at half a mile off the Beacon cliff, and have from 2 to 5 feet water over them at low ebbs. At the S.E. extremity, in 7 feet, is a *red spiral buoy*, with staff and ball.

The *Beach End buoy*, black, marks the limits of the shoal water of Landguard Point in 2½ fathoms.

The *Altar Bank* and *Flat* was a shoal lying to the northward of Landguard Point, separated from it by a very narrow but deep water channel. The depth on it, previously to the recent improvements, was from 7 to 12 feet, but it has been nearly altogether removed, and dredged to a depth of 15 to 18 feet.

The *Cod Bank* lies between the Eastern and Western Channels, to the northward of the Altar Banks, and has a depth of 9 to 11 feet; but its eastern end has been removed to form the channel between the Altar and Glutton buoys. The former *Glutton Shoal* is to the northward. This shoal has also been dredged away to a depth of 15 feet. Further within the entrance was the *Bone Shoal*, lying nearly N.N.W. from Landguard Fort, and above a mile from it.

Midway between the Bone and the Guard, off the point of Harwich, was the *Gristle Shoal*.

The *Guard Shelf* stretches to the eastward, and along the shore of Harwich, upon the western side of the harbour. Two *red* buoys in 15 feet water, marked " North Shelf " and " South Shelf," mark its limits.

DIRECTIONS for the HARBOUR.—The ENTRANCE OF FELIXSTOW or FELSTOW ROAD (the channel to Harwich) lies with Bawdsey church, N.N.E.; Landguard Fort, W.N.W. ¾ W.; and the buoy of the Cutler, E.N.E. ¼ E., distant 1½ miles. The fair course into the PITCHING GROUND is hence due West, giving the lightvessel on the Cork Ledge a good berth on the larboard hand, and *carefully avoiding the Cork Spit,* which lies within it on the same side.

From the Pitching Ground, the Cork Ledge light, bearing E. by S., leads between the buoys, through the best of the water, into the Rolling Ground, until Harwich lights are in a line, bearing N.W. by N.

Leading Mark for the Rolling Ground—*The Lighthouses* (*) *in one, bearing N.W. by N.*

The mark for sailing in toward Harwich, and *leading clear of the Rough,* on its North side, is the High light of Harwich just open to the right of Landguard Fort, and bearing N.W. by W. With this mark kept on until Bawdsey church bears N.E. ¼ E., you will be at the entrance of the Pitching Ground, and may thence steer, between the buoys, into the harbour.

Mark through the Rough Channel—*Harwich High Lighthouse to the right of Landguard Fort, N.W. by W., nearly.*

When rounding Shotley Point in order to cross from the Stour to the Orwell, keep the top of the High lighthouse open to the eastward of Harwich steeple, about midway along the roof of the church, S.S.W. ½ W.; or keep the Low lighthouse well open of the Ordnance pile jetty. Either of these marks will clear the Horse Bank in 12 feet at low water.

DIRECTIONS FOR ENTERING BY NIGHT.—Since the commencement of the breakwater intended for the improvement of the entrance to the harbour, a system of lights has been established, by which the entrance is much facilitated by night. The following directions given by the Trinity Corporation must be *carefully* attended to :—

It is to be observed, that the arrangement of the several lights for the harbour of Harwich is as follows, viz. :—

The lights in the High and Low light towers as heretofore exhibited ; and in the lower part of the High tower a light appearing of a *red* colour, or *white,* according to the line of direction on which it is seen.

The light from Landguard Fort will appear to vessels entering the harbour in succession as they proceed,—first, *red ;* and second, *white.*

Having reached the Rolling Grounds with the High light open to the westward of the Low light as heretofore, a *red* light will become visible in the lower part of the High lighthouse, and will so continue until the course between the Beach End and Cliff-foot buoys is open, when the said light will become bright and without colour, bearing by compass N.N.W. ¼ W., and being kept in sight, will lead through the entrance, until you have passed Landguard Fort, when the usual change of course to the northward and eastward for the anchorage will be requisite.

The light will also appear *red* immediately after vessels have passed to the S.W. of the *white* light, so that by tacking whenever the *red* light on either hand comes into view, they may readily and with certainty maintain their proper course in by the white light until they have reached Landguard Fort, as before stated.

In steering in on this course, when the vessel is to the northward of the ridge, a *red* light becomes visible on Languard Fort, bearing N.E.; and having opened the same, a W. by N. course must then be steered, until the lower *white* light in the high tower shall have been opened to the S.W. of the *red* light, and which *white* light being so kept will lead to the S.W. of the Beach End buoy, and between the Cliff-foot rock on the port or larboard hand, and the Altar Shoal on the starboard hand. When abreast of the Beach End buoy the *red* light in Landguard Fort will disappear, and be immediately succeeded by the *white* light therein, which will continue visible up to the harbour, and should be brought to bear E. by S. for the anchorage.

4.—GOLDMER'S GAT, WALLET, AND NAZE FLATS, TO HARWICH.
DESCRIPTION AND DIRECTIONS.

NAZE to HARWICH.—The passage over the Naze Flats to Harwich, called the MEDUSA CHANNEL, is bounded on the East by the *Stone Banks* and *Ridge;* and, on the West, by the *Naze Ledge, Pye Sand, Hallidays,* &c., of which the following is a description.

The STONE BANKS are irregular and extensive; on some parts there is a depth of only 6 feet over them at low water.

In 1821 a buoy was laid here, on the eastern side of the Medusa Channel, or Inner Passage, to Harwich. This buoy is *black*, with a white cross painted at the top, and a white band round the top and middle. It lies on the upper part of the bank or beach, between the West rocks and Harwich Naze, in 2½ fathoms, with the Naze tower bearing W.S.W. ½ W.; Harwich High light, N. ¼ W.; and a conspicuous tree just touching the highest and southernmost part of the Naze land, W.S.W. ½ W.

The NAZE LEDGE is the rocky and shoal ground which surrounds and extends from the Naze to a distance of 1½ miles S.E. ½ E. from the Naze tower. On the extremity without are 2 and 3 fathoms, but on some parts of the shoal within, only 5 feet at low ebbs.

The PYE SAND extends from Walton Stone Point 2¼ miles E.N.E. It is dry at low water, spring tides, and partly dry at half ebb tide. The North point lies with Harwich cliff N.N.E., distant 1½ miles. Between is the entrance of Hamford water, on the bar of which is a depth of 9 feet.

DIRECTIONS for HARWICH by the *Inner Channel.*—From off the beacon buoy on the Gunfleet Head, the leading mark for the channel, called *Goldmer's Gat,* is Walton Hall just open to the right of the Naze tower. With this mark run in, 3½ miles from the buoy, until you bring the High light of Harwich N. ¼ E. well open on the eastern side of the Beacon cliff at Harwich. You will now be at the entrance of the Medusa Channel, the mark for sailing through which is a large red brick house at Walton (within Landguard Fort), its length open to the left of Landguard Fort, and bearing nearly N.N.E. Having run thus until the eastern martello tower on Shotley Point comes its own breadth open North of the Ordnance pile jetty at Harwich (and which mark clears the Cliff-foot rocks in 11 feet at low water), you will come into the Rolling Ground, and thence proceed as before directed.

DIRECTIONS out of HARWICH *over the Naze,* through the MEDUSA CHANNEL.—Bring Landguard Fort on with the East side of Trimlies Wood, which leads from the Wallet, outside the Naze Flats, to the Stone Banks striped buoy. Keep the Fort on the East side of the wood, until the Naze Cliffs close on the Cork Land; then sheer to the eastward, and get the Fort on the middle or left of the wood, which will lead between the Ridge and Hallidays. The Low light on with the church spire clears the Hallidays; or, keep the easternmost martello tower on Shotley Land open with Harwich Jetty, about the width of the tower, which will clear the Cliff-foot rock, which is marked by the chequered buoy, and also very distinctly so by the breakwater and its beacon, whose direction continued touches the buoy. When Cliff House (Mr. Bagshaw's, formerly Mr. Billingsley's, West of the breakwater) is open twice its width, off the Beacon cliff, you are then without the rock; haul then to the westward, till you bring the Low light at Harwich on the chancel end of the church; and when the S.W. land appears, just showing itself open with the Naze land, then keep it so until the Low light comes on with the Cement mill at Harwich. This mark will carry you between the Flat of the Naze and the Stone Bank, until the tree on the Naze comes on the Naze tower; keeping this last mark on, leads you into a fairway into the Swin, through Goldmer's Gat.

Those coming through Goldmer's Gat for the Rolling Grounds and Harwich must be very attentive to the tides, and wait until they are well assured of having water sufficient for crossing the Naze. In order to proceed, keep Walton Hall just open to the right of the Naze tower, until you bring a white house on the declivity of a hill, rising from the West side of Walton Bay, a little open to the southward of the Naze cliff : keep on to the eastward with these marks, until the Low light of Harwich is in one with the chancel end of the church or with the High light, N. ¼ W.; either of these marks leads you up to an anchorage in the Rolling Grounds. With the Low light halfway between the church and High light, you will find the best ground and most water. You will be to the northward of the Ridge when Bawdsey Cliff and Felixstow Cliff are in one.

The WALLET.—The WALLET is the extensive space or channel between the Gunfleet Sand and the coast to the N.E. It is generally clear and even, the depths being from 5 to 7 fathoms; but there is a shoal in it called the *Copperas Ground*, of 3¼ and 3½ fathoms, the eastern part of which bears, from the East end of the Gunfleet, W. ¼ N. 5¾ miles, with the Gunfleet beacon S.S.E. ½ E. 2¼ miles. It extends thence 1¼ miles W.N.W. Between lies the channel of the Wallet and the East Knock of the Gunfleet. To the northward of the shoal there are gradual soundings to the shore, from 4 fathoms to 1 fathom; but W.N.W. ¼ W., 2 miles from it, is a shoal spot, called the *Tripod*, nearly dry at low water.

The WESTERN ENTRANCE into the WALLET, from the East Swin, is the Swash or SPITWAY between the Buxey and Gunfleet, which is pointed out by the buoys, called the *Buoys of the Spitway*, already described on page 47. Of these the southern or outer one is *black*; the northern or inner one *red*, with a *staff and ball*; both to be left to the South or larboard hand, as already shown in the note, page 47.

GOLDMER'S GAT.—The EASTERN PASSAGE into the WALLET is GOLD-MER'S GAT; the leading mark is that before mentioned, viz., Walton hall just open to the right of the Naze tower, whence you may haul round the Gunfleet, and anchor wherever agreeable at the back of that sand.

The best permanent anchorage is, however, stated to be where Great Clackton church is on with Little Holland hall, and Harwich cliff a little open to the right of Harwich Naze. Here, at the distance of about 4 miles W. ¾ N. from the Gunfleet buoy, there is exceedingly good riding with S.E., South, and S.W. winds, as thereabout the Gunfleet dries at the first two hours' ebb.

To SAIL OUT THROUGH THE GATWAY from the Wallet, bring the Naze tower N.W. ¾ N., and steer, with the flood tide, S.E. by E., with an ebb, S.E. by S., or otherwise according to wind and tide, with the leading mark before described, which will carry you in 6, 7, or 8 fathoms, until the water deepens to the southward of the sand. In working out, you may stand to the northward until Walton hall comes on with the tower, into 6 or 7 fathoms, and to the Gunfleet into 5 fathoms.

TIDES BETWEEN THE KING'S CHANNEL AND ORFORDNESS.

In HARWICH HARBOUR, or at the entrances of the rivers of Ipswich and Manning-tree, as well as at those of Woodbridge and Orford, it is high water, on the full and change, at 11h 50'. The rise at Harwich is 11½ feet; at Woodbridge Haven, 9½ feet; and Orford, 6¼ feet. At about a mile S.S.W. from Orfordness the stream turns, or alters its direction, at 11h 26'.

At Ipswich Quay it is high water, 12h 30'; rise, 6¼ feet: at Mistley Thorne Quay, 12h 25'; rise, 9¾ feet: at Woodbridge Quay, 12h 45'; rise, 7 feet: at Orford Quay, 12h 11'; rise, 6¾ feet.

SECTION VIII.

KING'S CHANNEL AND ORFORDNESS TO THE DOWNS.

DESCRIPTION.—The dangers which bound the tracks to the Downs from the King's Channel and Orfordness, and which have not yet been described, are the *Gabbards*, the *Galloper, Four-Mile Knolls*, and the *Falls*, on the eastern, and the *Longsand Head*, with the *Kentish Knock*, on the western, side.

GABBARDS.—The INNER GABBARD is a narrow, irregular shoal, having on its shoalest part near the middle only 12 feet at low water, and on a spot 1½ miles more to the southward 15 feet. On other parts the depths are 3½ to 4, 5, and 6 fathoms. The North end lies 15 miles S.E. ½ S. from the High light of Orfordness, and the sand thence trends 6 miles S.W. ¾ S. Near it on the eastern side are from 10 to 16 fathoms of water, and on the western side 9 to 15 fathoms.

The OUTER GABBARD is 4 miles to the eastward of the Inner Gabbard. It is a similar shoal, but divided into two parts by a narrow swashway. The North end is 18½ miles S.E. ¼ E. from the High light of Orfordness, and the general trend of the shoal is S.S.W. ¼ W., 3½ miles. On its shoalest part, at three-quarters of a mile from the North end, are 15 feet at low water. The soundings about it are from 6 to 12 and 15 fathoms.

By order of the Trinity House a buoy has been laid on the central part of each sand, in 2½ fathoms; that on the Inner Gabbard is *black*, and that on the Outer, *red and white* striped. They bear East and West from each other about 5 miles. Excepting at slack water, there is a constant rippling of the tide over the Gabbards, and by this the situation of each may be ascertained in hazy weather, when the buoys cannot be seen.

GALLOPER.—The North end of the Galloper lies S. by E. ¼ E. 20½ miles from Orfordness. The shoal thence extends S.W. ½ S. 4½ miles, from 7 to 7 fathoms. It is about half a mile broad in the broadest part, which is near the middle of the sand, and the least depth upon it is 7 feet at low water. From Orfordness the South end bears S. ¼ E. 23½ miles.

Since the year 1804 a vessel has been moored near the S.W. end of the sand, in which two *brilliant lights* are exhibited horizontally, from sunset to sunrise, at 32 feet above the level of the sea, and may be seen at 10 miles off. In order to prevent any mistake of this for the other lights in the vicinity, it is to be observed that the vessel has two masts, each surmounted by a red ball, with a light at each masthead, that it may be readily distinguished from the Sunk and Goodwin lights, the former of which is exhibited with one light only, and the latter with three lights.

The lightvessel was first moored within less than half a mile of the sand, in 13 fathoms, but it now lies in 15 fathoms at low water, the shoalest part of the sand bearing N.E. from the light, distant about 2 miles, where there are only 6 feet at low water. Upon the extremity of the shoal, southward of the light, a black buoy is placed, that the usual position of the vessel may be known, in case it should drift away, or be removed from its place.

From the lightvessel, situate in lat. 51° 45', lon. 1° 55' 50" E., the High lighthouse on Orfordness bears N. ¾ W. 24 miles; the North Foreland, nearly S.W. by W. ¼ W. 28 miles; and the buoy on the Longsand Head, N.W. by W. ½ W. 2 miles.

The FOUR-MILE KNOLLS are two small 4 fathom spots, the northernmost lying 4 miles S. by W. ¼ W. from the Galloper lightvessel, and the other about two-thirds of a mile southward of it; to the eastward there is a depth of 6 or 8 fathoms, and from 5½ to 8 fathoms to the distance of 1½ miles to the N.W. of the northernmost.

The FALLS is a long narrow bank or ridge, extending from the Four-mile Knolls as far as the South of the Goodwin Sands. It is divided into the Northern, Middle, and Southern Falls.

The NORTHERN FALLS extend from the Four-mile Knolls in a S.W. ¼ S. direction for the distance of 5 miles, with a depth varying between 7 and 10 fathoms, and is about one-quarter of a mile in breadth.

The northern end of the MIDDLE FALLS lies 8 miles S.W. by W. of the South extremity of the Northern Falls, and is connected to it by a narrow shoal of from 12 to 15 fathoms.

The SOUTHERN FALLS is the South extremity of the narrow ridge, which extends in nearly a straight line N.E. by N. and S.W. by S. 13½ miles. The depth on this narrow shoal, which varies in breadth from one-eighth to one-third of a mile, is from 4½ to 8 fathoms. The South extremity bears N.W. by N. 13 miles from the North Foreland lighthouse, and 7 miles from the North Sand Head lightvessel. The northern end of the Middle Fall bears West, 14½ miles from the North Foreland light.

LONGSAND.—From the Sunk lightvessel the bearing and distance to the Longsand Head are S.E. ½ E. 5½ miles, and from the N.E. buoy of the Gunfleet S.E. ½ S. 7⅓ miles. A considerable part dries at half ebb. Vessels should not, in passing, approach it nearer than in 10 fathoms. Off the Head the ground is sandy. From its extremity the N.E. end of the Kentish Knock lies nearly S. ½ E., distant 3 miles.

In February, 1826, by order of the Trinity House, a buoy was moored at the Longsand Head, in 6 fathoms; but in March, 1849, this was superseded by a *nun* buoy of large size, painted *black*, and surmounted by a staff, bearing a St. Andrew's cross, with the words "Longsand" marked on it, placed in 6¼ fathoms, with the Naze tower, midway between Walton Hall and the high tree, N.W. ½ N.; Sunk lightvessel, N.W. by W. ¼ W.; Kentish Knock lightvessel, South.

KENTISH KNOCK.—This shoal, lying nearly parallel to the outside of the Longsand, at the distance of 3 miles, seems to have grown up very much within the last few years, and it now occupies an extent of no less than 7 miles N.E. and S.W. Its greatest breadth, near the middle, is 1¼ miles. Some part dries at low water. From the South end the North Foreland lighthouse bears S.W. ¼ S. 13½ miles; and the East or beacon buoy of Margate Sand, S.W. by W. 10 miles.

A LIGHTVESSEL is placed on the eastern side of the Kentish Knock, 4¾ miles from the S.W. end, and 2¼ miles from the N.E. end, in 5 fathoms at low water, spring tides, with the North Foreland light S.W. westerly, 18 miles; the Sunk light, N. by W. ¼ W., 10 miles; and the Galloper light, E. by N., 11 miles. The light is from a single lantern; it *revolves* every minute, and burns at an elevation of 38 feet above the level of the sea. The ordinary ball upon the mast of the lightvessel is surmounted by a second ball of a smaller size, whereby it may be distinguished with certainty, under all circumstances, during the daytime.

WATCH BUOY.—Notice was also given, 4th September, 1829, that the Corporation had deemed it expedient to place a *Watch Buoy* near the beacon buoy; and that this buoy is laid in 5 fathoms, at low water, about a cable's length S.W. by S. from the beacon buoy. This buoy is *black*, with the head thereof *half white*, and is marked with the words *Kentish Knock*, and is 1 mile W. ½ N. from the lightvessel.

In March, 1849, a large *nun* buoy, coloured *red*, marked K.K. in large black letters, and surmounted by a staff and globe, was placed in 12 fathoms, off the South end of the Kentish Knock, with the Kentish Knock lightvessel N. by E., distant 7 miles; the Tongue light vessel, W. by S., distant 10¼ miles; the North Foreland lighthouse, with Broadstairs mill a ship's length to the westward of it, S.W. ¼ S.

A small *nun* buoy, painted *red*, and having K.K. on it in white letters, has also been laid in 7 fathoms water, three-quarters of a mile N.W. by N. from the before named large buoy.

DIRECTIONS.—*From the N.E. or beacon buoy of the Gunfleet* the bearing and distance to the buoy on the Longsand Head are S.E. ¼ S. 7¾ miles; and from the Sunk lightvessel S.E. ½ E. 5½ miles. The course and distance from the Gunfleet buoy to a fairway are, therefore, S.E. ½ E. 8 miles; making, however, a large allowance for the tide, which sets nearly on the beam. When clear of the Longsand Head, a course South or S. ½ E. will clear the Knock, whence you may proceed as hereafter directed.

From Hosley Bay and Orfordness.—If bound to the Downs from Hosley Bay, with an easterly wind, turn down to Orfordness with an ebb tide, and proceed thence to the eastward of the Shipwash. The course, in a fairway, from Hosley Bay to the Ness is agreeably to the former directions, E. by N. northerly, distance about 5 miles.

The High light on Orfordness, kept N.N.W., will lead clear of the lightvessel off the N.E. end of the Shipwash, and into 11 or 12 fathoms. In sailing off or along this sand, observe the precaution noticed in the description of it, by allowing for the set of the tide, the direction of which is about two points athwart the sand.

The course and distance hence, to the eastward of the Kentish Knock, will be nearly

S.S.W. 7 leagues; still continuing to make proper allowance for the tide, whether ebb or flood.

With contrary winds you may stand in towards the Shipwash to 12 and 14 fathoms, and off to 20; towards the Longsand Head to 9 and 10, and off to 20; and to the Knock into 12 and 13 fathoms.

The Sunk lightvessel will now bear about N.N.W. ¼ W., in which case the course and distance to the North Foreland will be S.W. ¼ W. nearly 6½ leagues; or to the Gull Stream, S.W. ¼ S. 7½ leagues.

The FLOATING LIGHT of the GOODWIN is principally intended for the use of vessels from the northward. Its uses have been more fully described on page 21.

This vessel exhibits *three brilliant lights* on separate masts, at 35 and 23 feet above the level of the sea; the mainmast being the highest. A red ball is hoisted on each mast by day, and a gong is sounded in snowy and foggy weather.

TIDES IN THE THAMES' MOUTH, ETC.

The tide off Orfordness and over the Shipwash sets as already described; the flood W.S.W. and ebb E.N.E.; and setting in this direction, it follows, that vessels passing from the Gunfleet to the Longsand must have it nearly on the beam. At the Longsand Head the first two hours of flood set W. by S. between it and the Kentish Knock; and with great velocity between it and the Sunk. The ebb in a contrary direction.

At Orfordness the flood tide continues to run until 11ʰ; see page 53. At the Longsand Head it flows at 11ʰ 30'; springs rise 15, and neaps about 10 feet. At the North Foreland it flows at 11ʰ; springs rise 10; and neaps 7 feet.

Between the North Foreland and the Kentish Knock the setting of the tide is extremely irregular; so much so that frequently, in the course of half a tide, the stream will set to every point in the compass. In these circular currents, or large whirlpools, the fishermen have sometimes found their nets coiled up in the most curious manner, and too often rendered useless; and as the whirls are not stationary, they have it not in their power to avoid them when driving off the Foreland.

Near the Galloper the tide flows, on the full and change, at 11ʰ 45', and runs at the rate of between 2 and 3 knots. The flood, for the first hour, sets from the N.E., afterward more from the East.

SECTION IX.

ORFORDNESS TO CROMER, INCLUDING YARMOUTH ROADS, ETC.

THE objects which appear on the coast described within the limits of this section are pleasing and interesting. In succession are seen the lighthouses of Orfordness, Lowestoff, Pakefield, Winterton, Hasborough, and Cromer; and, in the intervals, numerous churches, cultivated lands, and other cheerful scenery. The coasts are variable. From Orfordness, which is low, the land to the northward increases in height. The coasts of Suffolk and Norfolk to the southward of Hasborough are, however, rather low than otherwise; but Foulness and its adjoining coasts consist of a perpendicular cliff, which is, at Mundesley, from 50 to 60 feet in height.

SOUTHWOLD HARBOUR, in Sole Bay, is about 14 miles to the N.W. of Orfordness, and is formed by the channel of the river Blyth, where it enters the sea, at nearly right angles to the general line of coast. The direction of the harbour between the two piers is S.E. It is high water here, at full and change, at 10ʰ 15'. The best springs are a few days afterwards, at 2ʰ; thus the afternoon spring tides, and these only, are in good daylight throughout the year. The average rise of the tide is 5 feet 3 inches; a good spring, 6½ feet.

PAKEFIELD LIGHTHOUSE.—At the distance of 3 miles to the S.W. of Lowestoff-ness is the lighthouse within the cliff of *Pakefield*, which was established in 1832. This structure is white, and exhibits a *red* light. The height from the base to the lantern is only 23 feet; but from the elevation of the land the light is 68 feet above the level of the sea, and may be seen more than 4 leagues off. The angle of light is from S.E. by E. ¼ E. to S.E. ¾ S.

LOWESTOFF LIGHTHOUSES.—These two lighthouses stand within Lowestoff-ness, and in a line bear N. ¾ E. They are half a mile asunder, and exhibit brilliant fixed lights. The Low light stands near the beach, at 2 cables' length from the South-ness, and the High light on the high land, its lantern being 113 feet above high water.

In noticing Lowestoff church, hereafter, it is to be distinctly understood that the church meant is the old church, with a spire, to the N.W. of the town, and not the church of St. Peter, on the South side, which was built in 1834.

LOWESTOFF NEW HARBOUR.—The entrance of Lowestoff Harbour is nearly half a mile to the S.W. of the Low light. Within the piers, to the lock gates, there is a depth of only 3 to 9 feet at low water, with a shingle beach on either side, at the back of the piers: a warping buoy lies on the outside, and there are beacons within for the direction of vessels in the best water.

To facilitate the entrance into the harbour by night, *two red lights* are shown, one on each pier head, and kept burning from sunset to sunrise. At the entrance of the inner harbour *two green lights* are shown, which, brought in a line, vertical, leads into the inner channel: but vessels must not approach the bridge until the lower light is changed to red, which is a signal that the bridge is open. Sailing out at night one green light will be shown, which will be changed to red when the bridge is open.

A *red flag* will be hoisted on the lookout station of the inner harbour when the gates are open, and kept flying during the time vessels can enter the inner harbour. Vessels may enter the outer harbour at all times of tide, but they are not to attempt to enter the inner harbour unless the red flag is hoisted by day, and the two green lights shown by night.

Previous to closing the gates, a *black ball* will be hoisted.

GREAT YARMOUTH.—At the distance of 6 miles N. by E. ¼ E. from Lowestoff-ness is the entrance of Yarmouth Harbour. It is formed by the mouth of the Yare River, by which, were it not for the obstructions caused by the bridge at the head of the harbour, and some other impediments, sea-borne ships might reach the city of Norwich; and by the river Waveney, which also falls into the Yare, the large town of Beccles might have communication with the sea at Yarmouth, instead of the minor accommodation at Lowestoff, as is the case at present. The mouth of the haven, formed by piers, which is 209 feet wide, has generally 8 feet on the bar at low water, and vessels of 13 or 14 feet draught of water come in at ordinary high tide; vessels drawing 15 feet have at times entered the port.

SHOALS BETWEEN THORPNESS AND WINTERTONNESS, INCLUDING YARMOUTH ROADS.

DUNWICH BANK, which lies at a mile eastward from the shore of Dunwich, is a shoal of 3¾ and 4 fathoms. It is 1⅓ miles in length, trending N.E. by E. ½ E., and S.W. by W. ½ W.

BARNARD.—The next shoal, to the southward of Lowestoff Roads, is that called the *Barnard*; the South end of which lies at the distance of about three-quarters of a mile from the shore, S.E. by E. from Covehithe church. It extends thence N.E. 3 miles; is a quarter of a mile in breadth, and had but 4 feet on its shoalest part at low water, but the depth on it is improving. To steer clear of it, keep Southwold church at the least twice its apparent breadth open to the left of Easton houses, which stand within Easton Cliff. A *buoy, painted red,* is laid on the western side of this *sand,* in 6 fathoms.

Two buoys are laid, in 15 feet at low water, to the S.W. of the red buoy, which mark the sides of a narrow channel, lately formed between

The Coast to the southeard of Lowestoff when the lower lighthouse (b) bears W. ½ S., distant six-tenths of a mile.

(a) Kirkley Church. *(b) Lower Lighthouse (b) W. ½ S.*

Covehithe Point and the southern part of the Barnard. The first, on the S.W. side, striped black and white, is marked *Covehithe Point*. The other is a *black buoy*, with staff and ball, lying from the striped buoy E.N.E. ¾ E. The width of the channel between is 180 fathoms. Kessingland church leads through, when bearing N. ½ W. A buoy *chequered black and white*, with staff and ball, marked *North Barnard*, is laid off the *N.E. end* of this sand.

The course in the best water through Pakefield Gat is now N.N.W. ¾ W., and the line of the light has been altered to correspond therewith. It was announced in March, 1849, that the depth on the bar in the middle of the channel did not exceed 10 feet.

The NEWCOME, a bank of recent formation, extends in a N.E. by N. and S.W. by S. direction, to the southward of Lowestoff, and forms the passage called the INNER CHANNEL and LOWESTOFF SOUTH ROAD, sometimes called Abraham's Bosom. It is now 2¼ miles in length, and a part of it is nearly dry at low water. Toward the North end the bank is narrow, and is distinguished by the Stanford lightvessel, described hereafter. On the eastern side of the sand, and between it and the southern part of the Holm Sand, is the NEW STANFORD CHANNEL.

Another shoal, called LOWESTOFF INNER SHOAL, has also been formed off the *Southness* of Lowestoff. It now extends from near the Lowestoff Low lighthouse to the Stanford lightvessel; it has a depth of from 12 to 16 feet, and in one spot there is a depth of 11 feet.

The STANFORD PASSAGE, which was formerly the Inner Channel to and from Yarmouth Roads, became unfit for general navigation in 1836; but in January, 1843, notice was given that the Stanford Channel was again opened, and fit for navigation, as hereafter described.

Such buoys have since been placed; they consist of *four black buoys* on the Newcome, which, in proceeding northward, are to be left on the starboard or eastern side; and a *black buoy* on the *Inner Shoal*, off Lowestoff-ness, which is to be left on the port or western side.

The *first buoy*, called the *South buoy of the Newcome*, in 2¾ fathoms, is *black*, with a *staff and ball*.

The *second buoy on the Newcome*, called the *S.W. Newcome buoy*, lies in 4 fathoms at half a mile N. by E. from the South Newcome or beacon buoy.

The *third black buoy*, marked *N.W. Newcome*, lies in 4¼ fathoms, at three-quarters of a mile N.N.E. ¼ E. from the preceding or S.W. Newcome buoy.

The *fourth black buoy*, marked *N. Newcome*, lies in 3¾ fathoms, at nearly three-quarters of a mile N.E. ¾ E. from the N.W. buoy.

The *Inner Shoal buoy*, *black*, now lies in 14 feet.

The STANFORD LIGHTVESSEL now lies in 4 fathoms at low water, with Corton church and windmill in line, N. ¼ W.; and Lowestoff High lighthouse, N.N.W. ⅓ W.

INNER CHANNEL.—*Vessels approaching this channel from the southward* will leave the chequered beacon buoy off the N.E. end of the Barnard on the West or larboard side, and black beacon buoy of the South Newcome on the starboard side; and proceed in with Pakefield lighthouse bearing N.N.W. ¾ W., the depth being 21 feet and upwards, N.N.W. ½ W., as the latter will clear the South end of the Newcome in 15 feet; the course up to Lowestoff South road will then be to the N.W., leaving the black buoys on the Newcome to the East, or on the starboard hand. The Lowestoff Inner Shoal, marked by the buoy described above, lies athwart the South Road; and to proceed to the northward from this, when the North Newcome buoy bears about S.E., or Lowestoff Low light N.N.E., bring Pakefield church just open South of the village, bearing about W. by S., and pass out between the Inner Shoal and the Stanford lightvessel in 16 feet least water. Or you may pass to the West of the Inner Shoal, between it and Lowestoff-ness, in 18 or 20 feet water, by keeping Pakefield village open of Lowestoff Piers, or Pakefield church open of the village.

Vessels coming from the northward, after rounding the lightvessel to the westward, and bearing to the West, will be in the fairway to the southward, when Covehithe church comes over Kessingland fish houses; and by running southward on this bearing they will keep in 4 and 5 fathoms water, and can stand out between the Newcome and Barnard, when Pakefield mill and barn come in one, bearing N.N.W. ¼ W., or when Pakefield light bears N.N.W. ¾ W., as before mentioned. Vessels working and standing either toward the Barnard or Newcome must immediately tack on losing sight of Pakefield light. In going northward by night, a good mark is to keep Lowestoff Low light open East of the red pier lights.

The HOLM and CORTON, formerly distinct shoals, became united into one bank, nearly 7 miles in extent from North to South, but has again been cut through to the eastward of Lowestoff-ness by a broad channel, the *Corton Gatway,* having a depth of 4 to 5 fathoms. The Holm dries in extensive patches, for above 1¾ miles, in the part lying off Lowestoff-ness.

The eastern or seaward face of these shoals is now marked by *buoys,* as follows:—The southernmost of these black buoys, the *South Holm,* lies in 2¼ fathoms; Holm Hook buoy, N.N.E.

The *second of the black buoys* above mentioned, on the eastern edge of the Holm and Corton, is marked *S.E. Holm;* it lies in 6 fathoms, and bears S.E. by S. 2½ miles from Lowestoff church.

The *third black buoy,* called the *Middle Holm,* in 8 fathoms, bears from the S.E. Holm N.E. by E. easterly, 1⅝ miles.

The *fourth black buoy,* marked *S. Corton,* lies in 8 fathoms, at 1½ miles N.E. by N. from the Middle Holm.

The *fifth black buoy,* marked *S.E. Corton,* lies in 6 fathoms, at 1¼ miles N. ¾ E. from the N.E. Holm.

The *sixth black buoy,* marked *N.E. Corton,* lies in 4½ fathoms, at three-quarters of a mile N. ½ W. from the S.E. Corton.

The *seventh buoy* is chequered *black* and *white,* marked *Inner Kettlebottom,* in 6 fathoms.

The *eighth buoy* is *black,* marked *Outer Kettlebottom,* in 5 fathoms.

The STANFORD CHANNEL is nearly one-third of a mile wide, with 20 feet at its entrance, and 33 to 50 feet throughout at low water springs. Its southern entrance is between the *black South Holm buoy,* before described, and the *red buoy,* called the *East Newcome.* The *entrance of this channel,* between these buoys, is less than 2 cables' lengths in width.

The mark for the fairway between these buoys is the Stanford lightvessel, N.N.E. by compass, and having passed between them, run on a N.N.E. ½ E. course between the N.E. *Newcome buoy,* and the Holm Hook buoy.

The *Holm Hook* buoy, which is *chequered black and white,* lies in 6 fathoms, on the starboard side.

The *N.E. Newcome buoy, red,* lies in 5 fathoms, opposite the last.

Having come abreast of the Holm Hook buoy and N.E. Newcome buoy, bear away to the N.N.E. to pass the Stanford lightvessel to the eastward, and proceed into the Lowestoff North Road.

It is to be observed that the tides in the Stanford Channel set N.E. and S.W., and the course must be shaped accordingly.

The western edge of the *Corton Sand* is marked by three *chequered black and white buoys,* the *N.W. Holm,* the *North Holm,* and the *West Corton,* which of course are to be left to starboard in passing northward through Lowestoff North Road and Corton Road.

ST. NICHOLAS GAT has been much used as a channel way to the Yarmouth Roads; but in consequence of the shifting of the sands hereabout, it has so grown up that there is only 10 feet water where the principal channel existed. The buoys which marked it have therefore been taken up, and others substituted for the Hewett's Channel, St. Nicholas Gat being no longer practicable.

HEWETT'S CHANNEL, now the principal entrance into the Yarmouth Road, is a passage between the St. Nicholas or Kettlebottom Sand, and the southern part of the Scroby Bank. According to the examination in November, 1845, it is a clear channel of above half a mile wide, with a depth of from 7 to 10 fathoms, and is that now in general use. The SOUTH SCROBY SAND forms its eastern side, which is marked by four buoys, the southern a black monster buoy, the others black and white buoys. The St. Nicholas lightvessel marks its N.W. point.

The Corton and the Kettlebottom Sands, which form the western side of the Hewett's Channel, are now marked by the two buoys and the lightvessel following:—The *Inner Kettlebottom buoy*, which is placed near the former entrance of St. Nicholas Gat, is chequered *black* and *white*, and marked "Inner Kettlebottom." The *Outer Kettlebottom buoy*, painted *black*, and marked "Outer Kettlebottom," lies in 5 fathoms at low water.

The ST. NICHOLAS LIGHTVESSEL, which shows one bright fixed light, now lies at the *North* end of the Kettlebottom Sand in 10 fathoms. The vessel is painted *red*, with the name on the side; it has a single lantern, elevated 36 feet above the water, and during the day is distinguished by a *red ball* at the masthead, which, in the event of the vessel's driving from her proper station, will be taken down.

The outer buoy to the S.E. of the entrance is the South Scroby, a conspicuous black beacon nun buoy, of large size, and which lies in 3½ fathoms, at 2 miles S. by E. ¼ E. from the St. Nicholas lightvessel.

The South Scroby Spit buoy, chequered black and white, has been placed near a spit of sand, which has grown up about midway between the South Scroby and Scroby Fork buoys, having only 2¼ fathoms on it at low water.

The *Scroby Fork buoy, black and white striped*, lies in 5¾ fathoms, N. ½ W. 1½ miles from the *South Scroby*.

The *Scroby S.W. buoy, chequered black and white, with beacon*, in 3 fathoms, lies at two-thirds of a mile N.N.E. ¼ E. of the St. Nicholas lightvessel.

Caistor church and South mill in a line, bearing N. ¼ W., or Hemesby church, in one with the mill East of Caistor church, bearing due North, as shown by chart, lead through the middle of Hewett's Channel into Yarmouth Roads. By night the bearing of the lightvessel will indicate the proper course.

The SCROBY SAND, between the South Scroby and the North Scroby beacon buoys, is more than 7 miles in length: the bearing between these two buoys, which is the general direction of the bank, is N. by E. ¼ E. It alters considerably in its depth and figure, and now consists of three portions, the *South Scroby*, off the town of Yarmouth, a portion of which dries at low water, and the *Middle* and *North Scroby*, between that and the Cockle Gat. These patches have less than 2 feet water in many parts. Along the western side, which is slowly extending into Yarmouth Roads, there are eight buoys, the South, Spit, Fork, and S.W. Scroby, above described, and four black and white chequered buoys, as under:—

The *Scroby Elbow buoy*, black and white, in 11 fathoms water, W. by N ¼ N.; Caistor church, over the North end of a white house with a slated roof, N. by W. ⅓ W.; S.W. Scroby buoy, S. ¼ W.; West Scroby buoy, N.N.E. ¼ E.

The *West Scroby buoy*, chequered black and white, now lies in 10 fathoms water.

The *Middle Scroby buoy, chequered black and white*, lies in 5½ fathoms.

The *North buoy (a beacon buoy) of the Scroby, chequered black and white*, in 4 fathoms.

BARBER AND COCKLE.—The BARBER and COCKLE are two irregular but united shoals to the N.E. of Caistor, which forms *Hemesby Hole*, and the N.W. side of the Cockle Gat. They extend off Caistor Point in a N.E. direction. *Caistor Shoal* reaches for nearly half a mile off. The Barber is the southernmost, and within this is a swash-way, which we call *Hemesby Gat*: but this channel has now so grown up, that the depth of water therein at low water is reduced to 9 feet, and therefore it cannot longer be navigated with safety.

The *edge of the Barber* is distinguished by the following buoys: the first, a *black buoy*, marked "Caistor Shoal," has been laid in 6 fathoms water to the S.E. of this shoal.

The next, called the *Inner Barber*, is *black*, and in 8 fathoms water.

The *S.W. Cockle, chequered black and white*, lies in 6¼ fathoms.

The *Cockle Spit buoy, black*, lies in 4¼ fathoms.

The *N.E. Cockle buoy, black*, lies in 4 fathoms water.

COCKLE GAT.—The northern entrance to Yarmouth Roads is distinguished by the *Cockle lightvessel*, which shows a *revolving* light once in a minute, first exhibited on December 20th, 1843.

The SEA HEADS is a spit, 4 miles in length, which forks from the *Scroby* on the East, and extends in a direction N. by E.   In former years its depth was very inconsiderable, but it has nearly disappeared.

WINTERTON OVERFALLS, a ridge or bar extending in a N.N.W. direction, at the distance of a mile from the Cockle lightvessel and the Cockle Spit, has in one spot only 3½ fathoms.   This shoal has existed for many years, and there are strong overfalls on it with the ebb.

The CROSS SAND and NEWARP, the easternmost of the Yarmouth Banks, extend in a N.N.E. and S.S.W. direction, 8 miles, at the distance of about half a league eastward from the Scroby and Newcome Sea Heads.   The South end of the Cross Sand is now distinguished by a *black buoy,* in 12½ fathoms.

On the eastern edge of the Cross Sand, at 3 miles N.E. by N. from the South end, is another black buoy, called the *Middle Cross Sand buoy,* which lies in 11 fathoms.

The *N.E. Cross Sand buoy, black,* in 10 fathoms, is 2¾ miles to N.N.E. ¼ E. of the last named buoy.

The *North Cross Sand buoy* is now a *large black nun buoy, with a staff and ball.*   It is 1½ miles from the N.E. Cross Sand buoy, and S. by W. ¾ W., 2½ miles of the Newarp lightvessel.—*October* 10th, 1855.

NEWARP.—On the North end of the flat of the Newarp, at 4¾ miles N.N.E. from the North Cross Sand buoy, is a *red* buoy, lying with Winterton lighthouse, W.N.W. ¼ W., 6 miles.*

The NEWARP LIGHTVESSEL, with three fixed lights, is moored at the distance of a mile N.E. ¼ E. from the red buoy.   This vessel will be described in its place hereafter. Without it are several ripplings, but nothing that can take a ship up, as there is not less than 7 fathoms on any of them.

DIRECTIONS FOR SAILING FROM ORFORDNESS, THROUGH THE LOWESTOFF OR INNER CHANNEL, STANFORD CHANNEL, YARMOUTH ROADS, AND THE COCKLE GAT.

ORFORDNESS to the STANFORD.—In proceeding from Orfordness, you will avoid the Ridge, &c., by keeping Bawdsey Cliff, bearing W.S.W. ¼ W., well open of Orford beach, until Aldborough church bears N.N.W., when you will be about halfway between the black buoy on the Ridge and the S.W. end of Aldborough Knapes. From the last spot a direct course to the bar of the Stanford is N.E. ¼ N., and the distance 20½ miles.

Approach, on the West, no nearer to the Sizewell Bank than with Orford castle open to the southward of Aldborough town, and bearing S.W. by W. ½ W.; nor to Dunwich Bank nearer than with Covehithe church well open to the eastward of the N.E. end of Easton cliff.   Aldborough church open of Thorpness, S.W ¼ W., leads clear along the S.E. side of this bank, in 5 and 6 fathoms of water.

The mark leading clear of the South side of the Barnard is Southwold church, at the least twice its apparent breadth open to the left of Easton houses, S.W. by W. ½ W.

In SOLE BAY, or SOUTHWOLD BAY, between Sizewell Bank and the Barnard, there is good riding with offshore winds in 8 or 9 fathoms.   In approaching the Barnard go no nearer to it than in 9 fathoms, as it is steep, and there are 8 fathoms near to it on the eastern side.

It is to be observed that the flood sets strongly to the S.W. upon the Newcome, and the ebb, on the contrary, upon the Holm head.

Vessels from the N.E. may safely approach the parallel of Lowestoff, or 52° 28′ N., as the soundings are regular.   In this latitude they may steer boldly in, either by night or day, into 16 or 17 fathoms.   In the night time the high light may be seen 3 or 4 leagues off; and in the day the church with its spire steeple, and upper part of the town, at the distance of 7 leagues, if the weather be clear.

LOWESTOFF CHANNEL.—We have already given, in page 63, the marks for entering the Inner Channel, which are, Pakefield lighthouse bearing N.N.W. ¼ W.

* During the season of the herring fishery this buoy is taken up, and is replaced after its termination.

The course thence toward the Inner Shoal lies in the channel to the northward, N.E., and this course is to be continued until off the black North Newcome buoy; after which proceed as directed on page 63.

Having reached the Stanford lightvessel, you will have passed to the westward the four black buoys on the western edge of the Newcome; the general leading mark is, when within the channel and proceeding southward, Covehithe church, over the extremity of Kessingland fish houses, bearing S.W.

STANFOR CHANNEL.—This channel, which has been described on page 64, lies between the Holm and Newcome Sands, but from the shifting of the sands has grown up, and has now only 14 or 15 feet water between the buoys at the entrance. This southern entrance is marked by the South Holm buoy (black) on the starboard or eastern side, and the East Newcome buoy (red) on the larboard hand; these buoys are nearly 2 cables' lengths apart, and the mark for running through the channel is the Stanford lightvessel, bearing N. by E.

To come to Lowestoff South Road, this course must be continued until nearly up to the lightvessel; and when the entrance of Lowestoff harbour bears about W.N.W. $\frac{1}{2}$ W. haul round to the westward into the road; or if bound northward to Yarmouth Roads, &c., pass to the *eastward* of the lightvessel, and continue the course as directed.

CORTON ROADS lie between the Corton Sand and the shoal which extends along the coast to the North of Lowestoff-ness, and northward of Lowestoff North Road.

The western side of the Corton Sand is marked by the buoys described on page 64; and from off the N.W. Holm (formerly the S.W. Corton) chequered buoy, or from the North Holm (before the Middle Corton) buoy, which lies beyond the line of the other buoys, the mid-channel course will be, more or less, about N. by E., leaving the buoys as above on the starboard or eastern side. The breadth of the channel in this part is three-quarters of a mile, and the general depth 6 and 7 fathoms. Within this line on the West the black mill on Yarmouth Denes, on with the head of the town jetty, clears the bar which projects from the pier. For sailing along shore, between the Corton and the South pier head, the mark is, Nelson's column or monument, the hospital, chapel, and church of Yarmouth, all in one; but here the depth, at low water, will be only 2 fathoms.

YARMOUTH ROADS.—The anchorage in Yarmouth Roads is off the town. It is so extensive as to admit the largest fleet of ships. The ground is sandy, and ships in hard gales sometimes bring home their anchors, particularly if from the N.N.E. or S.S.W.

From mid-channel, off the Middle buoy of the Corton, to a berth off the new pier of Gorleston, the course and distance are N. by E. 4 miles. The greater part of the channel is 1¼ miles broad, and the soundings throughout are regular; so that you may in working stand to the shore into 5 and 4 fathoms, and to the Corton and St. Nicholas Banks to 8 and 7 fathoms. There is good room for turning to windward, and good anchorage all the way; but the best ground is in 6½ fathoms, with Corton church N.W. by N., and Lowestoff High light S.W. With an easterly wind you may ride nearer to the Corton Sand; with a northerly wind you may ride best to the N.E. of Yarmouth jetty.

In advancing toward Gorleston, you will see its new piers at the South end of Yarmouth Denes. By day a red flag, and by night a red light, is shown on the southern one. At a mile more to the North, on the Denes, stands the monument erected to the memory of Lord Nelson; it is a handsome column, on a broad basement, surmounted by a figure of Britannia, and which, as a mark, is equally ornamental and useful. Yarmouth church is nearly 1¼ miles more to the northward, and the town jetty midway between both. Northward of the jetty on the Denes are ten windmills.

HEWETT'S CHANNEL and St. Nicholas Gatway.—The last named of these channels was for many years the well known chief entrance to Yarmouth Roads; but in consequence of the ever-shifting character of the sands which shelter Yarmouth Roads, it has gradually declined in depth; and at last, in August, 1853, the depth in it being then only 10 feet, and some vessels having struck, the buoys marking it were removed; and thus the channel between the Corton and Scroby Sands, known by the name of the lamented surveyor, Captain Hewett, has become the entrance to this important roadstead.

HEWETT'S CHANNEL has been for a long time a much more open channel than the St. Nicholas Gat, and has a depth of 6½ to 9 fathoms. A mark that has been given for passing through this channel is Hemesby church in one with Caistor North mill : another is Caistor church and mill in one.

COCKLE GAT.—From the anchorage in Yarmouth Roads in 10 fathoms, which is two-thirds of a mile E.S.E. from the town jetty head, a N.N.E. ¼ E. course for 7 miles will carry you between the Cockle Gat lightvessel and the Cockle Spit buoy, which has recently removed in a westerly direction.   This course carries you nearly in mid-channel between the Scroby Sand and the Barber and Cockle Sands to the West, the buoys on which are described on page 65.

Ships bound from Yarmouth Roads through the Cockle Gat may pass safely to a berth by keeping Yarmouth jetty, Nelson's monument, and Gorleston barn* in a line, bearing S.W. ¼ S.   These marks lead through in the fairway, between the Scroby and Sea Heads on the East, and the Barber and Cockle on the West.

In working through with a turning wind, avoid standing too near the Scroby, for it is very steep.   So soon as you shoalen your water upon it, you should tack.   The flood tide sets strongly over the Scroby, and the ebb over the Barber.

From a position between the Cockle lightvessel and the Cockle Spit buoy you proceed to sea on a course N. ¼ E.; and with this course continued for 2¼ miles you will clear the Cockle with its buoys on one side, and some broken, uneven ground on the other, which extends about half a league from the Sea Heads to the N. by E., and over which are strong ripplings with the ebb stream.   You will now be off Winterton-ness, with the churches of Somerton and Martham in a line, bearing West, and may proceed according to circumstances.

HEMESBY HOLE is a channel formed by a swash in the sand called the *Barber*, but which has grown up, and is divided into two parts, called the *Inner Barber*, and the *Outer Barber*, each of which is marked by a black buoy.   The channel within is 3¼ miles in length, half a mile broad, and is limited on the West by a long, narrow shelf, called the *Hood*, extending parallel with the shore, as far as Winterton lighthouse; the opposite limit is the western edge of the Cockle Sand.

At the entrance is a bar, which has grown up to the depth of only 7 feet at low spring tide; but within and without are 5 fathoms, deepening northward to 8 and 10 fathoms. The course through is N. ¼ E. at three-quarters of a mile from shore.   Thus you leave the *white buoy* on the East or starboard side.

Off Winterton-ness is a narrow shelf, 1¼ miles in length, extending S. by E. ½ E. and N. by W. ½ W.   Its outer edge is half a mile from shore, and has on it 2 fathoms of water.   In order to furnish a convenient guide to vessels seeking shelter in Hemesby Hole, a buoy striped *black and white*, and marked " *Winterton-ness*," has been placed in 4 fathoms water.

HASBOROUGH GAT, AND THE COAST THENCE TO FOULNESS.

The Channel called HASBOROUGH GAT lies between the *Newarp*, &c., on the S.W., and the shoals called *Winterton Ridge, Hammond's Knoll*, and *Hasborough Sand*, on the N.E. side.   It is between 2 and 3 leagues in breadth, and has plenty of water for any ships, 14, 16, and 18, to 20 and 22 fathoms.

The NEWARP and other shoals, on the South side of the Gat, have already been described.   Off the North end of the Newarp, at the distance of a mile, is a *lightvessel*, exhibiting *three brilliant lights* upon separate masts, of which the central is the highest. The vessel lies with the Newarp buoy S.W. ¼ W., rather more than 1 mile.   When riding ebb, Martham church steeple appears open to the southward of Winterton steeple, twice the breadth of the latter, bearing W. by N.; Hasborough Lower lighthouse just open to the northward of the Higher lighthouse; Hasborough steeple, N.W.; Yarmouth church, S.W. by W. ¼ W.

HASBOROUGH SAND, from a *black buoy*, lying on its South end, to a *black and white buoy*, in quarters, on its North end, extends N.N.W. 9¼ miles; it is nearly 1 mile across, and 4 fathoms of water on one side to 4 fathoms on the other, at the broadest part: and in some places it almost dries at low water spring tides.   This sand, from the North end to within 4 miles of its South end, is steep on both sides; near the North

---

* Gorleston barn is three-quarters of a mile to the southward of Gorleston church.

end are, within a quarter of a mile of the outer and inner edges of the sand, from 15 to 17 fathoms of water.

LIGHTVESSEL.—From the month of January, 1832, a *lightvessel* has been moored near the North end of this sand, which vessel exhibits *two brilliant lights*, on separate masts, at 37 feet above the level of the sea; the vessel is moored in $13\frac{1}{2}$ fathoms, with Cromer lighthouse bearing W. by N. 11 miles distant; Hasborough High lighthouse, S.W. $\frac{1}{4}$ S.; North buoy of Hasborough Sand, E. by S., distant about 1 mile. On the sides of the vessel are the words " *Hasboro' light.*" The lights may be seen at 3 leagues off.

From the black buoy on the South end *of Hasborough Sand,* which lies in 7 fathoms, a narrow shoal of 4, 5, and 6 fathoms extends $3\frac{1}{2}$ miles N. by E. $\frac{1}{2}$ E., within which and Hasborough Sand the depths vary from 11 to 18 fathoms; and on its eastern edge are 8, 9, and 10 fathoms.

Middle Hasborough buoy.—A *buoy,* coloured *black* and *white* in *circular* stripes, has been placed near the middle of Hasborough Sand; on its western side is marked " Middle Hasborough," and lies in 6 fathoms, with Hasborough church, W. by S. $\frac{1}{4}$ S.; Hasborough lightvessel, N. by W. $\frac{1}{4}$ W.

HAMMOND'S KNOLL.—This is a narrow ridge of sand, extending 6 miles N. by W. $\frac{1}{4}$ W. and S. by E. $\frac{1}{4}$ E. Its South end, in 6 fathoms, bears S.E. by E. $\frac{1}{2}$ E., 4 miles from the black or South buoy on Hasborough Sand, and the soundings between the Knoll exceed 3 fathoms, in an extent of $2\frac{1}{2}$ miles. The eastern edge is very steep, and rises abruptly from 10 and 11 fathoms.

WINTERTON RIDGE, a shoal bearing a resemblance to Hammond's Knoll, extending nearly in the same direction, and equally steep on the eastern side, lies to the S.E. of that Knoll, at the distance of 2 miles. Upon it, it is said, there are only 8 feet of water (1842). The North end of the Ridge is on the same parallel as the South end of the Knoll: the depths between are 10 and 12 to 17 fathoms. From the North end the Ridge extends S. $\frac{1}{2}$ E. 4 miles.

From the South end of Winterton Ridge, in 5 fathoms, the Newarp lightvessel bears W. $\frac{1}{4}$ S. 7 miles; and the black buoy on the South end of Hasborough Sand, N.W. $\frac{1}{4}$ N. 8 miles.

SMITH'S KNOLL.—The South end of this bank lies E. $\frac{1}{2}$ S. from Yarmouth, 8 leagues distant; E. $\frac{1}{2}$ N. $7\frac{1}{2}$ leagues from the South end of St. Nicholas Bank; and E.S.E. 6 leagues from the floating light on the Newarp. Its form is serpentine, but its general direction is nearest to N. $\frac{1}{4}$ W., and its length, from 8 fathoms on each end, is 6 leagues. The shoalest spot on the bank is just in the middle of its length, where 2 fathoms near the eastern edge have been found, and at $2\frac{1}{4}$ miles each way from this spot are $3\frac{1}{2}$ fathoms. The greatest breadth near the middle is about a mile. The general soundings on the Knoll are of fine brown reddish sand, with red clay.

On advancing toward the South end on either side the soundings are fine reddish sand, with blue clay. The general soundings between it and the Ridge are from 15 to 20 fathoms. The sea hereabouts abounds with flat fish.

The eastern side of this Knoll is so steep that within three-quarters of a mile of it, in 4 fathoms, there is a depth of 27 fathoms; and ships coming in from sea, and getting quickly from 29 or 30 fathoms into shoal water, will certainly be upon the Knoll, as there is not so deep water to be found anywhere within it.

HASBOROUGH GAT.—From off Lowestoff a fair course along the back of the sands to Hasborough Gatway is N.E. by N. about 4 leagues, until the Newarp lightvessel bears N. $\frac{1}{4}$ E., and Winterton lighthouse N.W.; a N. by E. course, $5\frac{1}{2}$ miles farther, will bring you to the eastward of the lightvessel, until the leading mark for the Gat comes on; this mark is, the two lighthouses of Hasborough in one, bearing N.W.

SAILING IN THROUGH HASBOROUGH GATWAY.

In proceeding for the Gatway from the sea, the first object to be attended to is the lightvessel which lies off the North end of the Newarp; if you make her to the eastward of North you must steer to the eastward till you bring her to bear North, or N.N.W. When she bears N.N.W. you may safely steer for her, for the tide runs nearly in that direction; the flood sets S.S.E. and the ebb N.N.W. After passing the lightvessel, continue your course N.N.W., or more to the eastward, as you shall find occasion, until you see Hasborough lights on with each other ; they will then bear from you N.W. a little westerly. If you do not see Hasborough lights, you may take your soundings from the shore, in 12, 10, or 8 fathoms. Should you be a mile or two to the eastward of the floating light in passing it, the tide of ebb will set you in a fair direction through the Gatway.

If bound for Yarmouth Roads you must, after having passed the lightvessel, steer such a course as will (allowing for the cross of the tide) carry you to the Cockle Gat lightvessel, which lies on the fairway. Hence you may proceed through the Cockle Gat, leaving the black buoys of the Cockle on the starboard side, the buoys of the Barber starboard, and the buoys of the Scroby on the port side. The direct course toward Yarmouth will be S.W. ¾ S., with Nelson's monument on the Denes in a line with Gorleston barn, which barn stands at two-thirds of a mile southward from the church of Gorleston.

SAILING OUT THROUGH HASBOROUGH GATWAY.

If when off Hasborough you find that you cannot get through the Cockle Gat before dark, you may safely run through the Gatway, by bringing Hasborough lights in one, bearing then nearly N.W., and then steering to the S.E., so as to keep the lights on with each other, which will lead you a mile to the N.E. of the floating light. As the East side or edge of the Newarp, in 4 fathoms, bears S. by W. from the lightvessel, you must be careful in rounding her to the southward not to bring her to the eastward of North until you shall have passed the light to the distance of 4 miles; you may then steer S.S.W., which will carry you without the Cross Sand. If you have a half flood in your favour, with a brisk breeze, when you pass the floating light, you may steer S.S.W.; for the flood tide, by setting S.S.E., will certainly keep you clear of the Newarp. If you should have an ebb tide when you pass the lightvessel, you must be sure not to haul up too soon, for the ebb, by setting N.N.W., will steer you toward the sand, and it may, unless you have a fresh breeze, oblige you to come to an anchor.

If you are off Hasborough with the wind from the E.N.E., it will not be proper to proceed through the Gatway with the lights in one, but keep more to windward; and as the South end of Hasborough Sand bears E.S.E. ½ E. from the great light at Hasborough, you may, as soon as this light bears W.N.W., proceed with it in that direction. Should the wind blow so hard from the eastward as to render your weathering of the lightvessel improbable, and the keeping clear of the shore until daylight in the morning unlikely, the best way in such a case is to anchor off Hasborough, with the light bearing about W. by S., in 10 or 12 fathoms. You will then be above 3 miles from the shore, or nearly halfway between it and Hasborough Sand. You will ride much better here, under shelter from Hasborough Sand, than you would off Winterton, being less exposed to the sea, which sets through the Gatway.

WINTERTON TO FOULNESS.—In sailing to the northward from Wintertonness, the soundings are regular all the way to Foulness. The course from Wintertonness to Foulness is N.N.W., distance 19 miles; between in the fairway are 10, 11, and 12 fathoms. In turning to windward, you may stand toward the shore to what depth you please, and off to 14, 15, or 16 fathoms; but you must not stand farther off than to 16 or 17 fathoms, or you will be close to Hasborough Sand. The channel between this sand and the shore is 7½ miles wide.

FOULNESS, near Cromer, is distinguished by a lighthouse of stone, represented in the margin. As already shown, it exhibits a brilliant light, which revolves, and shows a face every minute. The light of this important structure may be seen, in clear weather, more than 7 leagues off.

In approaching Foulness, go no nearer to it than in 7 or 8 fathoms, as the ground is foul and rocky for a mile from the Ness, its outer extremity being marked by a *red buoy,* at a mile E.N.E. of the lighthouse. This foul ground extends thence 5 miles to the S.E., and terminates off Trimmingham.

Cromer Lighthouse.

TIDES BETWEEN ORFORDNESS AND FOULNESS.

At *Orfordness* the flood tide continues to run, on the change and full days of the moon, until 11ʰ, and the water rises 11 feet. The S.W. or flood stream makes about twenty-four minutes before low water on shore, and the N.E. or ebb stream about twenty-four minutes before high water. In *Alborough Bay* it is high water at 10ʰ 40′; spring tides rise 10, and neaps 6½ feet. Here the flood sets to the S.S.W., and the stream continues to run one hour and a half after the time of high water on shore.

Between Lowestoff and Orfordness the tide along shore sets parallel to the coast, but gales of wind from the N.W. so influence it, as to raise the flood from 2 to 3 feet above its ordinary level, and retard the return of the ebb: gales from the S.E. have a contrary effect. Ordinary springs rise from 7 to 8½ feet; neaps from 4 to 4¾ feet.

In *Lowestoff Roads* it flows at 9ʰ 10′; springs rise 7½, and neaps about 5 feet. The flood in the passage sets strongly to the S.W. upon the Newcome; and the ebb, contrariwise, upon the Holm, and through the Stanford Channel. It sets also nearly in the same direction, or a point more southerly, through St. Nicholas Gat, and over the Corton.

At Lowestoff-ness it is high water at 8ʰ 55′, but the flood stream runs to the southward for two hours after. The rise and fall on springs is 8½ feet; neaps, 6 feet.

At *Yarmouth* it is high water at 9ʰ 15′; springs rise 6 to 8 feet, and neaps 4 to 6 feet, but without the sands the flood runs until 10ʰ 40′. In the Cockle Gat the flood sets strongly over the Scroby, and the ebb over the Cockle and through Hemesby Gat.

The tide sets fairly into and out of *Hasborough Gatway;* the flood, S.S.E. southerly, and ends at 10ʰ 30′; the ebb runs in a contrary direction. The tides in the strongest springs run above 3¼ knots in an hour, and one tide will carry a ship about 4 leagues; a moderate spring not more than 3 leagues, and neap tides less than 2 leagues. Without Hasborough Sand the tides do not run so strong, and the flood sets more to the southward. On Hasborough Sand the water rises, at spring tides, about 10 feet.

Off Hasborough it is high water at 7ʰ 40′. Spring tides rise 11 feet, and neaps 7 feet. Here the flood stream runs to the southward until 10ʰ 15′.

Off Cromer it is high water at 7ʰ; but the flood stream runs to the southward until 10ʰ 15′. Spring tides rise 14 feet, and neaps 8¼ feet.

Near Winterton Ridge it is high water at 7ʰ 50′; but the flood stream runs to the southward until 10ʰ. Spring tides rise 10 feet; neaps, 6 feet.

Near Hammond's Knoll it is high water at 7ʰ 40′; but the flood stream runs to the southward until 10ʰ 30′. Spring tides rise 9¼ feet; neaps, 5½ feet.

On Smith's Knoll it is high water at 7ʰ 30′. Spring tides rise 9 feet, and neaps, 5 feet. At its northern extremity the flood stream sets E.S.E.; at its strength S. by E. and South, 1¾ miles; last quarter, S.W. Ebb stream contrariwise, 2¼ miles. At the middle first quarter flood stream sets S.S.E.; in its strength, S. by W. and S.W.; the last quarter veering to W.N.W.: the ebb, vice versâ. Flood stream continues to run to the southward two hours and a half or three hours after it is high water on the ground.

SECTION X.

CROMER TO LYNN AND BOSTON DEEPS.

THE navigation of the sea between Foulness and Flamborough Head is obstructed by the numerous shoal banks and overfalls shown in the Chart, which render it particularly dangerous to cruising ships. The coasts moreover are generally low, with the exception, however, of the cliff of Hunstanton, and of some other part of the coast of Norfolk, and also of Flamborough Head. Near Hunstanton the coast is a cliff of chalk and friable stone, nearly 80 feet in height; and Flamborough Head is a magnificent cliff of white limestone, ornamented with a handsome lighthouse, &c.

DESCRIPTION OF THE SHOALS.

Between Smith's Knoll and Hasborough Sand, which have been already described, and nearly mid-channel, there is a shoal of 3 fathoms, the South end of which lies with Hasborough lights W. ¼ N. 19 miles; and Cromer light, N.W. by W. ¼ W. 26 miles. It thence extends N.W. ¾ N. 3 miles, and has near to its N.W. extremity 6 fathoms of water.

LEMAN and OWER.—The Leman and Ower are two dangerous banks, which have been growing up for many years, and have now in some parts only 5 and 6 feet over them at low water. They lie nearly in a parallel direction, and the inner or western one, which is the *Leman*, is about 7½ leagues from the nearest coast, or that of Hasborough.

The LEMAN extends in an irregular form, about 15 miles, from N.N.W. ½ W. to S.S.E. ½ E. From its South end, in 4½ fathoms, Hasborough High light bears W. ¾ S. 25 miles; and Cromer lighthouse, W. by N. 30 miles. From its North end, Hasborough High light bears S.W. ½ W. 23½ miles; and Cromer lighthouse, W.S.W. ¾ W. at the same distance, or 23½ miles.

There are two remarkable elbows formed in this bank, and both convexing to the S.W.; the southern one is distinguished by its greater convexity, and the soundings of approach to it from the westward, when in a less depth than 5 fathoms, are very irregular; the northern elbow is the shoalest part of the Leman, and here a depth of 5 feet only, for a superficial extent of about a square quarter of a mile, exists. Between these elbows the prevailing depths are from 11 to 13 feet, and from each of them to the corresponding extremes of the bank the depth gradually increases to 4 fathoms, and thence to 6 and 7 fathoms. It is a very remarkable feature of this bank, that throughout its whole extent the shoalest water is on its extreme eastern edge.

When the stream of tide is running (ebb particularly), if the Leman does not show itself by breakers, occasioned by a running sea, it will be sure to do so by a "*smooth and rippling;*" and so remarkable is this effect, that the direction of the convexities are readily distinguished from each other, and serve as a most excellent departure.

It is high water on the Leman, on full and change of the moon, at 6ʰ, at which time the flood stream runs in its full strength. As a summary with respect to the tide, it may be observed that the flood stream springs up S.S.E. ¼ E., and terminates S.S.W. ¼ W.; that the ebb stream springs N.N.W. ¼ W., and terminates E.N.E.; that it is high and low water when the respective streams are running at their full strength, and that it is slack water by the stream between the third and fourth hours of flood and ebb.

The OWER is by far more dangerous and irregular than the Leman. This bank has likewise two remarkable elbows, which lie in one parallel of latitude; but unlike those of the Leman, the eastern of these two convexes to the N.E., the western to the S.W. By this difference, and their relative bearings, they may readily be distinguished from those of the Leman and from each other; that is, when breakers, or the strength of the stream, cause the back and these elbows to show themselves.

The southern extremity of the Ower bears from that of the Leman N. by E. ¾ E. 4½ miles; the northern extremity from that of the Leman, N.E. ½ E. 4 miles; and the shoal patch of the Ower from that of the Leman (the nearest parts of the banks), N.E. by E. ½ E. 3 miles.

From the North end of the Ower Hasborough High lighthouse bears S.W. ¼ W. 9½ leagues; the Cromer lighthouse, W.S.W. 9¼ leagues.

From the 1st of January, 1840, a LIGHTVESSEL has been moored in 16 fathoms, 2 miles to the westward of the shoal part of the Ower, in lat. 53° 8' 47", lon. 2° 2' 7" E. This vessel has two lanterns on separate masts, the foremost *revolving*, at 38 feet above the water; the aftermost fixed, at 27 feet. A ball by day at each masthead.

From the vessel the shoalest part of the Ower bears N. by W. ¼ W. about 2 miles, and that of the Leman W. by N. about 4 miles. The Trinity House notice states *that the light is to be considered as a warning light only, to indicate the position of the shoals, and should not be approached in any direction, either by night or by day.*

It is high water on the Ower, at full and change of moon, at 6ʰ 30'. A singular peculiarity in the tide about the Ower was observed; there was no sensible *rise* in the tide until three hours after low water, and when the ebb stream was nearly done, a sudden rise of 5 or 6 feet took place, so that nearly the whole rise of tide occurs in the last three hours of it.

To the EASTWARD of the Ower there are three similar parallel ridges, of which late examinations have clearly defined the character. With the exception of the first, they are not of a formidable character.

The WELL BANK, which is separated from the Ower by a channel 4 miles broad, with a depth of 10 to 16 fathoms, is about 12 miles in length, and has the same general directions as the Leman and Ower, the least depth on it being 3 fathoms, increasing from 5 to 8 at each end.

The BROKEN BANK, also parallel to the foregoing, is separated from the Well Bank by a channel of 14 to 20 fathoms, and 3 miles in breadth. The shoalest patch of 5 fathoms least water is not more than 3½ miles in length, and is narrow: the bank, within the 10 fathoms line, extends above 12 miles.

The SWARTE BANK, the outermost of these narrow strips of shoal water, is 14 miles from the Ower. It is more than 20 miles in length, and has a depth varying from 6 to 10 fathoms; the depths on either side being from 12 to 15 fathoms.

These peculiar shoal ridges follow the general trend of the adjacent coast, and in some degree also of the main tidal streams; they may owe their existence and peculiar formation to the combined efforts of tidal and other currents. Their forms, position, and relative bearings, are best understood by referring to the Chart.

SHERRINGHAM SHOAL.—At the distance of 5½ miles from the coast westward of Cromer, and nearly parallel thereto, the *Sherringham Shoal* extends N.W. ½ W. 5 miles. The depths on the eastern part, to the distance of a mile, are from 4 to 2 fathoms; those on its western part; to the distance of 2 miles, are rather more; but on the central part the depths vary from 20 to 14 feet, and in some spots to 10½ feet of water. In 1827 a *black* buoy was laid on its eastern part, in 4 fathoms, which lies with Cromer lighthouse, nearly South, 7⅓ miles; Blakeney church, W. ¾ S. 9½ miles; and the village of Lower Sherringham, S.W. by S.

DUDGEON.—At a distance of 8 leagues N. by W. from Foulness is a lightvessel, which rides a little to the westward of a shoal called the *Dudgeon*. This vessel exhibits one brilliant light.

The Dudgeon Shoal is divided into two parts, having 5 fathoms between them, and this swash is indicated by the lightvessel lying on its western or inner side. The shoalest spot has only 10 feet on it, and has a *black buoy* on it, lying 1¼ miles E.S.E. from the light. The N.W. portion of the bank, called the *North Ridges*, is, at its name indicates, a series of shoals, with from 3 to 4 fathoms on them, the N.W. end being about 4 miles N.W from the lightvessel.

RACE'S BANK.—To the West and S.W. of the Dudgeon is a shoal called *Race's Bank*, first discovered in 1801. It now occupies a space of 3 leagues in length, from N.N.W. to S.S.E.; in consequence of which, in March, 1826, a buoy was placed near each end. Of these, that on the southern end is *white*, and that on the northern end *red*.

OUTER DOWSING, &c.—The South end of the Outer Dowsing lies about 22 miles N. by E. ½ E. from Foulness: and the southern part of the shoal extends 3 miles N.N.E. and S.S.W. It is more than half a mile broad, and has one spot of 4½ fathoms, the rest from 5 to 6 and 7 fathoms. At 9½ miles from its South end is a shoal of 12 feet, and 5 miles farther is a second patch with the same depth. The shoalest portion of the Outer Dowsing, within the depth of 5 fathoms, is about 13 miles in length in a N. by W. direction, the entire shoal being 23 miles long.

The **SILVER PIT**, or *Little Silver Pit*, is a remarkable hollow which extends, as shown by the Chart, for 22 miles in a N.E. by E. direction, and from 1 to 1½ miles in breadth. The sides are very abrupt, falling suddenly from 8 and 15 fathoms to 30 and 50 fathoms. Its general direction is a continuation of Lynn Deeps.

INNER DOWSING.—Thirty-five miles N.N.W. ½ W. from Foulness, 13½ miles N.W. by W. from the Dudgeon, 20 miles S. by E. ½ E. from the Spurn Point, and 9 miles E. by S. from Trusthorpe, lies the North end of the Inner Dowsing, on which a *black buoy*, with a *staff and ball*, was placed in 1826, in a depth of 3¾ fathoms. The sand extends 5 miles S. by W. ½ W. from the buoy, and in the middle part is nearly half a mile broad. The least water on this sand is 4 feet at low water; although close to it, on the West side, are 10 fathoms; near the East side are 8 fathoms; and near the South end 4 fathoms. The South end lies 9 miles E. by S. from Ingoldmell church; between are 10, 9, 8, 7, 6, 4, and 3 fathoms, at low water.

The **DOCKING SAND,** which formerly appeared under the figure of a number of detached overfalls, now forms a regular bank, the southern side of which trends 6 miles in a N.W. by W. and S.E. by E. direction, with Addlethorpe church bearing nearly N.W. ¾ W.

The shallowest and nearest part of the Docking Sand, a portion of which is nearly dry at low water, bears from the buoy from N.E. by E. to E.S.E. ½ E., 1 mile; and this is the extreme breadth of the channel, the navigation of which it is the object of this buoy to facilitate. The depth on the bar, which connects the Burnham Flats with the Docking Sand, is 5 fathoms.

Addlethorpe and *Ingoldmell* or the *Sister Churches* in one, and bearing N.W. ¼ W., do not, as formerly represented, lead to the northward of the shoalest part of the Docking, for that line of direction does really cut off a considerable portion of the northern end of Burnham Flats, and leads over at a mile to the southward of the buoy, where, at the shoaler part, there are only 9 feet of water.

The North end of the Docking is distinguished by a *black and white chequered buoy*, in 4 fathoms of water, with Hunstanton lighthouse bearing S.W.; and the red buoy on the North end of Race's Shoal E. by N., 2½ miles distant. The shoal hereabout is very steep-to, having close to its N.W. side a depth of 10 fathoms, at about 2 cables' lengths from the buoy.

The BURNHAM FLATS are extensive grounds, which constitute the base of numerous shoals to the northward of the coast, between Wells and Hunstanton, and forming the East side of the great entrance to Lynn Deeps. The great Flat is of a triangular form, and spits which extend from it eastward are called the *Blakeney* and *Stukey Overfalls*.

At a mile to the S.W. from the S.W. end of the Docking Sand is a *red beacon buoy*, to mark the northern extremity of the Burnham Flats. This buoy lies in 4 fathoms, with Addlethorpe church, about twice its apparent breadth to the northward of Ingoldmell church, N.W. ¼ W., distant 11½ miles; Lynn Well lightvessel, W.S.W. ¼ W., 10½ miles; Hunstanton lighthouse, appearing on the extreme pitch of the cliff, S.W. ¼ W., 12½ miles.

At about 2 miles W. ½ N. from Burnham Flats buoy there is now a *black buoy*, marked *Burnham Ridge*, lying in 5 fathoms, with Ingoldmell church a sail's breadth open to the northward of Addlethorpe church, and bearing N.W.

On the western side of the Burnham Flats are the shoals named the *Woolpack*, the *Middle Bank*, and *Sunk*. On the South is the dangerous shoal called the *Bridgirdle*; beyond which, westward, extending 1½ leagues, is a tract of deeper water, called *Brancaster Roads*; and beyond this is a smaller tract of a similar description, called *The Bays*, which serves as an inshore passage for small vessels to Lynn Deeps, between the Sunk and Middle Bank, on one side, and the land on the other, called the *Gore Point*.

The WOOLPACK, lying on the western side of the Flats, has its southern edge at 6 miles from Hunstanton lighthouse, with that object bearing S.W. by W. to S.W., and a great part of it is dry at low water. The MIDDLE BANK lies between the Woolpack and Sunk, and some part of it dries 5 feet above water at low springs. The SUNK, more to the S.W., dries to the same height. Off the S.W. end of the latter is a *red buoy*, which lies with Hunstanton lighthouse bearing S.E. ¾ S., 3 miles distant, and is the first buoy on the eastern side of LYNN DEEPS.

The COAST of Norfolk is of moderate height and well wooded. The steeple of Blakeney church will be visible as you draw up with the Burnham Flats buoy on a clear day, on the extreme left; then the long level line of the dark woods of Holkham, with the square tower of Holkham church. Farther to the West, the Thornham wood and Docking steeple and Brancaster wood and steeple are conspicuous, with Hunstanton lighthouse appearing like a sail off the extreme point to the right, which, as you draw up, the remarkable cliff of white and red chalk on which it stands gradually rises into view.

Hunstanton lighthouse shows a bright light, but over the Roaring Middle Sand it is *red;* that is, when bearing E.S.E. and S.E. by E.

Between Foulness and Blakeney several parts of the coast are foul and rocky; as near Cromer, Sherringham, and Weybourn. From Cromer lighthouse the coast to Lower Sherringham rounds N.W. and N.W. by W. 4 miles, and it continues in the latter direction, 2½ miles farther, to the mill and church of Weybourn. At 2 miles westward of Weybourn is Salthouse; and at 2½ miles westward from Salthouse, the church and mill of Blakeney, which stand at nearly 3 miles S.S.E. from the entrance of Blakeney Harbour. *Off Salthouse*, at the distance of half a league from shore, is a bank of 2½ and 3 fathoms, called the *Pollard*, which is a mile in length, from E.S.E. to W.N.W.

BLAKENEY OVERFALLS.—The spit of sand called *Blakeney Overfalls*, stretching to the eastward (S.E. by E.) from the Burnham Flats, and nearly parallel with the coast between Blakeney and Burnham, is about 3 miles from the low water mark of the shore. Its eastern extremity lies with *Kelling and Salthouse churches* in one, bearing S. ¼ E. From this extremity the depths, to 3 miles westward, vary from 4 fathoms to 10 feet: but beyond this, to the West, is the KNOCK, which has on it, in one spot, only 8 feet of water.

The STUKEY or STIFFKEY OVERFALLS, extend in the direction of the coast near Wells, like a middle ground between Blakeney Overfalls and the shore : the channel way between them and the former is a mile wide, and its depths are 9, 8, 7, and 6 fathoms; while the Stukey Overfalls, on the South side of the channel, have only from 3 fathoms to 13 feet of water. A basin off Wells, called *Stukey* or *Stiffkey Road*, on the South of them, 3 miles long, has from 4 to 5 fathoms.

CLEY and BLAKENEY HARBOUR.—This harbour, and that of Wells, are the only safe retreat for vessels taken in a gale blowing upon the adjacent coast. Blakeney has a bar harbour, and the tide flows, on the full and change, at 6ʰ; but, without it, the stream runs to the southward and eastward three hours longer, which must be particularly attended to when going in.

If a ship be caught by a hard gale of wind at North or N.E., she may run boldly in, with sufficient tide, having the church at S. ¼ W. (Morston church, just open to the westward of the black boathouse); and when within 2 miles of the shore, bringing Morston church to S.W. ¼ W. will run her to the first buoy. A W.N.W. wind is the worst to come in with. But the bar often shifts, and though buoyed is dangerous to be attempted by a stranger, and therefore needs no particular directions here.

In making the harbour with a westerly wind, keep westerly, as the flood tide sets strongly to the eastward to within the second and third buoy. The harbour is safe for ships of 400 tons, in a gale of wind dead on the coast; and when boats cannot get off, a flag is hoisted on the church, at 9 feet water, as a signal that ships may run for the harbour.

The *Signal pole* is erected on the point: one ball denotes 8 feet water; two balls, 10 feet; and three balls, 12 feet. The same signals, with a flag over them, denote the depth over the *West Low*, which is not buoyed. In case of emergency, attend to the waving of flags by pilots on the point.

WESTWARD OF BLAKENEY, between it and Wells, is a shelf of sand about a mile broad, stretching off from shore, and towards which vessels ought not to approach nearer than in 4 fathoms.

WELLS HARBOUR.—The entrance of this harbour lies 5½ miles N.W. by W. from that of Blakeney. A red buoy, as a fairway buoy, marks the entrance; and within this, seven black buoys, on the edge of the western bank, denote the channel way into the harbour; and on the opposite side are four or five white buoys, for the same purpose.

Two large and conspicuous beacons, the West Scalp and Cape, which in a line bear S. by W., lead in a fair berth to the outer buoy, which is to be left on the starboard hand; and having run E.S.E. to the third black buoy, haul round W.S.W. to the 4th, 5th, and 6th buoys; on the fourth black buoy you will have two other beacons in a line, on which lanterns are kept lighted in the night; then keep away S.W. and South to the Scalp Beacon. The Low Cape and Eastern Beacon lead up to the Scalp, then South and S.E. up the river, with the Pool and Dolphin Beacons just open to the northward, round the lifeboat house, black (steep-to), and then steer about S.W. Having advanced to the last black buoy, you will be directed upward by two smaller (the Pool and Dolphin) beacons, which in a line bear S. ¼ E., until two others come on, bearing nearly S.E. The latter lead up into the harbour, toward a sunk beacon, which is to be left on the starboard side, and to the N.E. of which there is anchorage for light ships in soft mud.

The tide flows on the bar at 6ʰ 20′, on the full and change; but, as at Blakeney, runs to the eastward three hours after. The harbour is nearly dry at low water; but spring tides rise generally from 16 to 18 feet.

It is particularly to be observed that, in entering the harbour, sufficient allowance must be made for the tide, as the flood sets very strongly to the eastward.

In WELLS ROAD, or HOLKHAM BAY, vessels may anchor in 3 fathoms at low water, about 1½ miles from shore, with Wells church S. by E., Holkham church S.W. ¾ S., and the North part of the Scald Heads, a range of sandhills on the shore, W.N.W. Also, in 4 and 5 fathoms, good ground, at a mile more to the N.E., with Wells church S. ¾ W., and Holkham church S.W.

Here you will be in sight of the beautiful estate of the Earl of Leicester, including *Holkham Park*, between Wells and Burnham, with its column, &c.

Before hauling to the southward for the anchorage in Holkham Bay, after passing the Fairway buoy, bring a conspicuous detached clump of trees, named Dyke Row, just open to the westward of Wells Tower mill; then steer in till the Fairway buoy bears E.S.E., Holkham church, S.W. ½ S.

The BRIDEGIRDLE, or BRIDGIRDLE, a shoal partly dry at low water, lies to the northward of Burnham, at nearly a mile from the shore. It is in a horseshoe form, extends 1½ miles from S.E. by E. to N.W. by W., and is nearly a mile broad. Between the shoal and shore are from 9 to 3 feet only at low water, spring tides. With Holkham church and obelisk in one, S. ½ W., you will be clear of its eastern end, in 2 and 3 fathoms.

COASTERS, who are acquainted with the navigation of this part, on proceeding for Lynn from the eastward, commonly pass between *Burnham Flats* and the *Bridgirdle*. The course to this passage, from Blakeney and Stukey Overfalls, is N.W. by W. ¼ W., distance, 7 miles; that is, commencing when Blakeney church bears S. by E. ½ E. 5½ miles distant, and Wells church S.W. ¾ W. You may know when you have advanced to the Bridgirdle, by the mark above mentioned, Holkham church and obelisk in one.

When Brancaster mills, between the church and signal staff, bear S.W. by W. ¾ W., you will be off and near the N.W. extremity of the Bridgirdle, and may thence proceed W. by N. 3 miles into Brancaster Roads, until the church and mills, in a line, bear S.S.W. ½ W. At this spot are fine light sand and 13 to 15 feet at low water. Here, should the tide require it, you may anchor. Proceeding hence W.N.W. 2½ miles, you again cross the bank (but in this track there are one or two spots which have only one fathom on them), and reach *The Bays*. Here you have 2½ fathoms, with Hunstanton lighthouse S.W. by W. ¾ W., and Brancaster mills, midway between Titchwell and Brancaster churches, S. by E. ½ E.

From the last mentioned spot the course and distance through *The Bays* are West, 6 miles, which would lead over the bank, and to the southward of the *Sunk buoy*, noticed on page 74. In this course you leave the *Middle Bank* and *Sunk* on the starboard or North side. Thus, with the tide, you may gain Lynn Deeps; but it is a passage not to be recommended to strangers.

Near and upon the edge of the bank, at 2 miles S.S.W. ½ W. from the Sunk buoy, is the *black beacon buoy of the Ferrier*, lying with Hunstanton lighthouse E. by S. 2¾ miles. The depths near the edge of the bank are from 4½ to 6 fathoms. Hereabout you may have a pilot. *The pilot sloop* may be known by its broad vane; and if a red or blue jack be hoisted under the vane, it signifies that you are to make sail toward the vessel.

MIDDLE CHANNEL TO LYNN DEEPS.—*From Brancaster Roads* you may pass into Lynn Deeps through a sledway which exists between the *Middle Bank* and *Woolpack*. Starting from the spot whence Brancaster church and the mills are in one, your course and distance to gain the Deeps will be N.W. ¼ N. 4½ miles. The general depth over the bank is about 9 feet at low ebbs, but there are patches of 6 feet, which can be avoided. At the outlet you will be 5 miles to the E.N.E. from the buoy of the Sunk, and have 6 fathoms of water, but between them is the Burnham Ridge, marked by a black buoy, described on page 74.

DOCKING CHANNEL.—This channel to Boston and Lynn Deeps lies between the Docking Sand and Burnham Flats, and its N.W. extremity is denoted by the red beacon buoy, of which the mark is given on page 74. In order to take this channel, you may run out, over the tail of Blakeney Overfalls, with the churches of Salthouse and Kelling in one, bearing S. ¾ E., until you have advanced to the depth of 9 or 10 fathoms, sand and shells, about 7 miles from shore; whence Wells church bears S.W. by W. ½

W. The course hence will be N.W. ¾ W. 6½ miles, toward Burnham Flats, where you have 5 fathoms, coarse brown sand and shells. From the last spot the direct course to the Bar, between the Docking and Burnham Flats, is N.W. by N., and the distance 8 miles; here the depths are 5 and 6 to 10 fathoms, leaving the buoy on the South or larboard side.

The **N.E. CHANNEL** to Boston and Lynn Deeps is that between the Docking and *Inner Dowsing*. The last mentioned sand has been described in page 73. The chequered buoy on the North end of the Docking is, of course, to be left on the larboard or southern side. From Cromer lighthouse the bearing and distance of this buoy are nearly N.N.W. ¾ W. 28½ miles. You may cross over the western part of Sherringham Shoal in 6 or 7 fathoms, with Cromer lighthouse bearing S.S.E., and the course thence will be N.W. by N. Having passed the Docking buoy (*chequered*), the course into Lynn Deeps, passing the beacon buoy of Burnham Flats, will be S.W. and S.W. by W. (recollecting Burnham Ridge, of 3 fathoms, lying between the beacon buoy and the lightvessel, 1¼ miles from the former), until you come in sight of the lightvessel stationed in Lynn Well, between the Middle Bank on one side, and Long Sand on the other.

LYNN DEEPS IN GENERAL.—The estuary bearing this name is bounded on the East, as already stated, by the Docking Sand, Burnham Flats, and other shoals; on the West by the sand forming BOSTON DEEPS, called the *Dog's Head*, the *Long Sand*, the *Roger*, the *Gat Sands*, &c.; on the South by the banks forming the channels to the ports of Lynn, Wisbech, &c., which channels are narrow and intricate. Many of the banks are dry long before low water; as, for instance, the *Dog's Head*, the South part of which is elevated 6 feet above the surface at low spring ebbs; the eastern side of the *Long Sand*, 8 feet, although at a short distance without there are 9 fathoms of water; the N.E. part of the *Gat Sand*, 8 feet; and part of the southern shoals appear at times from 8 to 14 feet above water.

The LIGHTVESSEL in Lynn Well lies at a mile E.S.E. from the Hook of the Long Sand, and exhibits two lights, from separate lanterns of equal height. From the beacon buoy on the North end of Burnham Flats the vessel bears W.S.W. ¼ W. 10¼ miles. From the lightvessel Boston steeple bears W.N.W. ¾ W.; Snettisham church, S. ¼ W.; and Hunstanton lighthouse, S. ¾ E. Those coming into the Well from the Lincolnshire coast should bring the lightvessel to bear S.W. by W., which will carry them nearly a mile to the eastward of Lynn Knock; and after rounding the vessel to the southward, allowing for tide, they may steer W.S.W. ¼ W. 5 or 6 miles, and anchor for the night with the vessel E.N.E. ¼ E. in 9 or 10 fathoms, at low water. The flood sets W. by N., spring tides 4 or 5 miles an hour.

The best course into Lynn Deeps in the night, from the coast of Lincolnshire, is to bring Hunstanton light to bear S.S.W., which will carry you clear to the eastward of the Lynn Knock.

The *Lynn Knock* has in one spot only 4 feet water, and on it is a black beacon buoy, bearing N.E. ¼ N. 3¾ miles from the Lynn Well lightvessel, and 1¾ miles outside of the Dog's Head Sand, between which there is a depth of from 3 to 6 fathoms. Snettisham spire on with the West end of Hunstanton Cliff, bearing S. ¾ W., leads between the Dog's Head and Lynn Knock, but close to the former shoal. Snettisham spire and Hunstanton lighthouse in line S. by W. nearly, clears to the eastward of the Lynn Knock.

LYNN.—Since May, 1812, the old channel of Lynn, having grown up, has been totally disused; and fortunately the western channel, now the only one, has greatly improved, and is throughout regularly and closely buoyed.

The outer banks forming this channel are the *Roaring Middle* on the East, and the *Bell Sand* on the West. The N.E. extremity of the Roaring Middle* is 5¾ miles S.W. by W. from the lightvessel in the Well. In the same direction the shoal has on its N.W. extremity a buoy, painted *black* and *white* in quarters; above which, on the same sand, there are three *beacon* buoys, painted *black*, and numbered in succession on the head, 1, 2, 3.

On the opposite or western side of the channel, opposite the third beacon buoy of the Roaring Middle, is a *black* buoy, called *Wisbech Bar buoy*; and between the third and fourth, on the Bell Sand, is the *Bell buoy*, which is *white*, with a *staff and ball*.

---

* In the direction of the Roaring Middle Sand, the light at Hunstanton lighthouse is coloured *red*, between E.S.E. and S.E. by E.

The next buoy in succession above No. 3 on the Roaring Middle, and on the same side, is the Whiting Sand first buoy, *black*, above which are two other *black* buoys; the upper one lies on the westernmost part of the sand, a little to the eastward of which is the Whiting beacon. Opposite to the lower buoy of the Whiting is a *white* buoy off the N.E. point of the Westmark Knock, called the Little Bell buoy, above which is another small white buoy.

The direction of the channel to the buoys last mentioned, is S.W. ½ W., and its length from the first buoy, 3½ miles. It thence rounds more to the eastward, and serpentines up to Lynn, in a distance of 11½ miles. The succeeding buoys, &c., are as follows :—

Whiting, first buoy, *black*, larboard side. Westmark Knock, second buoy, *white*, starboard. Whiting, second buoy, *black*, larboard. Breast, *white*, starboard. Thief Sand, *black* buoy, larboard. Thief Sand life beacon, but which lies half a mile North and East of the present channel, larboard.

About 1 mile S.W. from the Thief life beacon is another on the Hull Sand, which is also a life beacon, as is that on the Whiting, before mentioned; which last are nearly as large as the first, which is described beneath. These three beacons are each about 1 mile from the other. The Hull Sand beacon to be left on the starboard side.

The direction of the channel here is S.E. and S.E. ½ S. into Bull Hole. A part of the Thief Sand dries, at low spring ebbs, to the height of 9 feet above the surface of the water. The channel hence northward, to the Deeps, increases in depth, and has from 3 to 7 fathoms, good ground of clay and sand.

Lloyd's buoy, *white*, starboard; opposite Lloyd's, black and staff on Boat Knock Side, at the Three Fathoms' Hole, larboard; channel between Black Shore and Lloyd's Sand, two beacons on Lloyd's Middle, starboard; and three *black* buoys, starboard; six beacons on Breast Sand, starboard; Daseley's Sand, two *black* buoys, larboard; then eight or nine *black* buoys, larboard, and seven *white* buoys, starboard, from Lower Breast to Marshes.

Here the channel winds more to the East, and the remaining buoys up to Lynn are uniformly black on the East or larboard, and white on the West or starboard side. To the distance of 4 miles below Lynn there is in general only 1 foot of water at low spring tides.

Lynn is connected by the East Anglian and Eastern Counties Railways with Yarmouth, London, &c.

WISBECH.—The entrance of WISBECH CHANNEL, from Wisbech Bar buoy, above mentioned, extends W. by S., 1½ miles; then S.W. by S., 1½ miles; and S. by W., 1¼ miles, to a white beacon buoy, which marks the entrance of the Wisbech Cut, which runs S.W. ¾ S., 2½ miles, and is marked by brush beacons on the western or starboard side, and by basket beacons on the larboard. The Cut then runs S.W. by S. across Sutton Marsh, for 2¼ miles, and thence to the town of Wisbech.

The *Bar buoy*, as already shown, is *black*; and with the two succeeding buoys, which are *red*, is to be left on the starboard side. Two other red buoys mark the West side of the channel, but the way in is to pass near to the three black buoys upon the western edge of the Westmark Knock on the opposite side.

The upper black buoy on Westmark Knock, a *nun buoy*, is called the *bringing up buoy*; a little below which ships ride in from 4 to 10 fathoms, and here they will get Wisbech pilots. The depth on the lower part of the Cut is from 8 to 9 feet; in the upper part, near Sutton bridge, where ships are moored, 10 feet at low water. Above the bringing up buoy the channel alters occasionally, in consequence of which the buoys are altered in their position as required. Wisbech (or Wisbeach) is connected with Lynn, &c., by a branch of the East Anglian Railway.

BOSTON.—THE CHANNEL to Boston Deeps is formed by the sands described on the Chart, which form also the northern side of LYNN WELL. The principal of these sands is that called the *Long Sand;* connected to which, on the N.E., is another, called the *Dog's Head;* and without these, on the eastern side, is that called the Lynn Knock, on which is a *black beacon buoy.* These, with the *Roger* to the westward, form the South side of the channel. On the northern side lie *Skegness Middle,* the *Outer* and *Inner Knock,* and the *Wainfleet Sand.* Besides these there is a middle ground or shoal, called the *Sculrig.*

The *Long Sand* lies in a curve. The greater part of it is steep-to, particularly near the Hook, on the South side, the part nearest to the lightvessel. The *Dog's Head* is narrow, but it is 4 miles in length, and its shoaler parts are covered at one-quarter flood; its direction is N.E. and S.W.

The *Outer* and *Inner Knock*, which now constitute but one bank, lie nearly midway between the Dog's Head and the shore of Wainfleet, in a similar direction. The extent is now more than 3 miles. The channel between the two banks is three-quarters of a mile in breadth.

Skegness Middle is a hook or spit of sand, dry at low water, which forks from the shore of Skegness at about half a league from the outer Knock. Several vessels from the northward have been lost by incautiously entering between it and the shore. Near its eastern side, and parallel with it, is a hole of 2½ and 3 fathoms.

BOSTON BAR forms a crescent, rounding northward, which connects the Dog's Head with the Outer Knock. From the chequered buoy on the North end of the Docking the bar bears W. by S. 12 miles; and from the red beacon buoy, on the North end of Burnham Flats, it bears W.N.W. ⅓ W. 7¾ miles. On the middle of the bar the present depth is 12 feet at low spring ebbs, but near it, both without and within, are 5 fathoms.

The WAINFLEET SAND and FRISKNEY FLAT are those extensive grounds which border the shore between Wainfleet and the River Witham or Boston River. The whole is dry at low water, and on its edge are *seven black buoys*.

The North end of Boston Bar, or of the *Outer Knock*, is distinguished by a very large *black beacon buoy*, on the S.E. or outside of which are 12 feet at low water, and this is consequently the best depth for crossing the bar. At half a mile S. by E. from the beacon buoy is a *red* buoy on the bar, or *Dog's Head*, which lies in 7 feet, to be left in passing on the larboard side.

At half a mile from the red buoy is a *black buoy*, in 4½ fathoms, near to which you pass, leaving it on the starboard side. The course in, to this buoy, is S.W. ¼ S., and the fairway course thence, between the Dog's Head and Knock, is S.W. by W. 3½ miles; the general depths 5 and 6 fathoms; thus leaving, on the larboard side, a *red* buoy near the Dog's Head, a *black* one near the middle of the Knock on the starboard side, and a *chequered black and white* one on the bar of Wainfleet Harbour, on the same side.

From the buoy last mentioned the edge of Wainfleet Sand trends nearly W.S.W. and W. by S., and is denoted by six *black* buoys, which mark the passage on the starboard side, while two *red* buoys on the middle ground, called the *Sculrig*, denote its larboard side. The general depths in the channel to the last black buoy, which is called the *High Horn buoy*, are 5½, 6, 5½, and 5 fathoms. The bottom is of sand and clay.

In the inlet called *Clay Hole*, at 2½ miles W.S.W. ¼ W. beyond High Horn buoy, is good anchorage at 2½ fathoms; two *red* buoys on the larboard side lead to this anchorage. Here a pilot for Boston may be taken.

The *Macaroni Channel* has latterly become the best channel for the port of Boston. It lies between the bank called the *Hook Hill*, on the West, and the *Trap*, with others, on the East. A white buoy on the Trap marks the entrance. There are four black buoys on the Hook hill, all to be left on the western or starboard side, and three red buoys on the opposite side. The depth here is 9 feet at low ebbs.

Boston South Channel is along the South side of the Trap. It has 4 or 5 fathoms of water, but is obstructed at each end by the general flat, on the West part of which only from 5 to 2 feet may be found.

As the BAR RIDGE of BOSTON DEEPS, above described, stretches across between the Dog's Head and Boston Knock, vessels bound in must wait for the tide, according to their draught. Here it is to be remarked that the bar is a shifting one, and the direct course over it may soon vary several points from that which has been described. To this due attention should be paid. The buoys may be shifted, but the rule is still to be observed; that is, always to leave the two black buoys on the starboard, and the two red ones on the larboard side; next, the two black buoys on the Knocks starboard, &c.

WAINFLEET ROAD and HARBOUR.—Those advancing from the northward toward Gibraltar Point, or Wainfleet harbour, must be very cautious, in coming along shore, not to approach so near as to get in between Skegness Middle and the Main. This may be avoided by not coming nearer than in 3½ fathoms.

When abreast the middle part of Skegness Middle, the northernmost Skegness house, which is readily known, bears W.N.W.; and with the southernmost Skegness house bearing W.N.W. you will be clear of the southernmost part of the sand, and may then run along shore at pleasure, in regular soundings, as far to the southward as Sykes' house, which is the southernmost house on that shore, and a very good mark for ships to bring up by, only observing to bring it to bear N.W., and let go your anchor in 3 or 3¼ fathoms at low water spring ebbs. The bottom is here good holding ground; the anchor will never draw home if kept clear, and a ship can always ride, let the wind be as it may.

If bound into Wainfleet Harbour, get under way at half flood, if spring tide, if not drawing more than 8 or 9 feet; or at the last quarter flood, if neap tide. In hauling round the point, you must pass as near to the buoy which lies on it as you can, lest the flood, which sets very strongly to the westward, should drive you on the Wainfleet Sand. When abreast the point, or even before you have advanced to it, you will see two beacons standing on the shore by the end of the sandhills; bring these beacons into a line, and keep them so until you are well shut in within the point, or abreast the upper beacon; then let go your anchor: after this get your small anchor and towline on the shore, and haul close up to the steep.

The tide flows at the point at 6ʰ on the full and change, and rises 16 to 18 and 20 feet.

Should night come on before you can gain a sight of the Skegness houses, when approaching from the northward, you may, by keeping the vessel in 4, 4½, and 5 fathoms, be sure of passing in between the Inner Knock and Main. Having advanced to the entrance you will have 5¼, 6, and 7 fathoms, and shoaling again to 5, 4½, 3½, and 3 fathoms; if in the middle of the channel the lead will stick very much, and thus you will always know when to bring up.

In the night or thick foggy weather ships in Lynn Well that cannot ride with southerly, S.S.W., and S.W. winds, may proceed to this place, and ride with great safety.

IF BOUND OUTWARD, to the southward, from LYNN, WISBECH, or BOSTON, when the water is low, it is recommended to every master of a vessel drawing above 9 or 10 feet of water to pass between the Docking Sand and Inner Dowsing, keeping over toward the latter; because without this precaution, when there is much swell on, and the tide low, in running out between the Docking and Dowsing your ship may strike on the Overfalls, as, if the weather be hazy, you cannot see the churches of Ingoldmell and Addlethorp to guide you clear of them. When running out, keep these churches well open to the northward; that is to say, the upper or northernmost church well open to the northward of the lower one, and you will thus pass out in the best of the water, and may then pursue your course according to circumstances.

BOSTON DEEPS TO THE HUMBER.—Between Boston Knock and the entrance of the Humber are several overfalls and flats, described hereafter. The direct course and distance from Boston Knock to that place, within the Inner Dowsing, are N.N.E. 9¼ leagues; but the safest course, to avoid the overfalls, &c., will be N.E. by N. 5¼ leagues, and thence N. by W. 4 leagues to the mouth of the river, making proper allowance for the tide, which sets as hereafter described.

When Grimsby church appears in a line with Clea church, bearing nearly N.W., you will be on the edge of the Sandhaile, and may, if going into the river, steer N.W. by N., in order to pass between the red buoy on the sand called the Bull, and the Spurn Point.

FROM THE HUMBER (SOUTHWARD) TO BOSTON AND LYNN DEEPS, ETC.

In proceeding toward LYNN WELL, from the Humber, care must be taken to avoid the *Sandhaile*, which is flat. When on the outer edge of the sand, in 5 fathoms of water, you will have Dimlington Cliffs, or high land, open to the eastward of Kilnsey church, which will lead you along it, in about 5 fathoms of water.

From the black beacon buoy on the North end of the Inner Dowsing to the lighthouses on Spurn Point is N. by W. ¾ W. 22 miles, and to the Spurn lightvessel is N. by W. 19 miles. These bearings pass inside and outside the *Protector Overfalls*, a number of detached shoals, having in many places, 9, 12, and 14 feet water, and extending from 5 to 8½ miles from the Inner Dowsing buoy, being 8 miles E.S.E. from Saltfleet.

Between these and Saltfleet are the *Saltfleet Overfalls*, having from 13 to 20 feet water on them, lying 4 miles off shore, between Saltfleet and Theddlethorpe.

Three miles to the southward of Saltfleet, and 1 mile from the shore at high water, or half a mile at low water, lies *Theddlethorpe Middle*. It has only 3 feet on it at low water. Without it, at the distance of about 1 mile, is an overfall, with only 3 fathoms, called *Theddle Overfalls*.

Two and a half miles nearly E. by S. from Trusthorpe church lies *Trusthorpe Overfall*, which has 20 feet at low spring ebb.

From 1 or 2 miles to the southward of Trusthorpe lie the *Clay Huts:* they are elevations of clay, with only 6 to 8 feet over them, lying nearly half a mile from the shore.

About 9½ miles E. by S. from Trusthorpe lies the northernmost end of the *Inner Dowsing*, upon which lies the black buoy, with staff and vane, mentioned in page 73. This shoal extends 6 miles N.N.E. and S.S.W., and the least water on it is 7 feet at low water.

WHEN BOUND TO BOSTON DEEPS, from the Humber, keep along shore in 5 or 6 fathoms, according as you have the wind and tide, until Addlethorpe church apparently comes within half a cable's length of Winthorpe church; you will then see Boston Knock buoys, and should keep nearest to the black ones, if the tide be low, as there is the deepest water on the Knock side. You leave the two red buoys on the Dog's Head on the larboard side, and all the black ones on the starboard. You may bring up anywhere in Boston Deeps, but the best roadstead is above the Sculrig.

WHEN BOUND TO LYNN OR WISBECH, keep along shore as above directed, until you are past Lynn Knock; and when you deepen your water to 9 or 10 fathoms, you may haul up to the S.W. or S.W. by S., according to wind and tide, until you have passed the lightvessel and the Hook of the Long Sand, and got Hunstanton light to bear S.E. by S.* You may then haul more to the W.S.W., until you get Hunstanton light to bear S.E. by E. ½ E. On that bearing you may run to the westward, until you get into 7 or 8 fathoms; and if in the night, bring up; but if in the day, you will come in sight of the buoys already described, and may proceed as the soundings direct. See the description, pages 77, 78.

IN WORKING UP LYNN WELL, from Lynn Knock, on the East side, next to the Middle and Sunk, you will have sticky ground, until you are up to the red beacon buoy on the West end of the Sunk; but all the way along the West side of the Well the bottom is of sand. When you have Hunstanton light from S. ¼ W. to S. by E. ¼ E., you should stand no farther from the eastern side than where you deepen into 20 fathoms of water; as you will have 18 fathoms near the Hook of the Long Sand, and may be on shore before you can haul in the lead. It is therefore best, particularly in the night, to stand over to the westward only until you get into the deep or middle channel; as to the eastward, you may stand into 14 or 16 fathoms with safety.

When you have gotten the light of Hunstanton to bear S.E., you may stand to the westward or eastward into 8 or 9 fathoms, and have nearly 3 miles across from S.E. to N.W.

Those who intend to take Lynn Well *during the night* should run with Hunstanton light S.S.W. until Lynn Well light bears S.W. by W.; then steer for the latter, and you will clear Lynn Knock at the full distance of three-quarters of a mile.

Pilots for Lynn, *Wisbech*, and *Boston* may respectively be found in Lynn West Channel, Wisbech Eye, and Clay Hole.

In sailing up, you must always allow, very particularly, for the strength and direction of the wind, &c., as well as for the tide, whether ebb or flood; as off Boston Knock buoys, Lynn Knock, and the Hook of the Long Sand, the spring tides of flood and ebb often run 5 miles an hour, and neaps, 2¼ miles. The perpendicular rise, with the former, is 4 fathoms; and with the latter, 14 feet.

TIDES.—Off Boston buoys the tides of flood and ebb run about W.S.W. and E.N.E. Off Lynn Knock, about W. by S. and E. by N. Off the Hook of the Long Sand, from W. by S. to West on the flood; the contrary on the ebb.

When the Long Sand is first overflowed on the flood, the tide runs very strongly from the eastward directly over it; so that, in light winds, when you cannot clear it, it is best to bring up in time.

* The mark leading clear of Lynn Knock on its eastern side, in about 7 fathoms, is Hunstanton lighthouse, on with Snettisham spire, S. by W. Snettisham spire on the West end of Hunstanton cliff, S. ¼ W., leads to the westward of Lynn Knock, and very close to the Dog's Head, or Boston Bar.

SECTION XI.

FOULNESS TO FLAMBOROUGH HEAD AND SCARBOROUGH, INCLUDING THE HUMBER.

The course from a fairway off Foulness, or from mid-channel between the North end of Hasborough Sand and Foulness to the Humber, westward of the Dudgeon lightvessel, will be first N. by W. ¾ W. about 9 leagues, and thence N.N.W. ½ W. 10 leagues. Or if to the eastward of the Dudgeon Shoal, N. ¼ W. 9 leagues, and thence N.W. ¼ N. nearly 11 leagues. Particular attention must, however, be paid to the set of the tides, especially when near the shoals.

The **RIVER HUMBER** is one of the most important inlets of the eastern coast of England, and is the estuary of the great rivers Trent, Aire, Ouse, and their tributaries, which drain so large an area of the N.E. portion of England; and by their navigation, and also by the system of canals connected with them, the commerce which is thus carried on to and from the North Sea is of great magnitude.

From the Spurn to the mouth of the river Trent the distance is about 35 sea miles, following the usual channel, and its breadth varies from 1 to 3 or 5 miles. The peculiar characteristics of the waters are their muddiness; they are constantly turbid, and the immense quantities of earthy matter brought into it by the rivers forming its head are chiefly confined to the estuary, but little reaching the sea, and the great part constantly adding to the mudbanks which line its otherwise picturesque shores.[*]

THE SPURN LIGHTHOUSES are the chief sea marks for the Humber. The High lighthouse shows a brilliant fixed light at 93 feet above high water, and has been fitted up with a beautiful new light room and lens apparatus. The brick tower (which was first constructed for a coal fire) was erected from the designs of the celebrated Smeaton.

The Low LIGHTHOUSE, a timber structure, formerly stood at 540 feet in a S.E. ½ S. direction from the High light; but the encroachment of the sea upon the Spurn Point having made the preservation of the Low light in its ordinary position both difficult and uncertain; and it having been ascertained, that the exhibition of a light situate to the N.W. of the High lighthouse would be equally effective for the purposes of navigation, the Low light has been exhibited, since August, 1851, from a building which has been set up to the N.W. of the High lighthouse, and that to the S.E. of it discontinued. The line of the two lights remains the same as before this alteration.

The SPURN FLOATING LIGHT is moored in 9 fathoms of water, between 3 and 4 miles without the Spurn Point; Dimlington Cliff, N. ¾ W. 7¼ miles; Kilnsea Beacon, N. by W. 5¼ miles; and the Spurn lighthouses, N.W. ¾ W. 3¼ miles. In this vessel a *revolving* light upon the improved principle is kept constantly exhibited in the night, and a red ball during the day. A gong is kept tolling during foggy weather. The revolving light has been in action from September 7, 1840.

SPURN POINT and STONY BINKS.—Off the Spurn Point, on a flat extending 3 miles to the eastward, are several hard spots, uncovered at low tides, and called the *Binks* or *Banks*. These lie between the shore and the lightvessel, &c., and they were buoyed with three *black nun buoys*, which now lie in a line East and West, by order of the Trinity House at Hull, in 1836, for the purpose of marking the channel between them and the floating light.

These banks and the shoals on each side of the river up to Hull are regularly buoyed with black buoys on the northern or starboard side in entering, and with red buoys on the port hand, or South side; and these buoys are regularly numbered, from 1, the outermost black buoy, to No. 12, on the North side of Hull road; and from No. 1, red buoy, on the Sandhaile, to No. 12, opposite Hull.

The *Outer Binks buoy*, No. 1, *black nun*, lies in 5 fathoms, with the light-tower of the Spurn bearing W. by N. ¼ N. 3½ miles distant, and Easington church, N. by W. ½ W.

---

[*] Those who feel interested in these subjects will find an excellent and detailed account of the Humber in the Transactions of the British Association for the Advancement of Science, for 1853. The meeting in that year was held at Hull.

The *Middle Binks buoy*, No. 2, *black nun*, with a *staff and ball*, lies in 6 fathoms, at 1⅓ miles from the outer buoy, No. 1, with the Spurn High light, N.W. by W. ¼ W.; Kilnsea South Cliff, N. by E.; the high land of Dimlington, North; and the buoy on the Chequer Shoal, S.W. ½ S.

The *Inner Binks buoy*, No. 3, *black nun*, lies in 5½ fathoms, 1⅓ miles from the Middle or beacon buoy, No. 2, with the Spurn High light bearing N.N.W. ½ W. 1¼ miles; and Kilnsea South Cliff, N.N.E. ½ E.

Chequer Shoal.—In the entrance of the river, and within the lightvessel, there is now a *chequered black and white buoy*, on a bank lately grown up, and which is called the *Chequer Shoal*. This buoy lies with the Spurn High light bearing N.N.W. ¾ W., distant about 2½ miles; Kilnsea beacon, N. by E.; and the Spurn lightvessel, E. ¼ N., 2 miles distant. There are from 3 to 5 fathoms of water over the shoal at a low spring ebb.

Bull Sand Floating Light.—By order of the Corporation of Trinity House, Hull, in 1832, a lightvessel was placed near the S.E. end of the *Bull Sand*, which displays one brilliant light. This vessel is moored in 4¼ fathoms, at about 1 mile from the Spurn Point, at a quarter of a mile from the extremity of the Bull Sand, with the Spurn High light bearing E.N.E. By day the vessel displays a blue flag, and a gong is sounded in dark and hazy weather.

Buoy on the Bull Sand.—A *red* can buoy, No. 2, on the eastern edge of the Bull Sand, lies in about 5 fathoms, at a quarter of a mile N.N.W. from the lightvessel; Clee mill, W.N.W. ¼ W.; Grimsby church, W.N.W.; and Patrington church, N. ¼ E. The *Bull Sand* is nearly 1¾ miles long, and has on its shoalest part 11 feet of water.

The southern side of the entrance of the river is bordered by an extensive bank which dries at low water for 1¼ to 1¾ miles off shore. This bank is called the Sandhaile, and the flat extending for 3 miles further, or 4 miles beyond Donna Nook, is called the *Sandhaile Flat.*

The SANDHAILE.—In November, 1839, a *red buoy*, now marked No. 1, the outermost of the buoys on the South side, was placed in 3 fathoms of water, on the edge of the Sandhaile Flat, at 2¼ miles S.W. ¼ W. from the floating light before described, with the Spurn High light bearing N. by W. ¾ W., and the beacon on Donna Nook S.W. ½ W., nearly 4 miles. The southern channel way into the river is therefore about midway between the lightvessel and the buoy.

Donna Nook *and Beacon.*—The Corporation of Trinity House at Hull have erected a beacon upon the low sandy point of the Lincoln shore, called *Donna Nook*, on the South side of the entrance into the Humber, as a distinguishing mark for the guidance of vessels entering the river from the southward. The beacon is 50 feet high, painted *red*, of a conical form, with a cap at the top, and may be seen in clear weather from a distance of 3 or 4 leagues. The outer edge of the Sandhaile, having 3½ fathoms over it, is 4 miles East from the beacon.

Clee Ness *and Beacon.*—Notice was given by the Corporation of the Trinity House, Hull, August 13, 1834, that a new beacon had been erected on Clee Common, for the use of vessels entering the Humber. The beacon is 60 feet high, of an octagonal form, and painted black. A vessel will clear the Inner Binks, &c., by keeping Grimsby church on with this beacon, and bearing N.W. by W. ½ W.

The CHANNEL into the Humber, between the outer black buoy of the Spurn Banks and the outer red buoy on the Sandhaile Flat, is 3 miles in width, and the depth between them varies from 15 to 4 fathoms. At 4 miles within the entrance the channel is 2¾ miles wide between the Spurn Point and the banks on the South side, and the depth between is 12 to 4 fathoms. The entrance is divided by the Chequer Shoal into two channels, the southern of which is the broadest.

In approaching the Humber from the *southward*, with the lights on the Spurn in one, bearing N.W. ½ N., they may be kept thus until the outer lightvessel bears N.E., when you will be nearly 1½ miles to the S.E. of the buoy on the Chequer Shoal. Then bear round to the *West*, and pass to the southward of the shoal in 12 and 15 fathoms water, till the High light bears N.N.E., whence you may steer northward up the Humber and haul into Hawk Road, or continue the western course until the Bull Sand lightvessel bears N.N.W., whence a N.W. ¼ N. course will carry you to the southward of the Bull Sand, and thence northward toward Grimsby Road. Or when, having approached the

Humber with the Spurn lights in one, the Killingholme lights are seen, if these be brought in one and this bearing kept on, it will lead up the river as far as Killingholme.

The river may be entered to the *northward* of the Spurn lightvessel; the direction of the channel being East and West parallel with the Spurn Banks buoys, which course leads between them and the Chequer Shoal, and kept on will lead to the point where the Killingholme lights come in one, whence you may proceed up the river on their line of bearing, as before stated. There is also a channel between the two outer black buoys, Nos. 1 and 2, which may be taken by bringing the beacon buoy No. 2 to bear W.S.W., and then steering for it into the main channel.

The HUMBER LIGHTHOUSES.—On the Lincolnshire coast, at about 12½ miles above the Spurn Point, the Corporation of Trinity House, Hull, have erected three lighthouses; these stand on the bank of the river, at South Killingholme: and at Paull, 3½ miles higher up, on the opposite side, is another, all of which exhibit brilliant fixed lights.

The lights at Killingholme are designated as the High light, the South Low light, and the North Low light; the former is about 50 feet, and the latter about 33 feet high. The light at Paull is about 30 feet.

The High light and the South Low light when in one bear N.W. ¼ N., and lead up the river from between the Sandhaile and the Binks off the Spurn. A *bright light* has been exhibited from the North Low lighthouse, recently erected about 300 yards N. by E. of the High light at Killingholme, and a bright light will also be shown from the High light, to serve as leading marks (being kept in one, and bearing S. by W.) from Killingholme to Paull, and particularly to enable vessels to clear the Hook of the Holme Sand, and the S.E. end of the Skitter Sand.—*January 3, 1852.*

When the two lights at Killingholme are in one, they will bear N.W. ¼ N., and will lead ships and vessels coming from sea in a clear course up the river from the Spurn, as before stated. On approaching them the light at Paull will be seen, when ships must alter their course to the northward, bringing the High light and North Low light in one; at the same time strict attention must be paid to the state of the tide. Vessels bound up to the port of Hull must be guided by the buoys and the lead round Skitter Sand.

In case of need, with Killingholme lights in one, a vessel may take the ground with safety, the bottom being mud.

Great attention must be paid to the setting of the tides, as the ebb runs strong over the Stony Binks, near the Spurn Point, from the southward, and the flood equally so in a contrary direction; therefore more *strict* attention must be given to the bearings than to the course steered, as all depends on the rate the ship is going. Spring tides run at the rate of about 5½ knots; neaps, 3 knots; but the ebbs in the freshes run with more rapidity.

A red buoy with *vane and spindle*, No. 3, on the point of *Clee Ness Sand*, lies 2½ miles E. ¼ N. of Clee Ness beacon, and 3¼ miles N.W. by W. ¼ W. from the Spurn lighthouse. In mid-channel between at the lowest depths are 7 and 8 fathoms.

The MIDDLE GROUNDS consist of several patches of from 17 to 21 feet least water, which extend for a distance of 5½ miles along the middle of the river above Spurn Point. These patches are respectively called the *Lower Middle, Middle,* and *Upper Middle,* and are marked by three buoys which lie in a line, N.W. ¼ N. and S.E. ¼ S., 1½ miles apart. The first of these on the Lower Middle, lies 1½ miles N.W. by W. from the High light-house on the Spurn Point. The Lower Middle Sand has 21 to 24 feet least water, and 3 fathoms between it and the Middle Shoal. In this space is a chequered buoy in 3½ fathoms, abreast of the No. 5 buoy on the North side of Hawk Road. The third buoy is at the S.E. end of the Middle Sand, in 3 fathoms, with the beacon on Clee Ness bearing S.W. by W. ½ W., and the red buoy No. 4 at the S.E. end of Grimsby Road S.W. ½ S., nearly a mile distant. The least water on the Middle is 17 feet, and the same depth is found on the Upper Middle 2 miles N.W. of the upper buoy. These banks are liable to shift.

The *black* buoy on the S.E. end of the *Burcom* lies 2 miles N.W. by W. from that off Clee Ness, 1 mile W. ¼ S. from the North buoy of the Middle, and 5½ miles N.W. ¼ W. from the Spurn Point. Its thwart mark is Grimsby church W.S.W. ¼ W. The sand extends from the buoy about 3½ miles to the N.W., and is a quarter of a mile broad. Between the buoy of this sand and that of Clee Ness are 5, 4, and 3 fathoms at low water; and between the latter and the Spurn Point are 5, 7, 8, and 7 fathoms. Between the Burcom and western shore are 5, 6, and 7 feet at low water, all the way through to Stallingboro' Creek.

In RUNNING INTO THE HUMBER, you must not borrow upon the Sandhaile, unless the wind be in the S.W. quarter; for it is to be observed that the N.E. part of the sand lies off so far from the shore, that it could not be weathered by vessels running along it in 3 or 4 fathoms, with a S.E. wind.

Having passed the Spurn, with a southerly or S.W. wind, and intending to anchor, the best place will be in *Grimsby Road*, which is 5 miles to the N.W. ¼ W. from the Spurn Point. In proceeding to this road you pass the floating light and buoy, the Bull, and the buoy of Clee Ness Sand, on the larboard side; and the buoys of the Middle on the starboard. You run N.W. by W. until Grimsby church tower bears W. by S., and the black buoy on the S.E. end of the *Burcom* Sand E. by N. half a mile.

Through the channel between the N.W. end of the Bull and the edge of Clee Ness Sand the flood tide sets strongly to the northward, and the ebb to the southward.

GREAT GRIMSBY, 16 miles East of New Holland, and 6¼ miles N.W. by W. of Spurn Point, one of the most ancient ports in the kingdom, had decayed in consequence of the rise of Hull, which has hitherto usurped almost all its foreign trade, Grimsby not being backed by a manufacturing population. In 1801 the first attempt was made to improve the natural harbour, and the Old Dock was opened. This was purchased by the Manchester, Sheffield, and Lincolnshire Railway Company, who, in 1845, obtained an Act for forming the new dock, the first stone of which was laid with great ceremony by Prince Albert on April 18, 1849. It was opened in May, 1852. The entrance tidal basin has an area of 15 acres; depth at low water springs, 9 feet; at neaps, 12½ feet; at high water springs, 27⅓ feet; at neaps, 24½ feet. The dock is entered by means of two locks, one of which is of the largest size; has an area of 25 acres, containing pure fresh water, of 25 to 20 feet depth. In constructing these works, 135 acres of land have been reclaimed, and every accommodation for steam and other shipping formed. The machinery of the cranes, lockgates, &c., are worked by hydraulic machinery, for which purpose a brick tower, 230 feet high, is erected between the lockgates as an accumulator of the hydraulic power, and is a very conspicuous object. It is the water terminus of the Manchester, Sheffield, and Lincolnshire Railway, which connects it directly with all the important seats of manufacture and trade, and to London, 173 miles distant, by Boston and Peterborough, or via Lincoln, 208 miles.

In Grimsby Road large ships lie, at a little without the stream of the Burcom buoy, in 5 or 6 fathoms. Small ships lie within the buoy, and a very little below it, in 9, 10, 11, or 12 feet at low water. It is requisite to observe the time of the tide at which you anchor, and whether spring or neap; as with spring tides the water rises here from 20 to 30 feet; and with neap tides, from 12 to 15 feet.

HAWK ROAD.—With N.E. and easterly winds the best roadstead in the Humber is in the *Hawk*, with the Spurn Point bearing S. by E. ¼ E. 1½ miles, in 5 or 6 fathoms at low water.

To RUN UP TO SUNK ROAD from the HAWK, steer N.W. ¼ N., with the Spurn lights in one, edging off and on Trinity Sand, on the N.E., in 6 and 7 fathoms; and you thus leave the Middle Sand, with its buoys, on the port hand, and the buoy No. 5 on the starboard side. The Spurn lights bearing S.E. ⅓ S. lead clear of the latter, and you may proceed with them thus until within a mile of Sunk Island. Here you may anchor on good ground in 6 or 7 fathoms, with Humberston church, on with Clee mill, bearing S. by W.

The coast of Sunk Island is bordered with sand to the distance of one-quarter to half a mile. Of this sand the spit or outer part is distinguished by a *black nun buoy* with *staff and ball* marked No. 6, lying with Patrington steeple N.E. by E. ¼ E., and Grimsby church tower, S. by W. At a short distance without this buoy the depth is 8 and 10 fathoms. At a mile below, or S.E. of No. 6 buoy, a spit runs off from the bank with 16 and 17 feet water on it, and 30 feet close inside it. Between this spit and the Upper Middle is *Sunk Road*.

At half a league above the Sunk Spit buoy there is good anchorage with Sunk chapel and Patrington steeple in a line, bearing E. ¾ N.

On leaving *Grimsby Road* for proceeding toward Hull, you leave the Burcom, or No. 5 buoy, on the port side, and thence follow the direction of that sand, with Killingholme church N.W. ¼ W. open to the eastward or right of the malt kiln, or large red house at the mouth of Stallingboro' Creek. This will lead within sight of the black beacon buoy of the Sunk Spit, No. 6, just described. In the mid-channel you will have 8, 9, and 10 fathoms.

If the wind be scant in the S.W. quarter, you may keep toward the Burcom in 5 or 6 fathoms; but higher up do not approach it nearer than in 7 fathoms. On approaching Stallingboro' Flat, which is steep, and extends to three-quarters of a mile from shore, steer for the black buoy on the *Holme Ridge*, next described, until Imingham church bears W. ½ N.

The FOUL HOLME SAND is a long spit, extending from the Cliffy Point near Paull town, or Paghill, 4½ miles South, where it terminates in the middle of the river. Its outer edge is marked by four black nun buoys, numbered from 7 to 10.

The lower black buoy, No. 7, lies in 3½ fathoms, with Ottringham church, a little more than a ship's length to the eastward of Stone Creek house, bearing N.E. by E.; Stallingboro' house, S.W. ½ S.; Paull church, N. ⅛ W.; and the Holme buoy, No. 8, a ship's length open to the northward of Roxham wood, bearing N.W. ¼ W.

In the bight to the eastward of the Holme Sand the water is shoal, there being only 3 and 2 fathoms, and is closed at its northern end. On the western side the tide sets strongly upon the sand; and here, in mid-channel, are 9 and 10 fathoms of water.

Should you be caught in the bight with a flood tide, you must immediately come to an anchor; and in a scant wind, if you cannot drive to the southward, let go an anchor promptly.

From abreast of the Holme buoy, No. 7, with Killingholme lighthouses in a line, you steer nearly N.W. until you have brought Grimsby church in a line with Stallingboro' kiln, and then with the mark on, or rather with Grimsby church a handspike's length open to the eastward of the kiln, upon a N. by W. course you reach *Whitebooth Road*, and may there anchor in 6 fathoms, with Grimsby church a sail's breadth open to the eastward of Stallingboro' kiln; Killingholme church, W.S.W.; Paull town, open to the northward of Paull Cliff, N. by E. ¼ E.; and Patrington church, E.S.E. Whitebooth Road lies abreast of the black buoy No. 10 on the West side of the Foul Holme Sand, but is separated from the main channel of the river by the *Halton Middle*, a narrow spit of 18 feet water.

From off Whitebooth Roads you proceed in the direction of N. by E. ¼ E. toward the lighthouse of Paull, which has been described in page 84. Or, in advancing upward, you steer for a short distance N. by E. toward Paull town, with the town at the North end of the cliff; and then, with Marfleet church on with the jetty, N. ¾ E. 3 miles. Paull Road lies close inshore, but the hardness of the ground and the rapidity of the tide make it the worst road in the Humber. Those acquainted with the navigation of this place should have a pilot from Grimsby Road, for the tides are so extremely rapid that were a ship to touch upon the sand, on either side of the channel, she would probably upset immediately upon taking the ground.

The *Skitter Sand* is that extensive bank, on the South and West sides of the river, which extends upward to beyond the western part of Hull, and southward to Whitebooth Road. In the bend of the river it extends nearly two-thirds over, and halfway over opposite to Hull. A great portion of the upper part is dry at low water, and on the lower part the depths are 2 and 3 fathoms: within it is a swash along shore. The Killingholme lights, described on page 84, will assist in avoiding it.

The edge of the Skitter is distinguished by six *red buoys*, numbered from 7 to 12, which lie at about three-quarters of a mile from each other; the first bearing W.S.W. from Paull lighthouse. Between the buoys numbered 9 and 10 is the *Hebbles lightvessel*, moored in 4 fathoms. This vessel lies with St. James's church its own breadth open of the West pier of the Humber Dock basin, and Sutton church midway between the two easternmost mills on the Holderness Road. It exhibits a red flag by day, and a fixed *red light* by night, at about 20 feet above the water. First lighted by the Trinity House at Hull, 28th of December, 1839.

On the opposite side, upon the shoals called the *Hebbles*, are two *black nun buoys*, Nos. 11 and 12. The lowermost of these is 1½ miles below the entrance of the Victoria Docks at Hull, and the last is about three-quarters of a mile from the same spot.

The proper place for anchoring in Hull Road is abreast of the citadel, or a little below it, in 5 or 6 fathoms of water. If you intend going into the harbour or the docks, you should, if the tide be then flowing, run on shore at the Dolphin Point, and get ready for warping in.

"**KINGSTON UPON HULL** takes the lead as the first port in the kingdom for inland trade, while its position with respect to the North Sea has made it the chief outlet for our manufactures to northern Europe, and raised it to the rank of the third port in the country for foreign traffic. The approaches by the deep but intricate channel of the Humber are admirably buoyed and lighted by the Hull Trinity Board. Floating docks to the extent of 23 acres already exist, and 15 acres in addition will soon be opened. The activity at the docks is not surpassed by that of any other port in the kingdom, seventy-five vessels having lately passed through the Humber Dock lock in a single tide. The tonnage of the vessels that have paid dock dues during the year 1845 amounted to 700,000 tons, and the whole income of the port, derived from tolls on shipping and goods borne by shipping, exceeds £75,000 a year.

" Commercially important as Hull appears to have been in the infancy of British commerce, it was not till 1775 that the Old Hull Dock was set on foot; the traffic still increasing, the Humber Dock was begun in 1807 ; more than twenty years elapsed, during which the trade almost doubled, when the Junction Dock was opened, in 1829, but not until Goole had been declared a bonding port. Great as was the increase of accommodation which was thus afforded, the trade more than kept pace with it, and ships are now much in want of dock room."

NEW HOLLAND is on the South bank of the Humber, opposite Hull, and is a terminus of the Manchester, Sheffield, and Lincolnshire Railway ; the ferry across the river is performed in fine steamboats in fifteen minutes. Formerly New Holland had but two houses. It has now a village of workpeople for the railway, and has also extensive timber ponds, deal yards, and a tidal basin. A pier, 1,500 feet in length, facilitates the passenger traffic.

SPURN POINT TO SCARBOROUGH.

IN SAILING OUT FROM THE HUMBER, for the northward, it will be requisite to attend to the directions given for entering the river.—The lights and buoys will be a sufficient direction for clearing the Binks, &c. Having then passed the Spurn Point and the Stone Bank, until you open Dimlington high land without the land to the southward of it, you may steer N. ¼ E. for Flamborough Head, the distance to which will be 11 leagues. If you come out of the Humber in the night time, so soon as you have passed the western part of the Stone Bank, &c., steer along to the eastward toward the light-vessel, until you find the water deepens to 10 and 12 fathoms. Hence you may proceed on a direct course for Flamborough Head. The ground without the Head is foul to the distance of 2 cables' lengths.*

BRIDLINGTON BAY, &c.—Within Flamborough Head, on the South side, is the bay called BRIDLINGTON or BURLINGTON BAY, in which lies the sand named the *Smithick*. The N.E. end of this shoal lies 1 mile S.W. by S. from Flamborough Head, and it extends thence to the W.S.W., increasing in breadth. On the N.E. part of the shoal there are only 1¾ fathoms at low water, but to the southward there are 3 and 4 fathoms. It is more fully described hereafter.

In the month of June, 1837, the Corporation of Trinity House, London, caused a *red buoy* to be placed off the N.E. end of the Smithick, in 4½ fathoms, with the following marks :—The southernmost windmill on Bridlington Cliff, in line with a white house, bearing W.N.W. ½ W.; Bridlington church, N.W. by W. ¾ W.; Flamborough windmill, N.W. by N. ; and Flamborough light-tower, N.N.E. ½ E.

A buoy, *chequered black and white*, has been placed in 4 fathoms, to mark the southern extremity of the Smithick shoal, with Flamborough new mill, touching the North edge of a hedge row, N. by E. ½ E. ; Flamborough lighthouse, N.E. ¾ N. ; Bridlington church, N.N.W. ¼ W.; Carnaby temple, N.W.—*March* 23, 1852.

There is very good riding within the Smithick, in any part of Burlington Bay; but the best place is with the Quay street open, bearing W.N.W., in 5 fathoms at low water.

BRIDLINGTON HARBOUR.—Before the close of the year 1840, the pier which

---

* The ancient landmark of the coast of Holderness, Owthorne church old spire, better known by the name of the Sister churches, was undermined by the sea, and fell to the ground with a tremendous crash, February, 1816.

forms the eastern side of the harbour, and extending about 600 feet in nearly a North and South direction, was almost completed ; and the trustees of the harbour have, since December, 1828, caused to be exhibited upon a staff, 100 feet within the South end of it, a red flag by day, and a light (but not a good one) by night. The flag or the lights are hoisted when there is a depth of 7 feet, with flood tide, at the entrance between the piers, and remain until the tide has ebbed to the same depth. The North pier, now completed, extends somewhat beyond the line of the new South pier, which will protect, in a degree, the entrance from the current, and allow vessels more easily to shoot in after rounding the pier, or working in with a North or head wind.

The new South pier runs from the western side of the harbour in an E. by N. direction for 1,300 feet, and will be raised 10 feet above high water level, leaving an entrance facing the South, which, though narrow, is as wide as can be allowed, in consequence of the roll of the sea setting into the harbour with South or N.E. winds. The swell inside the piers often caused great damage to the shipping moored in the former harbour, breaking the moorings, and deteriorated very considerably from its value as a port of refuge. The harbour is also protected, in some degree, by the Smithick Sand, which forms a kind of breakwater for the anchorage in the bay.

FLAMBOROUGH HEAD.—*The lighthouse on Flamborough Head*, 72 feet high, is erected at about 400 yards within its extreme point, close to a bluff on the South side of Silex Bay, which is the only place near the Head where a boat can land, and people ascend the cliff.

The light, 214 feet above the water, is *revolving*, and is triangular, with *three faces*, of seven reflectors each ; and in order to distinguish it from the revolving lights of *Tinmouth* and *Cromer*, which show a face every minute, it will exhibit a face every *two minutes*. One of the faces is coloured *red*, and the lights from that face being diminished will not, in hazy weather or at great distances, be visible so far or so strongly as the other two faces ; and when, in such cases, only two faces are seen, the interval of time between them will be *two* minutes and *four* minutes *alternately*, which will sufficiently distinguish this light from any other.

The Smithick Shoal may be said to extend within the limits represented by the dotted lines in the chart, encompassing every shoal which has less depth of water upon it than 3½ fathoms ; the shoalest parts of the Smithick are chalky or rocky ground, and are (as represented by the pilots and fishermen) dispersed over various parts of this shoal, but have not less than 10 feet upon any of them ; the North part of the shoal is narrow, but the South part is a broad extended flat ; for in taking a range of soundings toward Sewerby (bearing North), there was found a breadth of nearly 1 league, with not more than 4½ fathoms, nor less than 3½ fathoms, reduced to low water ; but the pilots' leading mark for running out of *Bridlington Bay*, clear of the South end, is 1 mile to the southward of this, having Bridlington church on with some houses near the West end of the South pier of Bridlington quay. The Smithick Sand has been proposed as the foundation of a breakwater, which would afford great shelter to the anchorage in Bridlington Bay.

In going into Bridlington Bay, between Flamborough Head and the Smithick, keep Sewerby hall just open without the bluff, near South Sea (a break or cove lying to the southward of Flamborough), until the light bears N.N.E., when you will be abreast of the North end of the shoal, and may steer toward Bridlington quay, for anchorage in the bay.

Gray's farm to the westward of the old tower upon the Head, or the lighthouse bearing North, will lead clear to the eastward of the Smithick.

From Flamborough Head to Scarborough the course is N.N.W. ¼ W., distance 5 leagues.

SCARBOROUGH.—The Bay of Scarborough, taken between the outermost point of Castle Headland and Nipe Point, is 2½ miles wide, and three-quarters of a mile deep, when taken in a straight line drawn between the above points ; if taken, however, between Flamborough Head, which is the extreme southern headland, and Castle Point, it is 18 miles wide and 1 mile deep.

The shores, generally speaking, are bold and abrupt on all sides, to high water mark being composed of cliffs of sandstone, varying from 50 to 150 feet in height ; from thence to low water the shores are flat, and ebb dry to a considerable distance. Towards the

N.W. end of the bay there are extensive sands, which at low water are bare for about 900 feet beyond high water mark, and three-quarters of a mile wide to the southward; they form a fine situation for bathing, and for the waves to expend themselves upon. From thence to the southward the shores are flat and rocky, and diminish in width until they unite with the bold perpendicular cliffs of Flamborough Head. The bay, for the most part, is clear of rocks beyond the line of low water, except the rock called Ramsdale Scar, situate about 1,000 feet to the South of the present harbour, and projecting out 1,100 feet at right angles to the shore, from low water of good spring tides, when there is little more than 12 feet upon its outer end: this rock forms a kind of natural break-water against the southerly seas to the harbour, although not sufficiently high to be effectual. The rest of the bay is clear of rocks, and affords good anchorage with the wind off shore from S. by E. to N.N.W., or about half of the compass.

The soundings taken in a line between the two landheads above mentioned vary from 5 to 6 fathoms at low water, decreasing from thence gradually towards the shore.

The bay is exposed direct to the East, and may be termed open from North to S.E., or twelve points of the compass. Gales from either of the above quarters send a very heavy sea into the bay, but the most severe come from N.E. to East, during which period the bay becomes dangerous and unsafe for anchorage, and frequent cases of shipwreck have occurred.

The main current of the flood tide sets from the northward, and when at the strongest runs at the rate of $2\frac{3}{4}$ miles per hour, and *vice versâ*. The main current of the ebb sets from the southward at $2\frac{1}{4}$ miles per hour, continuing nearly 6 hours each way.

The counter or eddy current commences close inshore, near the Spa, one hour before high water, setting to the northward, and continues in the same direction until two hours after low water, or nine hours, and during the remaining three hours it is barely perceptible; but when it blows strongly from South to S.E., it sets almost continually to the northward, passing close to the pierheads of the harbour, at the rate of $1\frac{1}{4}$ miles per hour; at this time the sands at the North end of the bay are chiefly in motion, and occasion inconvenience.

Spring tides rise 18 feet 6 inches; neaps, 7 to 9 feet; and equinoctial tides, 20 feet. These, however, are much influenced by particular winds, such as a strong northerly wind, succeeded suddenly by a southerly one, which occasions the highest tides, and with them a heavy sea.

The HARBOUR OF SCARBOROUGH may be properly described as consisting of three piers, namely, two eastern piers and one western pier, forming together an outer and an inner harbour, having the entrance of both pointing to the South.

The inner harbour contains about 9 acres, having at high water of spring tides $14\frac{1}{2}$ feet at the entrance, and 9 feet at neaps, and extraordinary tides from 16 to 17 feet. It cannot, therefore, under any circumstances, be termed accessible for vessels drawing more than 8 feet water until two-thirds flood at a medium tide, one-half flood at an equinoctial, and high water at a low neap tide.

The best times for going into this place are at half flood, or after the first quarter ebb, at which times the ships may be run aground; the bottom is clean sand. Should the wind, by being northerly at the time of your going in, render it necessary for you to stand over towards the Spa house, you must be careful to avoid the rocks, which lie at a considerable distance from the shore, to the southward of the Spa: stand in by the lead into not less than 15 feet, low water springs. The swell which comes round the pierhead, when northerly or easterly winds blow strongly, causes the ships in the harbour to range very much when they are afloat. At such times it is necessary to moor them with their cables to the dolphins or piers. Hempen cables are better than chains. Scarborough has a good outlet for ships bound to the southward, but for those bound to the northward warping buoys and every facility is afforded. You may anchor in Scarborough Wick, in 5 or 6 fathoms of water; but it is not safe to continue there long, of which there have been some fatal instances.

A *tide light*, upon a white tower on Vincent's Pierhead, is to be left on the starboard side when entering the harbour. It exhibits a red light, which may be seen at 10 miles off. Its height is 41 feet above the level of high water, and the light is kept on while there are 12 feet of water in the harbour. By day a *blue* flag is hoisted for the same period.

In coming from the northward with a fair wind and rounding the castle rock, keep the castle tower well in sight, and keep the Spa house open of the head of the pier, which will lead clear of the Gamble Stones, and then haul close round the pierhead into the harbour.

If you miss the pierhead with your warps, be ready to drop your anchor, or a ship risks driving to leeward into broken water.

SECTION XII.

TIDES.

IN the previous pages we have given a description of the tides which occur on each section of the coast. An account of the tidal phenomena and their causes will be found in our "Atlantic Memoir," 10th edition, 1853, pp. 165—170, to which work the reader is referred for an account of the tidal investigations and their results. In the "Directory for the English Channel," 11th edition, 1856, pp. 250—263, is a full description of the Channel tides, derived from these recent important observations, and in the "Directory for the North Sea," 1854, is given the conclusions of Professor Whewell, &c., on the subject of the tides of that sea.

The present brief extracts will be confined to the general subject of the tides of the S.W. portion of the North Sea, and are chiefly derived from the before mentioned works.

The Rev. Professor Whewell, in drawing his conclusions from the data which he in 1835 collected from the mass of observation, says: "It appears that we may best combine all the facts into a consistent scheme by dividing the German Ocean into two *rotatory* systems of tide waves; one occupying the space from Norfolk and Holland to Norway; and the other the space between the Netherlands and England. In the former space the cotidal lines, or those on which the tides are at the same time, revolve around a point where there is *no tide ;* for it is clear that at a point where all the cotidal lines meet, it is high water equally at all hours, that is, the tide vanishes. In the latter space we may suppose similarly a tideless centre, about which the cotidal lines revolve. . . . .

"This hypothesis of two rotatory systems in the German Ocean is recommended by its giving the most consistent and probable relations among the cotidal lines and the intervening spaces, as may be seen by reference to the chart; and I have therefore adopted it as the best approximation I can now obtain to the form of these lines.

"This theory is, indeed, nothing more than a representation of the facts of the case, yet it gives a view of the mechanism of the tides of the German Ocean different from any which has hitherto been suggested. The southern rotatory system, which exists between the coast of Suffolk and the Netherlands, may be conceived to be kept in constant circulation by impulses received from the adjacent tides; that is, an impulse at 6ʰ on the coast of Norfolk, and an impulse at 12ʰ on the coast of Belgium. Thus it resembles a watch or clock, which is kept in continual motion by a sustaining force applied at intervals. The larger rotatory system, lying between the East of Scotland and England and the coast of Germany and Denmark, does not, like the other, return into itself. We may conceive that, in this case, the tide wave is turned aside by the opposing coast of Norfolk and Germany, so as to be thrown back upon itself in the neighbourhood of the coasts of Jutland, after an interval of six hours. This would explain the vanishing of the tide in that region; for a tide at 12ʰ combined with a tide at 6ʰ are equivalent to no tide at all; the high water of the one filling up the low water of the other."[*]

The learned Professor's theory was verified by Capt. John Washington, R.N., on July 12, 1852, when in lat. 52° 15¾', lon. 3° 15' E., or about 56 miles from Lowestoft, on the extreme eastern edge of the space marked by Dr. Whewell as the point where the cotidal lines would meet; and by careful measuring through two whole ebbs and one flood the water was only found to fall 16 inches on two trials, and 18 inches on the third. Thus theory and fact were found to coincide.

Since that time, a most extended series of tidal observations was made under the direction of the British Admiralty, and these have been most ably discussed in the "Philo-

---

[*] "Phil. Trans., 1836," pp. 298, 299. Researches on the Tides: Sixth Series, by the Rev. Wm. Whewell, M.A., F.R.S.

sophical Transactions for 1851," by Rear Admiral F. W. Beechey, F.R.S. The following is a brief summary of the results arrived at:—

In the North Sea the general features of the streams correspond exactly with those of the English Channel, but the *direction* of the stream is reversed. As soon as the intermediate tide is passed, on coming from the westward, a ship enters the True Stream, which extends from the North Foreland to a line joining the Leman and Ower light and the Texel. To the northward between the Ower and the Texel a mixed tide occurs, similar to that which is experienced off the Start, occasioned by the Channel stream encountering that of the Offing Stream; and beyond these limits the time of slack water varies with the advance of the tidal hour, as at the entrance of the English Channel; and with this peculiarity also, that in a very short distance there occurs a difference of three hours in the time of slack water.

The True Stream will always carry a vessel *towards* the North Foreland while the water is *rising at Dover*, and *from it* while it is *falling at that place*. This stream sets nearly N.E. and S.W., except near the points where it partakes of the form of the land; and at the entrances of the Thames, where it is diverted from its course by the river. The annexed table will show these deviations, and the exact course of the stream in the North Sea, which, for the convenience of reference, is divided into compartments.

TABLE showing the MAGNETIC DIRECTION of the TIDAL STREAMS in the NORTH SEA, from the SPURN POINT to the NORTH FORELAND, at every hour of the tide at DOVER.

COMPARTMENT I.

Entrance to the Thames.

Hours.		Mouse Lightship.		Sunk Lightship.		Kentish Knock Lightship.		5 Miles North of North Foreland.		Galloper Lightvessel.	
		Course.	Rate.	Course.	Rate.	Course.	Rate.	Course.	Rate.	Course.	Rate.
After High Water, Dover.	1	W. by N.	Greatest rate, springs, 2·50 knots.	Slack.	Greatest rate, springs, 3·00 knots.	N.E.	Greatest rate, springs, 2·80 knots.	N.N.W. ¼ W.	1·80	N.E. ½ E.	Greatest rate, springs, 2·5 knots.
	2	Slack.		N.E. by E. ¾ E.		N.E.		N. ½ E.	1·20	N.E. by E.	
	3	E. ¾ S.		E.N.E. ¾ E.		N.E.		N.E. ½ E.	1·18	N.E. by E.	
	4	E. ½ S.		E.N.E. ½ E.		N.E.		E.S.E. ¾ E.	1·46	N.E. ¾ E.	
	5	E. ¼ S.		E.N.E. ¼ E.		N.E.		E.S.E. ¾ E.	1·60	N.E. by E.	
	6	E. ¼ S.		E.N.E. ¼ E.		N.E.		S.E. ½ E.	1·45	N.E. by E.	
Before High Water, Dover.	5	E. ¾ S.		.. .. ..		S.W. ½ S.		S.S.E. ½ E.	1·30	S. ¾ W.	
	4	Slack.		S.W. by W. ¾ W.		S.W. ½ S.		S. ¾ W.	1·30	S.W. ½ S.	
	3	W. ½ S.		S.W. by W. ¾ W.		S.W. ½ S.		S.W. ½ S.	1·60	S.W. by W.	
	2	W. ½ S.		W.S.W. ¾ W.		S.W. ½ S.		S.W. ¼ W.	1·65	S.W. by W. ½ W.	
	1	W. ¼ S.		W. ½ S.		S.W. ¼ S.		W.S.W.	1·40	W.S.W.	

COMPARTMENT II.

Between the mouth of the Thames and the coast of the Netherlands South of 52° N. latitude.

Hours.		West of 2° E.		Between 2° and 3° E.		East of 3° E.		REMARKS.
		Course.	Rate.	Course.	Rate.	Course.	Rate.	
After High Water, Dover.	1	N.E. ½ E.	Greatest rate, springs, { flood 2·50 / ebb 2·50 } knots.	E.N.E. ½ E.	Greatest rate, springs, { flood 2·50 to 3·0 / ebb 2·00 to 3·0 } knots.	N.E. by E. ¾ E.	Greatest rate, springs, 2·50 to 2·90 knots.	
	2	N.E. ½ E.		E.N.E.		N.E. by E.		
	3	N.E.		N.E.		N.E. ½ E.		
	4	N.E. by E. ½ E.		N.E. ½ E.		N.E. ½ E.		
	5	N.E. ½ E.		N.E. ½ E.		N.E. ½ E.		Stream from the Schelde N.W. by W. to 3° E. turning sharply to N.E.
	6	N.E. ½ E.		N.E.		N.N.E. ½ E.		Stream from the Schelde N.W. by W. to 2·30° E. turning sharply to N.N.E. ½ E.
Before High Water, Dover.	5	S.W. ¾ S.		S.W. by W. ¾ W.		W.S.W.		
	4	S.W.		S.W. ½ W.		S.W. ¾ W.		
	3	S.W.		S.W.		S.W. ½ W.		
	2	S.W.		S.W.		S.W. ½ W.		
	1	S.W. ½ S.		S.W.		S.W. ¼ W.		

COMPARTMENT III.

Between the latitude 52° and 53° N. and the English Coast as far as 2° E. longitude.

Hours.		Remarks.
After High Water, Dover. 1, 2, 3, 4, 5, 6	Stream runs northward.	Taking the directions of the land, except close to the banks, for which special instructions are necessary.
Before High Water, Dover. 5, 4, 3, 2, 1	Stream runs southward.	

Hours.	Shipwash Lightvessel. Course.	Rate.	Stanford Lightvessel. Course.	Rate.	St. Nicholas Gat Lightvessel. Course.	Rate.	Cockle Lightvessel. Course.	Rate.	Newarp Lightvessel. Course.	Rate.	Hasborough Lightvessel. Course.	Rate.
After High Water, Dover. 1	E.N.E. ½ E.		N.E. ¾ N.		N. ¾ E.		N.N.E.		N. ½ W.		N. by W. ½ W.	
2	E.N.E. ¼ E.		N.E. ¾ N.		N. ½ E.		N.N.E.		N. ¾ W.		N. by W. ¾ W.	
3	E.N.E. ½ E.		N.E. ¾ N.		N. ¼ E.		N.N.E.		N. ¾ W.		N. by W. ½ W.	
4	E.N.E. ¼ E.		N.E. ¼ N.		N. ¼ W.		N.N.E.		N. ¾ W.		N. by W. ¼ W.	
5	N.E. by E. ¾ E.		N.E. ¼ E.		N. ¾ W.		N.N.E.		N. ¼ W.		N. by W. ½ W.	
6	N.E.		Slack.		N. by W.		S. ¼ W.		N. ¼ E.		S. by E.	
							On the turn.					
Before High Water, Dover. 5	S.W. ¾ W.		S.W. ¾ S.		S. ½ E.		S. ½ W.		S. ½ E.		S. by E. ½ E.	
4	S.W. by W. ½ W.		S.W. ¾ S.		S. ¼ E.		S. ¼ W.		S. ¾ E.		S. by E. ½ E.	
3	S.W. by W. ¾ W.		S.W. ½ S.		S. ¼ W.		S. ¼ W.		S. ¾ E.		S. by E. ½ E.	
2	S.W. by W. ½ W.		S.W. by S.		S. ¾ W.		S. ½ W.		S. ¼ E.		S.S.E.	
1	S.W. by W. ¼ W.		S.S.W. ¾ W.		S. by W. ¼ W.		S. ¼ W.		S. ¼ E.		S. by E.	

COMPARTMENT IV.

Between the latitude 52° and 53° N. and longitude 2° to 3° E.

Hours.	S.W. Quarter.	Rate.	S.E. Quarter.	Rate.	N.E. Quarter.	Rate.	N.W. Quarter.	Rate.	Remarks.
After High Water, Dover. 1	N.E. ¼ N.	Greatest rate, springs, 2·25 knots.	N.E.	Greatest rate, springs, 1·60 knots.	N.E. ¾ N.*	knots. Greatest rate, springs, flood 1·40, ebb 1·40	N. by W.	knots. Greatest rate, springs, flood 2·60, ebb 3·00	* Turning sharply off for the Leman and Ower.
2	N.E. ½ N.		N.E. ½ N.		N.E. ¾ N.		N. ¼ E.		
3	N.E. ¼ N.		N.E. ¼ E.		N.N.E. ¼ E.		N.N.E. ¼ E.		
4	N.E.		N.E. ¼ N.		N.E. ½ E.		N. ½ W.		
5	N.E. ½ N.		N.E. ½ N.		N.E. ½ N.		N. ¾ W.		
6	N.E. ¾ N.		N.E. ¾ N.		N.E. by N.		N.N.E. ¼ E.		
Before High Water, Dover. 5	S.W. ½ S.		S.W. ¾ W.		S. ½ E.		S. ¾ W.		
4	S.W.		S.W. ¾ S.		South.		S. ¾ W.		
3	S.W. ½ S.		S.W. ½ S.		S. by W. ½ W.		S. by W.		
2	S.W.		S.W. ¾ S.		S.S.W. ¼ W.		S.S.W.		
1	S.W. ½ W.		S.W. ½ S.		S.W. ½ S.		S. by W. ¾ W.		

COMPARTMENT V.

Between the latitude 53° and 54° N., and from longitude 1° to 3° E.

Hours.	S.W. Quarter.	Rate.	S.E. Quarter.	Rate.	N.E. Quarter.	N.W. Quarter.	Leman and Ower Lightvessel. Course.	Rate.	Remarks.
After High Water, Dover. 1	N.N.W. ½ W.	Greatest rate, springs, flood 2·25, ebb 2·25 knots.	N. by W. ½ W.	Greatest rate, springs, flood 2·00, ebb 2·00 knots.	N.N.W. ¼ W.	N. ½ W.	N. by W. ¾ W.	Greatest rate, springs, 2·0 knots.	
2	N.W. ½ N.		N. by W. ¼ W.		North.	N. ¾ W.	N. by W. ¾ W.		
3	N.N.W. ½ W.		N. ½ E.		N. by E.	N. by W. ½ W.	N.N.W.		
4	N.N.W. ¼ W.		N. ¾ E.		N.N.E.	N.W. ½ W.	N.N.W.		
5	N.N.W. ¾ W.		N. ¾ E.		E.N.E.	S. by W. ¼ W.	N.N.W.		
6	.. .. ..		N.N.E. ¼ E.		S.E.	S. ¼ E.	Slack.		
Before High Water, Dover. 5	S.S.E. ¾ E.		S.S.E. ¾ E.		S.E. ½ S.	S. ½ E.	S.S.E.		Near the North point of Smith's Knoll the rates are, flood 2·6, ebb 3·0 knots.
4	S.S.E. ¾ E.		S.S.E. ¾ E.		S. ¾ E.	S. by E. ¼ E.	S.S.E.		
3	S.S.E. ½ E.		S. by E.		South.	S.S.E. ½ E.	S.S.E.		
2	S. by E.		S. ¼ E.		S. ¾ W.	E.S.E. ½ E.	S.S.E.		
1	S.S.E. ½ E.		S. by W.		South.	N.E. by N.	S.S.E.		

COMPARTMENT VI.

Between the latitude 53° and 54° N., and westward of longitude 1° E.

Hours.		Course.	Rate.	Spurn Lightvessel. Course.	Spurn Lightvessel. Rate.	Dudgeon Lightvessel. Course.	Dudgeon Lightvessel. Rate.
After High Water, Dover.	1	N. ¾ E.	Greatest rate, springs, { flood 2·50 / ebb 3·75 } knots.	E.N.E.	Greatest rate, springs, 4·35 knots.	N. by W. ½ W.	Greatest rate, springs, 2·5 knots.
	2	N.N.W. ½ W.		S.W. by S.		N.N.W.	
	3	.. .. ..		S.W. ½ S.		N.W. ¾ N.	
	4	S.W.		S.W.		W. ¾ S.	
	5	S.W. ½ W.		S.W.		S.W. ½ S.	
	6	S.W. ¾ S.		S.W.		S. ¼ E.	
Before High Water, Dover.	5	S. ¾ E.		S.W.		S. by E. ¾ E.	
	4	S. by E. ¾ E.		N.E. by E.		S.S.E.	
	3	S.S.W. ½ W.		N.E. by E. ½ E.		S.E.	
	2	N. by E. ½ E.		E.N.E.		E. ½ S.	
	1	N.N.E. ½ E.		E.N.E.		N.E. ½ N.	

COMPARTMENT VII.

On the parallel of 54° N.

Hours.		1° E. Course.	1° E. Rate.	2° E. Course.	2° E. Rate.	3° E. Course.	3° E. Rate.
After High Water, Dover.	1	N. by W. ½ W.		N.N.W. ½ W.		N.W. ½ W.	
	2	N. by W. ½ W.		N.W. ½ N.		N.W. by W. ½ W.	
	3	N.W. by N.		N.W. ½ W.		N.W. by W. ½ W.	
	4	S. ½ E.		W.N.W. ½ W.		N.W. ¾ N.	
	5	S. ½ E.		W. ½ S.		N. by W.	
	6	S.S.E.		S. by E.		E. by N.	
Before High Water, Dover.	5	S.E. ½ S.		S.E. ¾ S.		E.S.E. ¾ E.	
	4	S.E. by E.		S.E. ½ E.		E S.E. ½ E.	
	3	E. ½ S.		S.E. ½ E.		E.S.E. ¾ E.	
	2	N.E. ½ N.		S.E. by E. ½ E.		E.S.E.	
	1	N. by E. ½ E.		E.N.E. ½ E.		S. ¼ W.	

The hour of high water at Dover, on full and change days, is 11^h 10′.

It may be necessary to remark, in addition to the information afforded by the foregoing tables, as well as that given by the tidal arrows on the chart which accompanies this work, that the velocity and duration of these ebb and flood streams do not necessarily refer to the *rise* and *fall* of the water at the particular spot. It is frequently the case that at high or low water the stream is running at its greatest strength. Therefore, for the condition of the tide as to the depth of water, reference must be made to the previous portion of this work.

For the direction and rate at which the stream is running, it is only necessary to ascertain the state of the tide at Dover at the moment, and the tables and chart will at once indicate them.

SECTION XIII.

REGULATIONS AND RATES OF PILOTAGE.

The Act 17 and 18 Victoriæ, cap. 104, A.D. 1854, entitled the "*Merchant Shipping Act*," regulates the Mercantile Marine of the United Kingdom.

PART V.—*Pilotage* applies to the United Kingdom only.

§ 378. (Subject to any alteration to be made by the Trinity House.) Every master of a ship crossing from the westward, and bound to any place in the rivers Thames and Medway (unless she has a qualified pilot on board, or is exempted from compulsory pilotage) shall, on the arrival of such ship off Dungeness, and thenceforth until she pass the South buoy of the Brake, or a line to be drawn from Sandown castle to the said buoy, or until a qualified pilot has come on board, display and keep flying the usual signal for a pilot; and if any qualified pilot is within hail, or is approaching and within half a mile, and has the proper distinguishing flags (white and red horizontal) flying in his boat, such a master shall, by heaving-to in proper time, or shortening sail, or by any practical means consistent with the safety of his ship, facilitate such pilot getting on board, and shall give the charge of piloting his ship to such pilot; or if there are two or more of such pilots offering at the same time, to such one of them as may, according to the regulations of the time being in force, be entitled or required to take such charge; and if any such master fails to display or keep flying the usual signals for a pilot in manner hereinbefore required, or to facilitate any such qualified pilot as aforesaid getting on board as hereinbefore required, or to give the charge of piloting his ship to such pilot as hereinbefore mentioned in that behalf, he shall incur a penalty not exceeding double the sum which might have been demanded for the pilotage of his ship: such penalty to be paid to the Trinity House, and to be carried to the account of the Trinity House Pilot Fund.

§ 379. The following ships not carrying passengers shall be exempted from compulsory pilotage in the London district, and in the Trinity outport district; (that is to say :)—

(1.) Ships employed in the coasting trade of the United Kingdom.

(2.) Ships of not more than sixty tons burden.

(3.) Ships trading to Boulogne, or to any place in Europe North of Boulogne.

(4.) Ships from Guernsey, Jersey, Alderney, Sark, or Man, which are wholly laden with stone, the produce of those islands.

(5.) Ships navigating within the limits of the ports to which they belong.

(6.) Ships passing through the limits of any pilotage district on their voyages between two places both situate out of such limits, and not being bound to any place within such limits, nor anchoring therein.

§ 346. *Pilot boats* to be fitted with black sides, and while afloat, to carry a large flag at the masthead, or other conspicuous situation, which is to be half red and half white in horizontal stripes; the latter uppermost, and to have the name of the principal pilot on the stern, and the number on each bow.

(The pilot boats in the service of the pilots licensed by the Corporation of the Trinity House have been distinguished by night, since March 1, 1849, in the following manner: —In the *English Channel*, on the *East Coast of England*, and in the *River Thames*, by a *green light* at the masthead; and in addition thereto by a *flare-up light*, shown at intervals of fifteen minutes. Pilot boats in the service of the said pilots in the several ports of the *Bristol* and *St. George's Channels*, by a white light at the masthead, and a *flare-up light* at intervals of fifteen minutes.)

§ 356. If any boat or ship having a qualified pilot on board leads any ship without any qualified pilot on board, which cannot be boarded, the pilot so leading is entitled to full pilotage.

§ 357. No pilot to be taken, without his consent, to sea or beyond the limits for which he is licensed. If, from unavoidable circumstances, he is so taken, he is entitled to 10s. 6d. per day additional.

§ 362. An unqualified pilot may take charge of a ship, without incurring any penalty, either when no qualified pilot has offered to take charge of her, or when a ship is in distress, or under circumstances of necessity; or for changing the moorings of any ship in port, unless contrary to the regulations of the port.

The following notice was issued by the Trinity House, London, on the 13th November, 1855:—" Whereas the *buoys* and *beacons* placed by the Corporation of Trinity House for the guidance of shipping navigating on various parts of the coast of England, and especially in the channels leading to the port of London, have in repeated instances been negligently or wilfully broken away, or otherwise damaged and rendered unserviceable by vessels running foul of, or making fast to, and riding by the same:—And the *lightvessels* moored off different parts of the coast have also been frequently run on board of, and much damaged, with imminent risk of being broken from their moorings and lost;—And whereas, the safety of shipping, and of the lives and property embarked therein, requires that the said *lightvessels*, *buoys*, and *beacons*, should uninterruptedly preserve their respective stations,—masters, and other persons having charge of vessels, are hereby cautioned against the commission of such offences, and are desired to take notice, that by 'The Merchant Shipping Act,' 1854, sect. 414, it is enacted as follows, viz.:—'*Damage to lights, buoys, and beacons.*' If any person wilfully or negligently commits any of the following offences (that is to say,) 1. Injures any lighthouse or the lights exhibited therein, or any buoy or beacon; (2) removes, alters, or destroys any lightship, buoy or beacon; (3) rides by, makes fast to, or runs foul of, any lightship or buoy; he shall, in addition to the expenses of making good any damage so occasioned, incur a penalty not exceeding *fifty pounds*."

DUTIES payable to the TRINITY HOUSE, LONDON, for LIGHTS, &c., on the SOUTH-EASTERN COAST of ENGLAND, 1857.

	COASTERS.	OVERSEA.	
	Per Vessel.	British and Foreign, privileged.	Foreign, unprivileged.
		Sixteenths of 1d. per ton.	
Beachy Head ....One lighthouse	6d.	...	4	8
Dungeness ....Ditto	...	1	4	8
South Sand Head ....One floating light	...	1	4	8
Goodwin and Gull Stream...Two floating lights	6d.	...	8	16
Forelands ....Three lighthouses	...	2	4	8
Kentish Knock ....One floating light	...	1	4	8
Sunk and Galloper...........Two floating lights & buoys	...	2	8	16
Cork ....One floating light...........	...	1	2	4
Harwich ....Two lighthouses.............	...	1	4	16
N.E. Shipwash ....One floating light	...	1	2	4
Lowestoff ....Three lighthouses, one float-ing light......................	...	2	4	8
St. Nicholas Gat Buoys......		2	2	2
St. Nicholas Gat.............One floating light	...	1	2	4
Cockle Gat ....Ditto	...	1	2	4
Haisbro' and Newarp.........Two lighthouses and one floating light	...	2	4	8
Winterton and Orford ......Three lighthouses	...	3	8	8
Haisbro' Sand, North End...One floating light	...	1	4	8
Leman and Ower ....Ditto	...	...	8	16
Foulness ....One lighthouse	...	1	4	4
Dudgeon.....................One floating light	...	1	4	8
Spurn Shore ....Two lighthouses	...	1	8	16
Spurn Floating ....One floating light	...	1	...	...
Flamborough ....One lighthouse	...	1	4	8

FROM	TO	7 Ft. & under	8 Feet	9 Feet	10 Feet	11 Feet	12 Feet
		£ s. d.	£ s. d.	£ s. d.	£ s. d.	£ s. d.	£ s. d.
The Sea, Orfordness, or Hoseley Bay.	The Nore or Warps	3 13 0	4 2 9	4 12 0	5 1 3	5 5 9	6 5 0
The Sea, Orfordness, or Hoseley Bay	Gravesend, Chatham, Stangate Creek, or Blackstakes	4 12 0	5 7 9	6 3 3	6 18 0	7 11 9	8 5 6

Pilots duly licensed to conduct Vessels inwards above Gravesend, continuing in charge as far as any of the undermentioned places, are to be paid for the whole distance as follows, viz.:—

FROM	TO	7 Ft. & under	8 Feet	9 Feet	10 Feet	11 Feet	12 Feet
The Sea, Orfordness, or Hoseley Bay	Long Reach	4 16 6	5 12 3	6 8 0	7 2 6	7 18 3	8 14 9
	Woolwich or Blackwall	5 5 9	6 1 6	6 17 0	7 11 9	8 10 3	9 4 0
	Moorings, London Docks, City Canal, or St. Katherine's Docks	5 16 0	6 9 9	7 3 6	7 17 3	8 19 6	9 13 3
The Nore or Warps	The Sea, Orfordness, or Hoseley Bay	3 6 0	3 14 0	4 3 0	4 11 0	4 15 0	5 12 0
Gravesend, Chatham, Stangate Creek, or Blackstakes	Do. do. do.	4 3 0	4 17 0	5 11 0	6 4 0	6 16 0	7 9 0

Pilots duly licensed to conduct Vessels outwards beyond Gravesend, continuing in charge as far as any of the undermentioned places, are to be paid for the whole distance as follows, viz.:—

FROM	TO	7 Ft. & under	8 Feet	9 Feet	10 Feet	11 Feet	12 Feet
Long Reach	The Sea, Orfordness, or Hoseley Bay	4 7 0	5 1 0	5 15 0	6 8 0	7 3 0	7 17 0
Woolwich or Blackwall	Do. do. do.	4 15 0	5 9 0	6 4 0	6 16 0	7 13 0	8 6 0
Moorings, London Docks, City Canal, or St. Katherine's Docks	Do. do. do.	5 5 0	5 17 0	6 9 0	7 2 0	8 2 0	8 14 0
The Sea or the Downs, and vice versâ	The Nore or Warps	3 6 0	3 14 0	4 3 0	4 11 0	4 15 0	5 12 0
	Gravesend, Chatham, Stangate Creek, or Blackstakes	4 3 0	4 17 0	5 11 0	6 4 0	6 16 0	7 9 0

Pilots duly licensed to conduct Vessels beyond Gravesend, either inwards or outwards, and continuing in charge to or from any of the undermentioned places, as the case may be, are to be paid as follows, viz.:—

FROM	TO	7 Ft. & under	8 Feet	9 Feet	10 Feet	11 Feet	12 Feet
The Sea or the Downs, and vice versâ	Long Reach	4 7 0	5 1 0	5 15 0	6 8 8	7 3 0	7 17 0
	Woolwich or Blackwall	4 15 0	5 9 0	6 4 0	6 16 0	7 13 0	8 6 0
	Moorings, London Docks, City Canal, or St. Katherine's Docks	5 5 0	5 17 0	6 9 0	7 2 0	8 2 0	8 14 0
The Nore or Warps, and vice versâ	Gravesend, Stangate Creek, or Blackstakes	1 15 0	1 19 0	2 2 0	2 5 0	2 14 0	3 0 0
	Long Reach or Chatham	2 2 0	2 5 0	2 10 0	2 14 0	3 2 0	3 11 0
	Woolwich or Blackwall	2 10 0	2 15 0	3 1 0	3 6 0	3 14 0	4 1 0
	Moorings, London Docks, City Canal, or St. Katherine's Docks	2 18 0	3 4 0	3 10 0	3 14 0	4 7 0	4 15 0
Gravesend Reach, and vice versâ	Long Reach	0 9 0	0 13 0	0 18 0	1 3 0	1 7 0	1 11 0
	Woolwich or Blackwall	1 1 0	1 5 0	1 9 0	1 13 0	2 0 0	2 8 0
	Moorings, London Docks, City Canal, or St. Katherine's Docks	1 5 0	1 11 0	1 16 0	2 2 0	2 10 0	2 18 0
	Sheerness, Stangate Creek, or Blackstakes	2 10 0	2 13 0	2 15 0	2 18 0	3 6 0	3 14 0
	Chatham	2 18 0	3 1 0	3 4 0	3 6 0	3 14 0	4 3 0
Long Reach, and vice versâ	Woolwich or Blackwall	0 17 0	1 0 0	1 2 0	1 5 0	1 13 0	2 2 0
	Moorings, London Docks, City Canal, or St. Katherine's Docks	1 5 0	1 8 0	1 11 0	1 13 0	2 2 0	2 10 0
	Sheerness, Stangate Creek, or Blackstakes	2 18 0	3 1 0	3 3 0	3 6 0	3 14 0	4 3 0
	Chatham	3 6 0	3 10 0	3 12 0	3 14 0	4 3 0	4 11 0
Woolwich or Blackwall, and vice versâ	Moorings, London Docks, City Canal, or St. Katherine's Docks	0 17 0	1 0 0	1 2 0	1 5 0	1 7 0	1 9 0
	Sheerness, Stangate Creek, or Blackstakes	3 6 0	3 10 0	3 12 0	3 14 0	4 3 0	4 11 0
	Chatham	3 14 0	3 18 0	4 1 0	4 3 0	4 11 0	4 19 0

The several rates and prices specified above are subjected to a reduction of one-fourth part, in respect of be propelled by Steam or towed by a Steam Vessel for a part only of the distance for which any such or price as shall be proportionate to the distance so propelled or towed.

OF PILOTAGE

Strand, or acting as such under the authority of the Acts of Parliament 6 Geo. IV. cap. 125, and 16 and 17 within the limits, in the said Table mentioned.

13 Feet.	14 Feet.	15 Feet.	16 Feet.	17 Feet.	18 Feet.	19 Feet.	20 Feet.	21 Feet.	22 Feet	23 Ft. & upwards
£ s. d.	£ s. d.	£ s. d.	£ s. d.	£ s. d.	£ s. d.	£ s. d.	£ s. d.	£ s. d.	£ s. d.	£ s. d
6 13 0	7 7 3	7 16 6	8 14 9	9 8 6	10 17 0	11 10 0	12 17 6	14 5 3	16 11 3	18 8 0
8 19 6	9 13 3	10 0 7	11 0 9	11 14 6	14 1 6	16 13 0	19 6 6	21 5 0	23 3 9	25 2 3
9 8 6	10 0 0	10 16 3	11 10 0	13 3 6	15 9 0	18 11 9	21 5 0	23 0 0	24 16 9	26 13 6
10 2 0	11 0 9	11 14 6	12 8 6	14 3 6	16 5 0	19 11 0	22 1 6	24 16 9	27 12 0	30 7 3
10 11 6	11 10 0	12 8 6	13 2 3	14 14 6	17 0 6	20 10 3	23 4 6	25 18 9	28 13 0	31 7 0
6 0 0	6 13 0	7 1 0	7 17 0	8 10 0	9 16 0	10 7 0	11 12 0	12 17 0	14 18 0	16 11 0
8 2 0	8 14 0	9 6 0	9 19 0	10 11 0	12 13 0	15 0 0	17 18 0	19 3 0	20 17 0	2 12 0
8 10 0	9 0 0	9 15 0	10 7 0	11 17 0	13 18 0	16 14 0	19 3 0	20 14 0	22 7 0	21 0 0
9 2 0	9 19 0	10 11 0	11 4 0	12 15 0	14 13 0	17 12 0	19 17 0	22 7 0	24 17 0	27 7 0
9 10 0	10 7 0	11 4 0	11 16 0	13 5 0	15 6 0	18 19 0	20 18 0	23 7 0	25 16 0	28 5 0
6 0 0	6 13 0	7 1 0	7 17 0	8 10 0	9 16 0	10 7 0	11 12 0	12 17 0	14 18 0	16 11 0
8 2 0	8 14 0	9 6 0	9 19 0	10 11 0	12 13 0	15 0 0	17 18 0	19 3 0	20 17 0	22 12 0
8 10 0	9 0 0	9 15 0	10 7 0	11 17 0	13 18 0	16 14 0	19 3 0	20 14 0	22 7 0	24 0 0
9 2 0	9 19 0	10 11 0	11 4 0	12 15 0	14 13 0	17 12 0	19 17 0	22 7 0	24 17 0	27 7 0
9 10 0	10 7 0	11 4 0	11 16 0	13 5 0	15 6 0	18 19 0	20 18 0	23 7 0	25 16 0	28 5 0
3 5 0	3 8 0	3 14 0	4 1 0	4 11 0	5 5 0	5 16 0	6 19 0	7 17 0	8 14 0	9 11 0
3 14 0	3 18 0	4 4 0	4 15 0	5 5 0	6 2 0	7 9 0	8 14 0	9 11 0	10 9 0	11 10 0
4 9 0	4 18 0	5 5 0	5 12 0	6 8 0	7 7 0	8 6 0	10 9 0	11 6 0	12 9 0	13 11 0
5 4 0	5 12 0	6 0 0	6 8 0	7 5 0	8 6 0	9 19 0	11 12 0	12 9 0	13 5 0	14 2 0
1 15 0	1 19 0	2 4 0	2 8 0	2 12 0	2 16 0	3 0 0	3 4 0	4 3 0	5 0 0	5 16 0
2 16 0	3 4 0	3 11 0	3 17 0	4 4 0	4 11 0	5 12 0	6 16 0	8 2 0	8 14 0	9 6 0
3 6 0	3 14 0	4 3 0	4 11 0	4 19 0	5 8 0	6 13 0	7 17 0	9 2 0	10 7 0	11 12 0
4 3 0	4 11 0	4 19 0	5 8 0	5 16 0	6 4 0	6 13 0	7 1 0	7 9 0	7 17 0	8 5 0
4 11 0	4 19 0	5 8 0	5 16 0	6 4 0	6 13 0	7 1 0	7 9 0	7 17 0	8 5 0	8 13 0
2 10 0	2 18 0	3 6 0	3 14 0	4 3 0	4 13 0	5 5 0	5 16 0	7 9 0	8 6 0	9 3 0
2 18 0	3 6 0	3 14 0	4 3 0	4 13 0	5 5 0	5 16 0	6 13 0	8 6 0	9 19 0	11 12 0
4 11 0	4 19 0	5 8 0	5 16 0	6 4 0	6 13 0	7 2 0	7 9 0	7 17 0	8 5 0	8 13 0
4 19 0	5 8 0	5 16 0	6 4 0	6 13 0	7 1 0	7 9 0	7 17 0	8 6 0	8 14 0	9 2 0
1 13 0	1 17 0	2 2 0	2 5 0	2 10 0	2 14 0	2 18 0	3 2 0	3 6 0	3 10 0	3 14 0
4 19 0	5 8 0	5 16 0	6 4 0	6 13 0	7 1 0	7 9 0	7 17 0	8 5 0	8 13 0	9 1 0
5 8 0	5 16 0	6 4 0	6 13 0	7 1 0	7 9 0	7 17 0	8 6 4	8 14 0	9 2 0	9 10 0

Vessels propelled by Steam and Vessels towed by Steam Vessels, provided that if any such Vessel shall
rate or price may be payable, the reduction of one-fourth shall be made on such part only of the said rate

Vessels not exceeding 70 tons, chiefly laden inwards with fish, corn, or other provisions, are to pay during the summer months, viz.: from Lady-day to Michaelmas-day inclusive, the following rates only, viz. :—

From sea to London or *vice versâ*	£4 14 6
„ Gravesend to London or *vice versâ* .	1 5 0

Vessels exceeding 70 tons and not exceeding 100 tons, chiefly laden inwards with fish, corn, or other provisions, are to pay during the summer months. viz.: from Lady-day to Michaelmas-day inclusive, the following rates for the outward voyage, viz. :—

From London to Gravesend	£1 5 0
„ Do. to the Nore.	2 18 0
„ Do. to the sea	5 5 0

A pilot taking charge of a foreign vessel, on board of which there may not be any individual qualified to interpret his orders, shall be authorized to employ a person to assist him as leadsman or interpreter; provided it be distinctly understood that the necessity for the employment of such person shall be proved to the satisfaction of the Corporation of Trinity House, in which case only the following rates shall be chargeable in addition to the regular pilotage, viz. :—

For the whole run from sea to Gravesend . . .	£2 10 0
„ Ditto from Gravesend to sea . . .	1 0 0

Ships not having British registers are to pay one-fourth more than ships having British registers, except when such first mentioned ships shall be chiefly laden with fish, corn, or other provisions; or shall, by any order of Her Majesty's Most Honourable Privy Council, be privileged to enter the ports of this kingdom, upon paying the same duties of tonnage as are paid by British ships; in which case such ships and vessels not having British registers, shall pay the like rates of pilotage only as are payable by ships having British registers.

The additional rate, for intermediate portions of a foot in the draft, to be regulated as follows, viz. :—

For 3 inches and under	No addition.
For more than 3 inches and under 9 inches. .	The medium between the two rates.
For 9 inches and upwards.	The rate for the next foot.

For removing a ship or vessel from moorings into a dry or wet dock :—

For a ship under 300 tons	£0 15 0
Ditto of 300 to 600 tons	1 1 0
Ditto of 600 to 1000 tons . . .	1 11 6
Ditto above 1000 tons	2 2 0

In the Thames, above Gravesend,—

For a boat of a class carrying an anchor of above 4 cwt., with a corresponding tow line			£2 2 0
Ditto	Ditto	2 cwt.	1 1 3
Ditto	Ditto	under 2 cwt.	0 15 6

Per trip, for the whole distance from Gravesend to London, and in proportion for any part of that distance.

And for each man's service in those boats, 8*s.* per tide.

For putting a pilot on board, and for pilotage of ships and vessels to the anchorage in the Downs.*	60 Tons, and under 150.			150 Tons, and under 250.			250 Tons, and under 400.			400 Tons, and under 600.			600 Tons, and upwards.		
	£	*s.*	*d.*	£	*s.*	*d.*	£	*s.*	*d.*	£	*s.*	*d.*	£	*s.*	*d.*
From off Dungeness to off Folkestone, the Church bearing N.N.W. by compass	1	16	0	2	14	0	3	3	0	3	12	0	4	14	6
From off Folkestone to the South Foreland; the lights in one.	1	7	0	1	16	0	2	5	0	2	14	0	3	15	6
From off the South Foreland to the Downs	1	2	6	1	2	6	1	7	0	1	16	0	2	17	0

Approved by Her Majesty in Council, 18th February, 1854.

* When the pilot is put on board by a boat from the shore, one-seventh to the pilot, and the remaining six-sevenths to the boat and crew.

LOCAL DUTIES.

	Coasters.	OVERSEA.	
		British and Foreign, privileged.	Foreign, unprivileged.
		Per vessel.	
Thames River.—Sea Reach lights. On all vessels, on their *upward passages only*, passing by or through Sea Reach :—			
Of 50 and under 100 tons......	6d.	6d.	1s.
100 „ 200 „	1s.	1s.	2s.
200 „ 300 „	1s. 6d.	1s. 6d.	3s.
300 „ 400 „	2s.	2s.	4s.
400 „ 500 „	2s. 6d.	2s. 6d.	5s.
500 and upwards	3s.	3s.	6s.
Nore.—Floating light. On all vessels passing the light, on their *upward passages only* :—			
Under 100 tons	1s.	1s.	2s.
Of 100 and under 200 tons......	2s.	2s.	4s.
200 „ 300 „	3s.	3s.	6s.
300 „ 400 „	4s.	4s.	8s.
400 „ 500 „	5s.	5s.	10s.
500 and upwards	6s.	6s.	12s.
Trinity Duties.—Buoyage and beaconage. On all vessels *entering* the port of London from any port beyond Leigh or Faversham, with goods or passengers .... per ton	½d.	½d.	
Wholly laden with coals .... do.	¼d.	...	
On all vessels *entering* the port of London......... do.	...	1d.	2d.
On all vessels *entering* the ports of Sheerness, Rochester, Faversham, Leigh, Maldon, Colchester, Harwich, Ipswich, Woodbridge, or Aldborough .... per ton	¼d.	¼d.	1d.
Woodbridge buoys.—On all vessels *entering* the port of Woodbridge, under 50 tons .... per vessel.	1s.	1s.	1s.
Of 50 and under 100 tons .... do.	2s.	2s.	2s.
100 tons and upwards............... do.	3s.	3s.	3s.
Hunstanton, one lighthouse.—On all vessels passing to or from the ports of Lynn, Wisbeach, or Wells ; or to or from the port of Boston, southward, 4d. per 20 tons, or 1d. per 5 tons.			
Lynn Well.—Floating light. On all vessels passing to or from the ports of Lynn or Wisbeach, or to or from the port of Boston, if navigated to the southward of the Long Sand; also on all vessels entering or departing from Lynn Deeps, southward of the Long Sand.. per ton	½d.	1d.	2d.

These duties on coasting and other vessels were established by Order in Council, 26th of June, 1855, as shown in the extensive tables published by authority, and which exhibit all the consolidated duties from one port to another in England and Wales.

ABATEMENT.

Until Her Majesty, with the advice of her Privy Council, may see fit otherwise to determine, there shall be allowed to every person paying such tolls (being those specified in the foregoing tables), an abatement or discount upon the amount payable by him ; which abatement or discount shall in the case of every OVERSEA vessel be TWENTY-FIVE per cent.

And in the case of every COASTING vessel be TEN per cent.

REGULATIONS AND EXEMPTIONS.

The duties for certain lights on the East coast, viz., those between Flamborough and the Kentish Knock, in the foregoing list, both inclusive (with the exception of the Leman and Ower), are payable once only for the whole voyage out and home; but a single passage, whether coastwise or oversea, subjects a vessel to full dues ; and a vessel having paid inwards on a coasting voyage is not exempt from full duties, if she proceeds outwards with an oversea cargo.

The duties for the Spurn Floating, Gunfleet, Swin Middle, Maplin, and Mouse, are payable once only for the whole voyage out and home, upon the same conditions as before stated. The duties for the Tongue and Girdler (Prince's Channel) are payable for each time of passing, or by all vessels which shall navigate by, or pass, the North Foreland on their voyages to or from any port or place within, or at the entrance of, the rivers Thames or Medway; but vessels navigating any of the channels to the southward of the Queen's Channel, are not to be charged therewith.

Vessels *bonâ fide* belonging to Her Majesty, and those under 20 tons register, are exempt; as also are British and foreign privileged vessels when navigating wholly in ballast, and without having any passengers on board; but foreign unprivileged vessels in ballast are liable to all lights which they may pass on the English coasts, with the exception of the North and South Forelands.

Vessels are to be charged for one passage only in a day, although any number of passages more than one may be made; the day to be computed from midnight to the midnight following.

The charges are leviable for the course usually taken from or to the respective ports. Should any vessel have been charged light duties, and thereafter have made any variations on their voyage which entitle them to a return, or subject them to an increase of the duties for the voyage actually performed, the collectors are authorized to make such return, or levy such increase respectively, on satisfactory evidence being produced of such voyage having been made in the manner represented.

Vessels are not chargeable with any light which they may pass or receive benefit from by reason of their being driven out of their course by stress of weather.

Vessels from foreign port to foreign port, without touching at any port or roadstead in the United Kingdom, are exempt from all dues; as also all vessels which may put into any such port or roadstead, on account of stress of weather, or for the purpose of repairing damage, or of obtaining such supplies of provisions or other necessaries as shall be actually required for the safety of the vessel, or the support of her crew; excepting such as shall break bulk, or take in cargo other than such necessary supplies, as aforesaid; and excepting also such as shall remain in port longer than the time required for obtaining such supplies; or longer than the time which the reparation of damage, or the state of the weather, may render unavoidable, or which shall receive orders or information relative to the destination of such vessel.

Vessels on *oversea* destinations are to be charged at the port of *clearance*.

All vessels, smacks, and boats belonging to the United Kingdom, while actually employed in catching fish within soundings, are exempt; but this exemption does not extend to vessels carrying to port fish caught by other vessels, or otherwise procured. Vessels employed as regular ferry boats, on any ferry established by Act of Parliament, are exempt.

Steam tugs employed solely in towing other vessels, and having no goods or passengers on board, are exempt. The duties in each case to be levied on the vessel towed.

The duties on *coasting* voyages are to be collected at the port of *delivery*.

These duties may be recovered by distress, according to Clause 401, Act 17 and 18 Vic., c. 104.

INDEX.

Mr. LAURIE

BEGS TO SUBMIT THE FOLLOWING RECENTLY PUBLISHED WORKS TO
PUBLIC NOTICE.

1. THE NORTH SEA. 2 Sheets, with Directions, 8s.
2. THE SOUTHERN PART OF THE NORTH SEA. 8s.
3. THE EAST COAST OF ENGLAND AND SCOTLAND, from Flamborough Head to the Orkneys, and thence to Cape Wrath. 3 Sheets, with Directions, 10s.6d.
4. THE THAMES AND MEDWAY. 2 Sheets, with Directions, 8s.
5. HARBOUR AND ENVIRONS OF HARWICH. 1 Sheet, 5s.
6. HOLY ISLAND, &c. 1 Large Sheet, 5s.
7. HARTLEPOOL BAY AND TOWN. 3s.
8. THE COASTS OF FRANCE, BELGIUM, AND THE NETHERLANDS, from Boulogne to the Texel. 9s.
9. THE STRAIT OF DOVER. 6s.
10. THE COASTS OF HOLLAND, GERMANY, AND DENMARK, from the Texel to the River Hever. 6s.
11. THE COASTS OF FRANCE, BELGIUM, AND THE NETHERLANDS, from Dieppe to the Texel. 12s.
12. THE CATTEGAT, &c. With Directions, 12s.
13. THE SOUND AND DANISH GROUNDS. 5s.
14. THE ATLANTIC, OR WESTERN OCEAN. 4 Sheets, 16s.
15. DITTO DITTO 2 Sheets, 8s.
16. THE ENGLISH CHANNEL. 3 Sheets, with Directions (*new*), 12s.
17. GUERNSEY, JERSEY, &c. 1 Sheet, with Directions, 5s.
18. THE EASTERN HARBOURS OF THE ENGLISH CHANNEL. 1 Sheet, 5s.
19. THE CENTRAL HARBOURS OF DITTO 1 Sheet, 5s.
20. THE WESTERN HARBOURS OF DITTO 1 Sheet, 5s.
21. THE ISLE OF WIGHT, &c., from Surveys of Capt. Sheringham, &c. 1 Sheet, 5s.
22. THE BRISTOL CHANNEL (*from the late Surveys*). 2 Sheets, with Directions, 8s.
23. ST. GEORGE'S CHANNEL, AND BRISTOL CHANNEL (*new*). 3 Sheets, with Directions, 12s.
24. THE BAY OF BISCAY. 2 Sheets, with Directions, 8s.
25. SPAIN AND PORTUGAL. 2 Sheets, with Directions, 8s.
26. THE MEDITERRANEAN SEA. 3 Sheets, with Directions, 14s.
27. THE ARCHIPELAGO, &c. 2 Sheets, 10s. 6d.
28. THE AZORES. 1 Sheet, 5s.
29. THE CANARIES. 1 Sheet, 5s.
30. THE ETHIOPIC, OR SOUTH ATLANTIC OCEAN. 4 Sheets, 16s.
31. DITTO DITTO 2 Sheets, 8s.
32. THE BRITISH ISLES TO THE CAPE OF GOOD HOPE. 2 Sheets, 10s. 6d.
33. NORTH ATLANTIC MEMOIR, Descriptive and Explanatory, New Edit., 14s.
34. SOUTH ATLANTIC DITTO DITTO 14s.
35. THE INDIAN AND PACIFIC OCEANS. Comprised in 12 Sheets. £3.
36. THE NORTHERN PART OF THE INDIAN OCEAN. 3 Sheets, 16s.
37. THE SOUTHERN PART OF DITTO. 3 Sheets, 16s.
38. THE NORTH PACIFIC OCEAN. 3 Sheets, 14s.
39. THE SOUTH PACIFIC. 3 Sheets, 14s.
40. THE COAST OF CHINA, FROM CANTON TO NANKING. 3 Sheets, 14s.
41. THE DIRECTORY FOR THE PACIFIC OCEAN. 2 vols. royal 8vo., £3.

London: J. & W. Rider, Printers, 14, Bartholomew Close.

CPSIA information can be obtained at www.ICGtesting.com
Printed in the USA
LVOW111934210812

295317LV00007B/97/P